Fines & Fees

Fines will be assessed for all overdue
materials. Fees for lost materials will be
the cost of the item + a processing fee.

**WASHTENAW COMMUNITY COLLEGE
LEARNING RESOURCE CENTER**

SMART
MONEY MOVES FOR
AFRICAN AMERICANS

SMART MONEY MOVES

F O R

AFRICAN AMERICANS

KELVIN E. BOSTON

Foreword by Dennis Kimbro

G. P. PUTNAM'S SONS   NEW YORK

G. P. Putnam's Sons
Publishers Since 1838
200 Madison Avenue
New York, NY 10016

Library of Congress Cataloging-in-Publication Data
Boston, Kelvin E.
    Smart money moves for African Americans / by Kelvin E. Boston :
    foreword by Dennis Kimbro.
        p.   cm.
    Includes bibliographical references and index.
    ISBN 0-399-14028-X
    1. Afro-Americans—Finance, Personal.   I. Title.
HG179.B5847   1996
332.024'0396073—dc20   95-37409   CIP

Book design by Ann Gold

Printed in the United States of America

10   9   8   7   6   5   4   3   2   1

This book is printed on acid-free paper. ∞

To Astor Boston, my mother;
Ella Williams and Willabe Williams, my godparents;
and the Reverend Merrick Collier, Mollie Barringer,
and Minor Barringer, my lifelong friends and mentors.
All saw something of value in me even when I did not see it in myself.

CONTENTS

"At the bottom of education, at the bottom of politics, even at the bottom of religion, there must be economic independence."
—Booker T. Washington, ca. 1903

ACKNOWLEDGMENTS

Writing a book is more than a notion. I learned this after missing too many deadlines concerning *Smart Money Moves for African Americans.* This project would have been further delayed were it not for the assistance and support of many generous individuals. First I must thank my literary agent, Denise Stinson, who asked me to consider this project, and then not only helped me package it, but also closed the deal. Next I must thank my literary angel from Putnam, Irene Prokop. Irene not only lent her guidance to the project, but most importantly, never gave up on it—even after I missed too many deadlines. Then there was Marcia Hayden, the editor who helped pull the final manuscript together and deliver it to Putnam. I know that God blessed me with this trio, who together represent one of the best literary production teams in America.

I have come to realize that the rest of my team was also God sent. They include the financial scholar, Leon Lebreque, and the entire staff at Educational Technology, Inc. They gave me a great deal of information about taxes, credit management, and real estate. Then there was Carl Norris, who graciously shared his knowledge about small business development. Likewise, I was fortunate to have Sidney Madlock of American Express Financial Services, who shared with me the finer points about life insurance; Robert McNatt, for his editorial assistance; and Dennis Kimbro, for taking the time to write the foreword.

I will also be forever grateful for the advice from several African American financial advisors (Gail Mason, Jane McNamara, Evelyn Johnston, Glinda Bridgforth, Gwen Cohen, Terri Price) for their input on the chapter concerning women. On my list of valuable assistants, I must recognize Deborah Atkinson, Dante James, Joe Madison Gray, Glenda Gill, Sharon Banks, Rhonda English, Marilyn Meredith, Frank Washington, Erica Caver, Julia Matthews, and Vanessa Foster.

Lastly I must thank the following people for supporting *The Color of Money* television series. They are Don Barden (Barden Cablevision), Jerry Trainor (WTVS-56 Detroit), Robert Johnson (Black Entertainment Television), and the loyal viewers of *The Color of Money* series. Without their support, this book would have never been written, and as with everything I do, I must give honor and thanks to God for giving me the mission to help others learn to live with financial dignity.

FOREWORD

by Dennis Kimbro

While addressing a business group in Chicago, I received a phone call from my Atlanta home. My wife informed me that Kelvin Boston, host of the nationally syndicated television show, *The Color of Money*, wanted me to write the foreword to his book, *Smart Money Moves for African Americans*. Ordinarily, my wife wouldn't concern me with such matters, particularly before I was to make a major presentation, but she was openly excited. "I was sure you wanted this message right away," she explained, "since you speak so enthusiastically about the importance of Kelvin's show."

I was honored and thrilled to have Kelvin ask me to pen a few pages to introduce this magnificent book. You see, the content of *Smart Money Moves for African Americans* has been a source of inspiration for me as long as I can remember.

While I was still a young man, my father died. Even though he had attended college and worked nonstop for nearly thirty years, he died absolutely broke. I will never forget thinking how, in a country loaded with opportunities and possibilities, anyone could work so hard during his or her life and end up with nothing. As tears streamed down my face, I promised myself that it would never happen to me. No matter how long or hard I had to search, no matter how many books I had to read or how many people I had to ask, I was determined to find the key to financial success and prosperity.

Why is this important to you? Because Kelvin Boston has placed the keys to financial prosperity within your grasp. Here he outlines a blueprint that offers lifetime security and economic well-being. When it comes to money, Kelvin knows his field. If Kelvin shares a financial strategy, you can count on it. If he offers advice, read carefully. You will find these money moves both easy to understand and easy to apply. You can use these strategies to pry open financial doors and give yourself more time to secure your dreams.

Smart Money Moves for African Americans breaks new ground by examining the basics of financial planning from an African American perspective. This book also shows African Americans how to use their resources to increase their net worth. At the same time, *Smart Money Moves for African Americans* presents a viable blueprint for economic self-determination for African Americans.

It's a much needed reference guide for African Americans. Within its covers Kelvin gives many financial strategies that have been overlooked. In Chapter 4, he explains the major reasons why African Americans should invest in stock mutual funds. In Chapter 6, there is a call to arms for African American entrepreneurs, and in Chapter 10, he explores the financial myths that place self-imposed limitations on many African American breadwinners. These wealth-building money moves are explained along with other strategies on home ownership, financial planning, and money issues facing African American women. His insights are informative and inspirational, and his ideas have never been presented in such a straightforward manner. For these reasons, *Smart Money Moves for African Americans* will be referred to often; it is the financial success guide for African Americans.

Making financial decisions is like standing in a room full of doors, knowing that behind one is the reward you seek but behind so many others lie the financial pitfalls you hope to avoid. For example, do you work hard for your money or is your money working hard for you? Does the month outlast your money? Are you still waiting for your ship to come in? Do you live on that far away fantasy island "Some Day Isle?" Someday I'll start saving . . . Someday I'll launch my own business . . . Someday I'll reach my financial goals. Does the thought of money seem to bring undue stress? Without sleight of hand or spinning mirrors, *Smart Money Moves for African Americans* suggests ways in which you can take the lead in strengthening your personal bottom line.

In the past, the African American community had to rely on its own resources to survive. Hence, Kelvin spends little time on racism and discrimination, choosing instead to devote his efforts to those things we can change. His priority is personal economic development, and he suggests ways in which each of us can invest in ourselves as well as in our system of economic free enterprise.

As you read through the pages of this book, keep in mind a well-worn maxim: People get in trouble in life not because they wanted too much. They land in trouble because they settled for too little. Thanks, Kelvin. We no longer have any reason to accept anything less than what is personally possible.

For those of you who are being introduced to the financial acumen of Kelvin Boston for the first time, prepare yourselves for a wonderful and prosperous experience. Don't let Kelvin's laid-back conversational style fool you. *Smart Money Moves for African Americans* is packed with sound financial advice. *Smart Money Moves for African Americans* is not only a smart move, but also the right move!

INTRODUCTION

Where there is no vision, the
people perish.
　　　—Proverbs 29:18

Designed to show African Americans how to increase their net worth, *Smart Money Moves for African Americans* explains how to invest profitably in financial planning, life insurance, home ownership, stock ownership, business ownership, and human resources. I also show you smart ways to manage the challenges of your income taxes and to control consumer credit.

Many who read and adhere to the Smart Money Moves strategy will increase their net worths substantially. Our major objective is to help you increase your net worth by $200,000 to $500,000. The information in this book will show you how you can reach this financial goal by using only 10 percent of your income and using proven moderately conservative investments.

The result is that, in ten to twenty years, you could have a net worth of over a half million dollars. Some of the people who read this book will reach this goal sooner because they will start or purchase a small business. In either case, the good news is that by following the Smart Money Moves outlined in this book, you and your family can enjoy your financial dreams.

As noted by Frank Levy, the author of *From Dollars and Dreams: The Changing American Income Distributions:* "While today's middle-class dream does not carry a precise price tag, it exists in popular consciousness and has come to include a single-family home, one or two cars (including a new one), a washing machine and dryer, a color TV, raising and educating children, providing a period for retirement, and so on."

Many African American households have already implemented plans that will help them secure a financially comfortable lifestyle. In the chapters you are about to read, you will learn about the smart money moves these individuals made. Additionally, I will introduce you to several seasoned African American investors, persons who may be like you in many ways—they work for a living and want to enjoy financial success. However, they may be unlike you in that they are already enjoying the rewards of investing in the American free-enterprise system.

When writing *Smart Money Moves* I tried to present the information in a candid and concise manner. I also tried to limit the use of financial, legal, and economic jargon. Unfortunately, I could not remove all the financial, legal, and economic terminology without losing some important wealth-building concepts. Nevertheless, I don't think that you will let a few technical terms or charts deter you from completing *Smart Money Moves*. Your perseverance will be quickly rewarded, especially after you use the information to increase your family's financial well-being.

In Chapter One, you will receive your travel itinerary outlining the route you take, the journey from bondage to abundance. In Chapters Two through Ten, you will learn how to make the financially rewarding smart money moves. In Chapter Eleven, you will see how, combined, the smart money moves can increase your net worth.

Written from an African American viewpoint, *Smart Money Moves* meshes a fascination about the wealth-building process with a fear of investing in stocks and other business operations. Sometimes, I whipped this fear, and sometimes this fear whipped me.

Yet, in spite of my fear, I have always benefited. I have experienced this wealth-building paradox on numerous occasions, and the fascination has often helped me increase my net worth.

Hence, it is from this perspective—a compendium exposing the yearnings of my soul as well as the socially abused, religiously nurtured, politically underestimated, economically intimidated, and financially fascinated souls of African Americans—that I present for your consideration *Smart Money Moves for African Americans*.

Dr. W. E. B. Du Bois wrote that "The problem of the twentieth century will be the problem of the color line—the relation of the darker and the lighter races. . . ." I wonder what Dr. Du Bois would have to say about the state of my soul and "the souls of black folks" today. His poignant predictions have become a painful reality for many whites and African Americans.

Unfortunately, it appears that Dr. Du Bois's observation about the twentieth century may also be true of the twenty-first century—with one noticeable difference. In the twenty-first century, the color of the almighty dollar will be added to the list of factors separating "the darker and the lighter races."

Therefore, as African Americans we can remember our historic past and sing the words of Mahalia Jackson:

> *"You know my soul looks back in wonder:*
> *How did I make it over?"*

Still, faced with the grim economic realities of the future, our soul asks what will we do?

No amount of wealth can solve the race problem in America. Nevertheless, by increasing the wealth of individual African Americans, we can reduce their financial suffering. Furthermore, by increasing the wealth of all African Americans, we can reduce the great economic divide that now separates African Americans from the rest of America.

Hence, while *Smart Money Moves for African Americans* will not solve all of America's problems, this money management manual represents part of the answer to the major problem facing African Americans today—the need to develop a systematic way of increasing the collective wealth of African Americans families.

Unlike many personal economic development plans promulgated in the African American community, *Smart Money Moves for African Americans* is not a get-rich-quick-scheme for the masses. To the contrary, *Smart Money Moves for African Americans,* is a lifetime wealth-building strategy for African Americans.

This strategy represents the economic evolution of African Americans. This program of personal economic emancipation was a long time in coming. A social odyssey that began in slavery, found its way through the deep wilderness of the civil rights movement, and continues today.

The foundation of this strategy is the American dream and the American free-enterprise system. However, the social and spiritual principle of the strategy is rooted in the hope of African Americans and summarized in these words of Dr. Martin Luther King, Jr., who told an audience of 250,000 during the 1963 March on Washington, "America has given the Negro people a bad check, which has come back marked 'insufficient funds.' But we refuse to believe that the bank of justice is bankrupt. We refuse to believe that there are insufficient funds in the great vaults of opportunity of this nation."

And so we present *Smart Money Moves for African Americans* as an economic strategy for African Americans' future financial success. In so doing, we also present Dr. King's symbolic promissory note. Affirming his belief that once his check is honored, African American families will enjoy "the riches of freedom and the security of justice."

FROM BONDAGE TO ABUNDANCE

He which soweth sparingly, shall reap also
sparingly; and he which soweth bountifully shall
reap also bountifully.
                              —2nd Corinthians 9:6

"Eternal vigilance is the price you must pay for freedom," former United States representative Shirley Chisholm told me in an interview for my television program, *The Color of Money*. These words would later forge my understanding that "eternal vigilance" is also the price African Americans must pay for financial freedom. Until paid, we will never really enjoy the "life, liberty, and the pursuit of happiness" promised in the United States Declaration of Independence, nor will we completely enjoy our American citizenship until the majority of African American households secure financial freedom. Therefore, to complete the odyssey to American citizenship, as descendants of former African slaves, we must move beyond America's voting booths and continue our journey to abundance.

In many respects we are being guided on this journey by successful African American entrepreneurs, motivational speakers, and media personalities. Similar to the conductors on the underground railroad, these modern day conductors are quietly showing all African Americans the way to financial freedom. Their call to get on board can be heard from national television programs, major newspapers, convention floors, and best-selling books. These pathfinders include economists Dennis Kimbro, Thomas Sowell, and Walter Williams; national talk show hosts Oprah Winfrey, Tony Brown, and Les Brown; charismatic spiritual leaders Johnnie Coleman, Iyanla Vanzant, and the Reverend Ike (Frederick J.

Eikerenkoetter II); and successful businessmen Wally "Famous" Amos, Earl Graves, and John H. Johnson. These scouts are safeguarding the passageways to prosperity for African Americans and for all people of color.

It is exciting to watch the masses enthusiastically respond to the call of these conductors to board the train to abundance. It is also fascinating to watch these conductors as they prepare African Americans for their long ride to financial freedom.

Although many of us are already boarding the abundance train, many more of us need to buy a ticket and prepare our families for financial freedom. Let's consider the reasons why. Only 7.5 percent of African American households earn $50,000 or more. These households represent African American families with the most ability to control their financial destinies. Their income allows them the opportunity to reach many of their financial goals. They have the financial resources to send their children to college, make a down payment on a home, and retire with financial dignity. While many African American families in this socioeconomic group obtain these financial goals, recent findings indicate that far too many do not.

Many African American households in this high-income bracket experience the same money management problems faced by the majority of African American families, who on average earn $21,162. These problems include the inability to save a portion of their income, plan for their financial future, invest in appreciating assets, control their income tax obligation, fight inflation, and find reasonably priced insurance.

As a result, lower- and middle-income African American families commit the greatest financial error that they can make: they fail to substantially increase their net worth over time. If their financial goals are met, it is due in part to the support of a family member, a subsidy check from the government, or a lucky break. Hence, both lower- and middle-income groups need to develop a financial strategy that will help them obtain concrete financial objectives.

African American families cannot afford to miss the train headed toward financial success. Those households that do will find themselves waiting at a train stop with no shelter against the harsh winds of economic uncertainty. According to the July 1994 edition of *Black Enterprise* magazine, African Americans have a net worth of $10,651 while the average white American has a net worth of $51,191. These numbers represent a $1.065 billion wealth deficit between white and African Americans. There is also a gap in mutual fund investments, interest earning accounts, home equity, and real estate.

**CHART 1: BLACKS OWNED A SIGNIFICANTLY
SMALLER SHARE OF WEALTH PER CAPITA THAN WHITES**

	Net Worth	Interest Earnings	Stocks Mutual Funds	Home Equity	Rental Property
Black	$10,651	872	115	416	7,196
White	$51,191	7,308	3,420	4,561	21,627

Chart 1 graphically illustrates the disparity of net worth per capita that exists between African and white Americans. It highlights the fact that African Americans own a significantly smaller share of wealth than their white counterparts. In net worth African Americans own $10,651, whites own $51,191; in interest income African Americans earn $872, whites earn $7,308; in ownership of mutual funds African Americans own $115, whites own $3,420; in home equity African Americans own $416, whites own $4,561; and in rental property African Americans own $7,196 compared to $21,627 owned by whites.

Such findings explain why The National Urban League's 1994 *State of Black America Report* stated that "There has been little significant improvement in the quality of life for blacks since 1980." Additionally, these figures show that most African American households do not have any savings, liquid assets, or appreciating property that could sustain them during an emergency, divorce, employment interruption, or uninsured calamity. In short, in the 1990s the average African American family does not have the financial resources to control its financial future. These economic circumstances should motivate more African Americans to jump aboard the abundance train.

SYSTEMATIC PLANNING TO INCREASE NET WORTH

What can African American families do to control their financial futures? The answer is simple and important. They must increase their families' net worth. In doing so these households can

1. Utilize income the family already controls.
2. Help reach important financial goals.
3. Reduce the impact of financial hardships.

4. Decrease the wealth deficit with white America.

5. Reduce the numbers of "working poor" African American families.

An important aspect of the net worth–building program outlined in this book will be its reliance on utilizing resources the African American community already controls. These resources include our income combined with our human resources, that is, our intellectual, physical, and spiritual capital.

By pursuing a strategy to increase their family wealth, African Americans can also control their economic destinies and reach their financial dreams. Only recently have African American families turned their attention to increasing their net worth. In the past, most of us were too busy fighting racism to worry about our net worth. Additionally, few African American families had the financial resources to save, invest, or manage money. Until the passage of the 1964 Civil Right Acts, most African Americans worked in low-paying jobs with meager pension benefits; few of us had much disposable income. A landmark exposé by *Money* magazine in 1989, entitled "Race and Money," documented the results of this legacy.

The article showed how job discrimination, housing segregation, and redlining against African Americans contributed to our lack of financial resources. These race-related factors, restricted "the income-generating opportunities blacks had and therefore limited their ability to save, provide for their families, or leave sizable estates to their heirs."

Systematically increasing your family's net worth is not complicated. Nevertheless, as with so many things in life, you cannot achieve this goal if you do not know how to do it. This point is particularly true for African Americans who are rarely privy to information that would improve their financial well-being.

THE FINANCIAL MISEDUCATION
OF AFRICAN AMERICANS

The teaching of basic money management concepts was not a major interest of the African American church, the Civil Rights movement, or the American public school system. This is an important observation given the significant role these institutions played in shaping the economic views of African Americans.

The church and the Civil Rights movement championed many campaigns that opened employment and business opportunities to African Americans. However, after opening these doors, neither group taught its followers what to do with their new sources of revenue.

Furthermore, while preaching "about the hereafter" the African American church rarely promoted the idea of accumulating earthly possessions; in fact, it championed living a pious life and waiting to receive "God's riches in heaven."

A few nontraditional religious organizations and leaders, such as The Universal Negro Improvement Association, The Nation of Islam, and several African American New Age Churches, have stressed the importance of economic self-determination. However, they have not been able to influence the majority of African Americans churchgoers to become financially secure. Thus, while a small number of non-traditional African American worshipers were instructed that "God wants you to enjoy an abundant life *now*," the majority of African American churchgoers were taught that money was "the root of all evil" and to store their "treasures up in heaven."

Given the traditional African American church's position on money, one can understand why African American ministers never became strong advocates of individual prosperity. However, trying to understand why African American civil rights leaders did not advocate prosperity is another matter. With the exception of Booker T. Washington, who preached a gospel of hard work, thrift, business organization, and industrial education in the late 1800s, no other national African American leader has advocated the importance of creating "personal wealth." Economic empowerment was not the main thrust of the civil rights movement or of its leaders.

Let's remember, however, that the segregated America of the 1950s and 1960s looked nothing like the pseudo politically correct America we live in today. There was a time when racial hatred, segregation, and disenfranchisement were the norm in America. Were it not for the African American church's spiritual leadership and the civil rights leaders' political agenda during those turbulent times, today we could not turn our attention to increasing our net worth.

When considering the financial miseducation of African Americans, we should not forget the contributions of the public school system. Surely, the public schools would teach African American children how to manage their money. Such, however, is not the case.

The primary job of the public school system has been, and continues to be, to teach children the basics needed to enter America's work force. Apparently, the public school system does not consider money management a basic requirement for entering this work force for any of our children.

Therefore, a paradox has developed whereby African American children are taught the American dream but are not taught how to secure that dream. This dilemma has occurred because few public schools teach students the role the American dollar plays in securing the dream, nor do schools teach them a systematic approach for building financial security.

Public schools do a good job of teaching children about independence and a poor job of teaching them about investing. They do a good job of teaching children about the principles of American freedom, but a poor job of teaching them about the principles of the American free enterprise system.

The tragedy of this paradox is the confusion it creates in the minds of African American children who graduate from public schools without the financial skills they need to compete successfully. Many African American high school graduates have no idea of the financial responsibilities they will face in life; therefore, many are forced into the job market armed only with a false sense of financial reality and a distorted expectation of living the American dream.

Consequently, the public schools, the churches, and the civil rights organizations all contributed to teaching African Americans that all men are created equal but failed to teach us the importance of creating wealth. In so doing, each institution contributed to the financial miseducation of African Americans.

This lack of financial information has kept many of us from enjoying the American dream. Instead many African American families have learned to cope with experiencing the American nightmare instead. For many families, poverty has become a normal way of living. Scraping pennies has become a habit, and maintaining the status quo is easier than trying to break out of the cycle of poverty. Consequently many of these families unconsciously leave their heirs a tradition of poverty, which is passed along from one generation to the next.

Nevertheless, there is good news for the millions of African Americans who represent the poor, working poor, and nearly working poor. The good news is that we can still enjoy the fruits of the American dream once we learn how to use our financial resources effectively.

SEVEN SMART MONEY MOVES TO OBTAIN THE AMERICAN DREAM

The major focus of this book is to teach you how to use your financial resources effectively and how to take seven smart money moves that will help your family increase its net worth and financial well-being. We will devote a chapter to each of these smart money moves described briefly below.

1. CREATE A WEALTH-BUILDING PLAN

A wealth-building plan is a financial plan in which the major goal is to increase a household's net worth to $200,000 to $250,000. Unlike most financial plans that center on a specific lifestyle goal—a vacation, new home, or retirement—the wealth-building financial plan goal is to increase the household's net worth. Additionally, while the net worth goal timetable is ten to fifteen years, the wealth-building plan is a lifetime plan. Therefore, after showing you how to achieve your net worth goal you will learn how to double your net worth every ten years.

2. INVEST IN YOUR DREAMS EVERY PAYDAY

Mark and Jo Ann Skousen wrote in *High Finance on a Low Budget,* "Saving must become an immutable rule in life." According to Mark, who has also appeared on *The Color of Money* show, "Saving must come first, before the rent, before taxes, even before food for the baby." Adopting the Skousens' appreciation for the importance of saving, I believe that every payday is your day to save a dollar and a dream.

Additionally, it is important for African Americans to save a portion of our annual $300 billion income so that we will be able to sustain our own institutions, organizations, and causes. The ultimate success of increasing our net worth will depend on African American households developing the habit of long-term investing.

3. OWN YOUR HOME

"Most Americans count their home as their most valuable possession, but segregation means that African Americans build less home equity," reported Farai Chideya in her book *Don't Believe the Hype: Fighting Cultural Misinformation About African Americans.* Additionally, many African Americans who do own homes do not view them as investments. Therefore, few African Americans are willing to use their homes as equity to purchase other homes that may be appreciating faster. Our reluctance to use our home equity to purchase higher priced homes limits our ability to increase our net worth. Nevertheless, given the tax benefits and the opportunity for appreciation, home ownership can be a powerful tool in creating wealth for many African American households.

4. INVEST IN THE STOCK MARKET

Historically, investing in stocks has provided an average return of 14 percent annually. Chart 2, "Stocks, Bonds, Bills, Inflation, Real Estate, and Gold," prepared by Ibbotson Associates, illustrates how one dollar grows after being invested in gold, treasury bills, real estate, government bonds, and large company stocks. The investment with the best return over an eighteen-year period was large company stocks, producing an annual compound return of 14.21 percent.

Ironically, African Americans own very few stocks compared to white Americans; in fact, according to the U.S. Bureau of the Census, on average we own approximately $115 worth of stocks. In order to increase our net worth, African Americans will need to understand how to select, invest, and maintain a portfolio of stocks or stock mutual funds.

5. INSURE YOUR DREAMS

In *Don't Believe the Hype,* Chideya states, "Due to factors ranging from violence to poor access to health care, African Americans live an average of six years less than whites." This statement illustrates the need for African Americans to understand how to protect our financial dreams, using low-cost term-insurance and disability-insurance plans.

6. OWN A BUSINESS ENTERPRISE

One of the most alarming situations today is the small number of African American entrepreneurs. At last count by the U.S. Bureau of the Census, this number was less than 425,000. This fact is alarming because few African Americans can make vast fortunes without owning a business. Today most millionaires are not born, they are self-motivated, hardworking entrepreneurs.

Entrepreneurship offers the greatest opportunity to build and maintain wealth in America. If African Americans want to participate in the great bounty of America's free-enterprise system, then more of us will have to join the ranks of the African American entrepreneur.

CHART 2:
STOCKS, BONDS, BILLS, INFLATION, REAL ESTATE, AND GOLD, 1975–1993

Growth of $1 Invested at Year–End 1975*

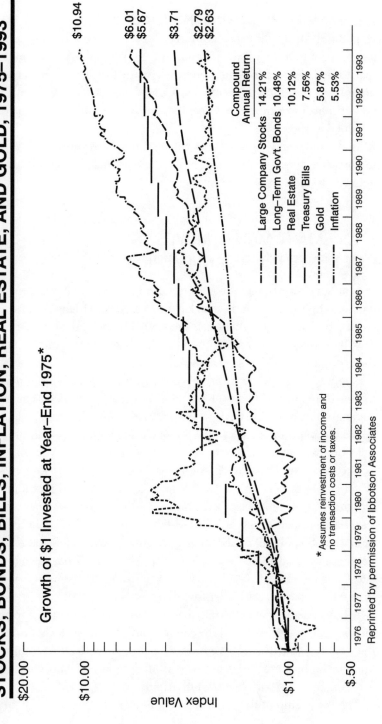

	Compound Annual Return
Large Company Stocks	14.21%
Long–Term Govt. Bonds	10.48%
Real Estate	10.12%
Treasury Bills	7.56%
Gold	5.87%
Inflation	5.53%

$10.94
$6.01
$5.67
$3.71
$2.79
$2.63

Index Value

$20.00
$10.00
$1.00
$.50

1976 1977 1978 1979 1980 1981 1982 1983 1984 1985 1986 1987 1988 1989 1990 1991 1992 1993

* Assumes reinvestment of income and
no transaction costs or taxes.

Reprinted by permission of Ibbotson Associates

7. MAXIMIZE YOUR HUMAN RESOURCES

In addition to the financial resources African Americans own, we also have access to an enormous amount of intellectual, physical, and spiritual capital. For various reasons we have historically undervalued and underused our human resources. Consequently once we understand how to maximize our human capital, we will be able to reach our net worth goals sooner.

In the following chapters you will learn the steps you will need to take to complete these seven smart money moves: making these moves will help you to increase your family's net worth.

HOW SMART MONEY MOVES CAN BENEFIT AFRICAN AMERICANS

We cannot overestimate the importance of African American families increasing their net worth. Every dollar invested by African Americans decreases the wealth gap that exists between African and white Americans. This by-product of net worth building holds enormous implications for the economic future of African Americans.

Many of us believe that earning a decent income is all that is necessary to win the game of financial success. As such, many economists often compare the annual earnings of Blacks and Whites. This rationale undermines the importance of saving and increasing your net worth over time. Let's briefly review the economic advantage of increasing your net worth.

According to Dr. Claude Anderson, author of *Black Labor, White Wealth,* "On the eve of the Civil War, records indicated that more than 50 percent of free blacks were paupers; all free blacks collectively held less than one-half of one percent of the nation's wealth . . . in the 1960s more than 55 percent of all blacks were still impoverished and . . . barely held one percent of the nation's wealth." Not much has changed. The latest census indicates that African American per capita net worth is $10,651 compared to $51,191 for whites.

Mr. Anderson's data illustrate that African Americans' efforts to achieve income parity with their white counterparts has done little to decrease the wealth gap with white America. It is time for us to focus more attention on the importance of net worth building as an important factor in achieving income parity with white America.

The ownership of more net worth–building assets will greatly improve the economic fortunes of the African American community, for we will not just be saving money, we will be investing in stocks, homes, and businesses. Furthermore, while individual African American households are increasing their personal net worths, we will simultaneously be increasing the collective economic power of African Americans across the nation.

Whenever I consider the importance of African American families increasing their net worth, I remember a former financial planning client of mine, Melvin James. Melvin is an African American auto worker, who for two years personally delivered to me his monthly mutual fund investment of $150. He could have mailed it to my office or had it automatically deducted from his checking account, but because of his resolve to become financially independent, he chose to deliver it personally.

His monthly visit gave us the opportunity to catch up on the latest happenings in the stock market and Mr. James's life. One day while sitting in my office, I asked him why he was so conscientious. Melvin turned to me and said, "Because I do not want to be a poor, old, black man living in America." The thought of joining the ranks of millions of other poor African American senior citizens terrified Melvin, and his terror was—and is—still justified. Today, 60 percent of all African American seniors depend on social security. Many of them will tell you that they are living, but few of them will tell you that they are living well.

Melvin understood that the only way not to join the ranks of poor seniors was to systematically increase his net worth. Based upon his resolve to invest regularly, I know he will achieve his goal. More African Americans can also achieve their financial goals if they concentrate on systematically increasing their net worth.

Mr. James felt that he was lucky to find an African American financial planner. We met while I was working for IDS/American Express, a national financial planning company. Unfortunately, millions of African Americans do not have the opportunity to work with an African American investment advisor who can personally answer their money questions. Unlike our white counterparts, most African American families do not have access to such a professional or organization for investment advice. According to the June 1994 issue of *Black Enterprise* magazine, there are only 2 mutual funds, 36 commercial banks, 18 saving and loans,

23 insurance companies and 13 investment banks owned by African Americans today. These ninety-two establishments represent African America's financial elite—a great accomplishment to be sure—yet there are not enough of these organizations to teach thirty million African Americans how to manage their combined annual gross income of $325 billion. Therefore, I hope that you will use this book to jump-start your plan to achieve financial success.

Consider *Smart Money Moves for African Americans* as your family's boarding pass on the train bound for financial freedom. Be mindful of the economic journey you are about to make. Make a commitment to stay on the train—a train that pulled out of a station called *Bondage* many years ago and will not stop until it reaches a station called *Abundance*.

ESTABLISH A WEALTH-BUILDING PLAN

Lazy hands make a man poor, but diligent hands bring wealth.

—Proverbs 10:4

Every dollar comes into our lives for a reason, a season, or a lifetime. We choose which of our dollars to spend in a season and which of our dollars to save for a lifetime in order to achieve what financial planners refer to as a "long-term goal." Long-term goals include saving for college, raising the down payment on a house, or investing for retirement.

Once a dollar is spent, it is gone forever—like a season past. Consequently, it's important to do everything to hold on to a portion of your earnings.

Understanding how dollars can be divided into seasonal and lifetime resources is important because only funds invested for the long term can help you increase your net worth. Hence, when I discuss investing, I will refer to investing *lifetime* dollars. These dollars, or funds, should be invested for five years or more.

You can review some of the most common areas in which dollars can be used for seasonal purposes and lifetime investments in Chart 3, "Seasonal and Lifetime Dollars." This chart also illustrates how lifetime investments help families increase their net worth. But more importantly, this chart will help you understand why you should keep a portion of your earnings for long-term investments.

CHART 3: SEASONAL AND LIFETIME DOLLARS

Seasonal dollars are usually spent soon after they are received and never seen again. We use our seasonal dollars to pay for food items, make rent payments, purchase gifts, take vacations, and pay our taxes.

On the other hand, lifetime dollars are the dollars we keep for five to ten years. These dollars meet our long-term financial goals because they are our investments, retirement accounts, and businesses.

The following chart explains the uses of seasonal and lifetime dollars, and it will help you understand the difference between the two.

SEASONAL AND LIFETIME DOLLARS

Seasonal Dollars Usage	Impact on Net Worth
Current expenses	none
Food	none
Credit cards	none
Car lease	none
Term insurance	none
Entertainment	none
Gifts	none
Vacations	none
Clothing	none

Lifetime Dollars Usage	Impact on Net Worth
Investments	positive
Business ownership	positive
Mortgage payments	positive
Car payments	positive
Retirement plans	positive
Whole life insurance	positive
Fine art	positive

Most of the dollars African Americans earn remain in their possession for only a short period of time. This time frame may be hours, days, or weeks depending upon when the monthly bills are due. Hence, most African American households use their earnings in a particular season, and as a result, only a few African American households ever benefit from having long-term investments.

In the previous chapter, Chart 1 illustrated that African Americans have one tenth the net worth of white Americans. We should also note, as Farai Chideya wrote in her book *Don't Believe the Hype:* "Net worth reflects not only earnings, but also family savings accumulated over time."

The ability of an African American household to possess long-term investments has also been hindered by their trappings of success. Audrey Edwards wrote in an article for *Essence* magazine that African Americans tend to invest in the trappings of success—"Clothes, expensive cars, electronic equipment, household gadgets, fine liquor—rather than the substance of success." The author also writes: "This is due largely to a history of deprivation that has resulted in African Americans needing to make a visible statement about economic success." When you consider the lack of their long-term investment capital and their huge investment in the trappings of success, you can understand why African American households have few appreciating assets. Thus, in spite of the fact that the average African American household will control over $1 million in earnings over a forty-year period, that household does not have a plan to accumulate wealth. One way to reverse this trend is for more African American households to make long-term investments.

Likewise, to substantially increase your family's net worth, you will need to identify the financial resources that you can invest for a lifetime. For this reason, you should understand which dollars you want to spend in a season and which dollars you need to invest for a lifetime. By allocating both seasonal and lifetime dollars, you acknowledge that there is a time for spending and a time for saving. But more importantly, such allocations will enable you to enjoy the benefits of having both seasonal expenditures and lifetime investments.

Whenever I consider giving up on one of my long-term investments, I remember a story that the successful entrepreneur Arthur likes to tell.

Arthur's story begins when he was working part-time to complete his college education. He had completed a tour of duty in the armed forces, he was married with a family, and he was also working full-time at an auto plant.

One day, a security guard noticed Arthur's college textbooks and asked him how long it would take him to finish school. Arthur told him that he could take only a couple of credits per semester because of his responsibilities. The guard snickered and said, "At this rate it will take you at least five years to finish your college education." His inflection seemed to indicate that this was a waste of Arthur's time.

The unflappable Arthur responded, "That's okay, because if I'm lucky, I'll be here anyway." The reference was that Arthur would still be living, but living better having earned his college degree. Today, Arthur is recognized as one of the most influential African American entrepreneurs and civic leaders in the United States.

Adopting a long-term investment philosophy can be difficult at times. One of the biggest challenges is being able to stay focused on your long-term goals. One financial tool that can reduce this anxiety and help you stay focused is a financial plan.

CREATE A FINANCIAL PLAN

A financial plan is usually a computer-generated document prepared by an insurance or investment professional. Its purpose is to evaluate the likelihood of your reaching your financial goals given your age, asset allocation, and tax obligation. Most financial plans concentrate on specific goals like funding a college education, planning for retirement, and reducing the impact of estate taxes.

When your financial advisor returns your plan, he or she will amaze you with many tables, charts and graphics. But, do not be overwhelmed! What you really want to know is what will it take financially to reach your goals and what you need to do to get there. The plan will provide the answer. A conscientious planner will take the time to carefully explain and design a plan of action to help you reach your stated goals.

All computer printouts are not financial plans, and all financial advisors are not financial planners. Anyone with a computer and financial software can print a chart that can forecast financial projections, but a sound financial plan is more than just a compilation of numeric charts. A sound financial plan should list your stated goals; give a timetable to reach your goals; have financial projections related to your stated goals and asset allocation; evaluate your need for disability, life, and liability insurance; make investment recommendations related to your goals; and give income tax management strategies. As you can see, some of this information will be computer generated and some of the information will be prepared by your financial planner.

In fact, the financial plan is really a tool for your financial advisor to evaluate your financial situation and then help plan a course of action to assist you in reaching your financial goals. A planner works in much the same way as a medical doctor who reviews your medical charts to diagnose your medical problem and plan a treatment.

Care should be taken when looking for a competent financial planner. In most states there are no laws for accrediting financial planners. Unfortunately, many unsavory characters have used the title of financial planner and offered misleading financial information to unsuspecting people. And it isn't only people of moderate means who are duped. Sadly, we read about star athletes or entertainers who incur huge losses because they are so busy making money that they fail to exercise care in overseeing their investment advisors. Muhammad Ali, Aretha Franklin, and Kareem Abdul-Jabbar are just three who have lost large sums because their money was mismanaged.

You may not have their millions, but what you could lose might be even more painful to you. Financial planners are well aware of the bad apples in their midst and have begun to set standards for legitimate practitioners of the craft, just as doctors and lawyers do.

One of the leading groups that sets standards is the Institute of Certified Financial Planners. Practitioners who pass the organization's six-part course in financial planning are allowed to call themselves Certified Financial Planners, or CFPs. At the very least they will have the minimum qualifications to address your financial planning needs. At best, these professionals can draw on their experience and resources to be outstanding guides for you. The CFP designation, as with the M.D. or the J.D., is no absolute guarantee of competence; it is, however, the most widely recognized financial planning credential currently used. The institute is located in Denver, Colorado, and has trained thousands of financial planners, who work either independently, at banks, or at brokerage houses. You will find their national toll-free number in the *Resource Guide*.

Since accountants have traditionally been a source of financial advice for people, it isn't surprising that the American Institute of Certified Public Accountants also runs a program for accountants who want to offer financial services. These CPAs can become Accredited Personal Financial Specialists, who engage in the full range of financial planning services. To find out more about African American CPA firms, refer to the *Resource Guide*.

The International Association for Financial Planning (IAFP) in Atlanta, Georgia, can refer you to financial planners in your area. This organiza-

tion requires less extensive training for its planners, but all IAFP planners have advanced training in accounting or insurance.

Finally, the National Association of Personal Financial Advisors in
Buffalo Grove, Illinois, can refer you to financial planners who work
strictly on a fee-only basis. Fee-only planners charge you only for putting
together a financial plan; they will not sell you stocks, mutual funds, insurance, or any other product on which they would earn a commission.

There are also several large national financial planning companies,
the two largest being American Express Financial Advisors, a division of
the American Express company, and Merrill Lynch, that's right—Merrill
Lynch. Many traditional brokerage-service companies, such as Merrill
Lynch, offer financial planning services to their customers. Unfortunately,
you usually have to be a customer first, but it is easy enough to call and
just ask to speak to the financial planning department. Also, many large
banks have financial planning departments—banks usually refer to their
financial planners as private bankers. All too often, though, banks prefer
to work with the high rollers (doctors, lawyers, and entrepreneurs) and
may require substantial net worth.

Probably the best way to find a good planner is to ask for referrals
from friends and relatives. Then interview at least three prospective candidates. It is important to find someone you feel comfortable with because you will be working with your planner for some time as well as
providing some intimate financial information. Some of the questions
you may want to ask potential advisors are:

1. How long have you been in the business?
2. Do you specialize in any product or service?
3. How are you compensated?
4. What services does your company provide?
5. Will other members of your company help prepare my plan?
6. How many clients do you have?
7. What is the average net worth or portfolio of your client base?
8. How many of your clients have financial plans?
9. Can I see some of the financial plans you have prepared?
10. How many of your clients have stayed with you through the past
    five years?

On the issue of compensation remember that there are no free
lunches on Wall Street. You are about to enter a world where you must

pay for the services that you receive. Do not expect free advice from anyone, and if it is offered to you, consider it very carefully before taking any action. Most financial planners earn their living from collecting fees for designing financial plans, implementing the plans, or receiving commissions on the insurance and investment products they sell. Either way, you will pay for their services.

There has been a debate in the industry over whether fee-only planners are more objective than commission-compensation planners. Personally, I believe that it depends on the integrity of the planner and his or her ability to always put the clients' needs first. Therefore, unless you have strong feelings about the subject, I would suggest that you interview at least three financial planners and carefully decide which one you want to help you plan your financial future.

Most of the superior financial tools tend to share the following characteristics: they are easy to understand, lack glamour, and are readily available to the general public. For these same reasons they are normally underappreciated. One such tool is a financial plan. Over the years many people have underutilized this great financial tool. Many investment advisors have used plans only to justify selling expensive insurance and investment products to their clients, and many families let their financial plans collect dust on their bookshelves. I believe that no other investment tool will be more important than your financial plan. A written financial plan is the first investment a family should make. It is also the best!

Here are some more reasons why I believe so strongly in financial plans:

- Financial plans can help a family clarify and achieve numerous financial goals.
- Financial plans can help a family determine where its money is being spent.
- Financial plans are affordable (in the range of $300 to $1,000).
- Financial plans can help families develop a sound tax management strategy.
- Financial plans can be tax deductible.
- Financial plans can serve as a map to your financial goals.
- Financial plans can help organize the family's financial resources.
- Financial plans can help spouses discuss their financial situation in a nonthreatening manner.
- Financial plans can help a family understand its real insurance needs.

- Financial plans can help a family understand the financial commit-ment necessary to meet its financial goals.
- Financial plans can help plan major purchases.
- Financial plans can help determine the most effective way to invest resources.
- Financial plans can establish the size of a family's estate and net worth.
- Financial plans set implementation timelines.
- Financial plans help monitor and review financial progress.

A financial plan is one of the few investments that everyone needs, re-gardless of whether she or he is single or married, young or old, just starting out with a small monthly accumulation program or a high-income earner with a large estate. Your financial situation does not matter; if you do not have a financial plan you are not being all you can be, financially speaking.

TURN A FINANCIAL PLAN
INTO A WEALTH-BUILDING PLAN

Financial plans force people to put their goals in writing. Writing down your financial goals will help you clarify what you want to achieve in life and when you want to achieve it. Having goals also gives meaning to your efforts to save money.

African American households use financial goals all the time to plan major purchases. For example, many people who have never been able to save a dime for anything will find a way to save when they know that they need $1,000 for the down payment for a new car. Suddenly, the goal becomes achievable and saving is easier because they have a goal. The same thing can be seen when African Americans use the layaway plan to buy clothes at department stores or buy major purchases for Christmas or Kwanzaa.

To turn your financial plan into a wealth-building plan, one of your goals must be financial security. You will meet this goal when you in-crease your net worth to $200,000. Your stated timetable to achieve this goal should be ten to twenty years.

FINANCIAL OBSTACLES

There are many obstacles to financial planning process. Some of these include:

- Risks.
- Taxes.
- Inflation.
- Day-to-day expenses.

We encounter risks in everything we do. There are financial risks, such as premature death, disability, or possibly having to pay a large settlement as a result of litigation. Proper planning through risk management can reduce the effects of these risks. We will review this topic in more detail in Chapter 5, "Insure your Financial Future."

Taxes also hinder us from obtaining our goals. We are taxed on the wages we earn. We are taxed on most interest we receive. Even worse, we are taxed again at death if our estate is large (above $600,000). Proper tax planning and estate planning can reduce these risks.

Inflation is also an obstacle to effective planning. Inflation constantly affects our cash flow; as the prices of goods rise, we must spend more than we expected. Inflation has an impact on reaching our goals of college funding and retirement planning. Inflation also affects the real rate of return on our investments. Inflation is an obstacle we cannot ignore. Later when we consider our investment options, we will do so keeping the risk of inflation in mind.

Everyday living can affect the financial planning process. Surveys have indicated that the number one reason people don't plan financially is they see it as too large a task. Another expression sums it up quite well: Why do today what I can do tomorrow? Most people fall into another category: All their intentions are good, they make some plans, but something always happens to detour their efforts. The story goes something like this for a young couple. "Once we get settled in we can start to save money." Then the kids come along and they say: "Once the kids are grown we'll really be able to save some money." Then the kids go to college and they say: "Once the kids graduate, we will be on easy street and be able to save all kinds of money." By then it's time to retire. By starting on a plan and following through, we can overcome this obstacle called procrastination.

The first step in planning for your financial future is to find out where you are right now. To find your "financial starting line," take an inventory of your assets and liabilities and determine your net worth. You can calculate your net worth by using Chart 4, "Figuring Your Net Worth." It is designed to help you list the value of your assets and liabilities.

CHART 4: FIGURING YOUR NET WORTH

PROPERTY ASSETS

$	Residence
$	Vacation Home
$	Furnishings
$	Automobiles
$	Art, jewelry, or other valuables

EQUITY ASSETS

$	Stocks
$	Equity mutual funds
$	Variable annuities
$	Limited partnerships
$	Rental real estate
$	Business interests

FIXED ASSETS

$	U.S. government bonds and agency securities
$	Municipal bonds
$	Corporate bonds
$	Face amount certificates
$	Fixed-dollar annuities
$	Other fixed assets

CASH RESERVE ASSETS

$	Checking accounts
$	Savings accounts
$	Money-market funds
$	Certificates of deposit
$	Other cash reserve accounts
$	Total assets

LIABILITIES

$	Home mortgage
$	Other mortgage
$	Automobile loans
$	Bank loans
$	Personal loans
$	Charge account debt
$	Other debts
$	Total liabilities

NET WORTH

$	Total assets
$	Total liabilities
$	Net worth (subtract your liabilities from your assets)

Reprinted by permission of Educational Technologies, Inc.

Set a goal for yourself
What would you like your net worth to be

$_____ in 5 years?

$_____ in 10 years?

Assets can be divided into liquid assets, deferred assets, and hard assets. Liquid assets can be converted to cash in a minimum amount of time and with little or no penalty. Example of liquid assets are cash, savings accounts, checking accounts, money market funds, securities, and mutual funds. Deferred assets are assets purchased or acquired for tax purposes or for future use (such as for retirement). Types of deferred assets include IRAs, 401(k) plans, Keogh accounts, pension funds, and profit-sharing plans. The last category, hard assets, includes personal property, tangibles (works of art, recreational vehicles, automobiles), and real estate. Hard assets are more difficult to convert to cash than liquid assets.

Personal property includes items such as clothing, small appliances, video cameras, VCRs, radios, and tools. Listing personal property can be tedious, but it is important. (Can you list everything in one room of your home in case it is broken into or burned?) An alternative to making a list is to take pictures or videotape your possessions.

After you have listed all your assets (the items you own), the next step is to list your liabilities (the amount you owe). Liabilities can be divided into three categories: consumer debt, mortgage debt, and other debt. Consumer debt lost its tax deductibility in the Tax Reform Act of 1986. Most mortgage debt, however, is still 100 percent deductible from your income tax. Mortgage interest reaches a limit when the combined acquisition and home equity debt exceeds the lesser of $1,100,000 or the fair market value of your home. Acquisition and home equity debt can be combined in one mortgage, and you don't need to take out two separate loans to deduct the maximum allowable interest.

THE "NO-BUDGET" BUDGET

Many people begin the new year by making a resolution to save more money. To reach this goal the first thing they do is put the family on a budget. But going on a budget is the wrong financial move to make. According to Mark and Jo Ann Skousen, authors of the best seller *High Finance on a Low Budget,* budgets just don't work for most Americans.

When they appeared on *The Color of Money* Mark and Jo Ann shared with me several of the major reasons why most budgets fail:

1. Strict allocation-type budgets are self-defeating.
2. Most people make unrealistic budget allocations.
3. Budgets are too confining and simply aren't fun.
4. Sticking to a budget requires lots of hard work and discipline.

So, if you are serious about building your nest egg, don't make the mistake of trying to live on a strict budget. There is a more effective way to control your spending and saving habits.

This strategy popularized by the Skousens requires a family to make note of every dollar it spends for twenty-one days and then analyze the expenditures. Mark and Jo Ann have found that many people are shocked to learn how much they spend regularly on impulsive purchases like eating out, cigarettes, magazines, cosmetics, snacks, and lottery tickets. Cutting back on such items is an easier way to save money than trying to live on a budget.

Mark shared with me the story of a doctor who had overextended his credit, was robbing Peter to pay Paul, and had no savings account. Mark instructed the man to save $1,000 a month in a money market account. A year later the doctor called Mark to complain that the system had failed. He was still in debt, and he was still living on a tight budget. The only difference was that now he also had $12,000 in the bank, and he didn't know what to do with it.

The Skousen's refer to this wealth-building strategy as the "no-budget" budget. They believe that it is more important for families to know where their money is going than to spend indiscriminately. Their experience has shown them that people who cut the waste from their monthly expenditures do not need to establish a formal budget.

What I like about the Skousen's no-budget budget is that anyone can use it as a way to start spending less and saving more. Use Chart 5, the Monthly Budget Worksheet, on the following pages to see where your money is going.

CHART 5: MONTHLY BUDGET WORKSHEET

INCOME:

Husband _____

Wife _____

Interest income _____

Investments/Dividends _____

Other income _____

Total Net Income (1) $_____

EXPENSES:

House payments $_____

Property taxes (if not included in house payment)   _____

Home insurance   _____

Utilities   _____

Auto insurance   _____

Health insurance (if applicable)   _____

Life insurance (if applicable)   _____

Other installment loans (e.g., boat, RV)   _____

Charge card payment   _____

Other debts   _____

Automobile operating costs (gas, oil, tune-ups)   _____

Food/Family expense   _____

Meals away from home   _____

Clothing   _____

Entertainment   _____

Gifts   _____

Charitable contributions   _____

Total expenses (2) $_____

SAVINGS:

IRA (Husband) $_____

IRA (Wife)   _____

Pension contribution   _____

Savings account deposit   _____

Emergency fund deposit   _____

Education fund deposit	_____
Total savings contribution (3)	$_____
Total net income (1)	$_____
(Minus) Total **Expenses** (2) and **Savings** (3)	_____
(Equals) Surplus or (Deficit)	$_____

If your budget shows a surplus, that's great! If you show a deficit and are having trouble balancing your budget, you may have to cut back on nonessential living expenses temporarily. This doesn't mean that you have to give up on buying a new car, but you may have to wait until you have paid off some of your other consumer debt. We know that with proper planning and budgeting, an individual can save a few extra dollars each and every year.

Compare your personal financial scenario to the average expenditures by middle-income Americans for typical expenses.

CHART 6: FAMILY INCOME EXPENSE PERCENTAGES

Item	National Average
Food	13.9%
Clothing	5.6%
Automobile	16.1%
Housing	30.8%
Insurance	1.1%
Entertainment	4.9%
Personal care products & services	1.3%
Education	1.4%
Health care	5.3%
Other	2.5%
Total	**82.9%**

To see how African American spending compares to that of white Americans look at Chart 7, "Blacks Earn Less, Spend More." By deciding to spend less in the areas of food, clothing, and utilities, for example, you will have more money to spend in the long term.

CHART 7: BLACKS EARN LESS, SPEND MORE

LIVING EXPENSES   EXPENSES AS A PERCENTAGE OF INCOME

	Blacks	National Average
Food (at home and away)	15.4%	13.9%
Housing:		
Shelter (owned and rented)	18.3	17.6
Utilities	9.1	6.4
Household operations and supplies	2.5	3.0
Furniture and equipment	3.0	3.8
Clothing	7.2	5.6
Transportation:		
Car purchase	6.5	7.1
Gas, oil	3.3	3.2
Other vehicle-related expenses	5.7	5.8
Entertainment	3.3	4.9
Personal care products and services	1.7	1.3
Education	0.8	1.4
Health care	3.9	5.3
Life and other personal insurance	1.3	1.1
Miscellaneous	2.4	2.5
Total Annual Living Expenses	**84.4**	**82.9**

Reprinted by permission of Black Enterprise Research, 1994

SAVE 10 PERCENT OF YOUR INCOME

I believe it's imperative for African Americans to save more of their disposable income. In general, it would be a smart money move to save 10 percent or more of your take-home pay. For example, your weekly take-home pay is $435.00. If you were to save $43.50 per week or 10 percent for thirty years at 8 percent interest, you could accumulate over $282,000. By saving 12 percent of your take-home pay, you could accumulate over $339,000, and by saving 15 percent of your take-home pay, you could accumulate over $424,000. Of course, the higher the interest rate, the faster your savings can grow.

African Americans must save at twice the rate as white Americans.

Why? Because African Americans, who have less disposable income, must save more of that income just to keep pace with white America. According to Mark Skousen, whites on average save 5 percent of their income. With this being the case, African Americans must save at least 10 percent of their income. This represents an effective way to reduce the wealth gap that exists between African and white Americans.

Example:

African American family earning $25,000 saves   10% = $2,500
White family earning $50,000 saves: 5% = $2,500

African American family earning $50,000 saves: 10% = $5,000
White family earning $100,000 saves: 5% = $5,000

This example illustrates why African Americans must save 10 percent of their incomes to keep pace with their white counterparts who save only 5 percent of their incomes. This may not seem fair, but who says fair has anything to do with accumulating wealth? On the other hand, saving and investing have everything to do with wealth accumulation. Instead of debating fairness, let's get busy finding 10 percent of our earnings to save and invest.

You can find more money to save by reducing certain (nonessential) regular expenditures. For example, I have friends who were surprised at the monthly entertainment expenses they charge on their credit cards. It was not uncommon for them to spend $100 to $200 a month entertaining friends at the local drinking establishments. Portions of these funds could be used for seasonal or lifetime investments. I know this to be true because when they have pressing financial needs, my friends do not visit the local drinking establishments—they stay home! Maybe the following cost-saving ideas will help you reduce your current outlay and find that 10 percent you need to save.

Food
- Use coupons.
- Shop in bulk.
- Consider generics.
- Use a shopping list!
- Don't shop when hungry.

- Compare restaurant prices.
- Take advantage of sales and promotions.
- Share expense of annual family gatherings.
- Buy second-shelf liquor instead of always going top shelf.

Clothing
- Watch for sales.
- Use a shopping list.
- Buy directly from manufacturer or factory outlet.
- Shop off season.
- Combine pieces of an outfit for multiple wear.

Automobile
- Compare car insurance prices.
- Increase car insurance deductible amount.
- Change collision type (broad, basic, limited, none).
- Check for car insurance discounts.
  - Multiple car
  - Alarm
  - Nonsmoker
  - Antilock brakes
  - Miles driven
  - Senior citizen
  - Good driver

- Schedule preventative maintenance.
- Buy a less expensive car or a used car.

Housing
- Compare homeowner's insurance policies.
- Increase deductible.
- Don't overinsure.
- Check for discounts.
  - Nonsmoker
  - Smoke alarm
  - Deadbolt lock
  - Fire extinguisher
  - Burglar alarm
  - Senior citizen

– Multipolicy
– New construction

- Know replacement cost on house contents.
- Take an energy audit.
  - Turn down the thermostat.
  - Increase insulation.
  - Furnace and air conditioning maintenance.
  - Replace filters regularly.
  - Use lower-wattage light bulbs.
  - Use shower head water restrictor.
  - Use appliance or lighting timers.
  - Check proper roof ventilation.

- Time property tax payments for income tax advantage.
- Reduce or eliminate escrow costs.
- Reduce or eliminate mortgage term insurance.
- Set specific mortgage payoff schedule.
- Consider accelerating mortgage payments.
- Make selective improvements.
  - Keep all receipts for tax purposes.
  - Safeguard against home improvements loan overcommitments.

- Compare household supply prices.
- Buy household supplies in bulk.

Insurance
- Consider term versus whole life.
- Consider policy loans on cash-value policies.
- Use policy dividends properly.
- Consider long-term care or Medicare supplement.
- Make proper use of waiting periods and deductibles on disability.
- Coordinate all coverages with employee benefits.
- Compare three companies for all policies.
- Stop smoking cigarettes.

Entertainment
- Take advantage of discounts.
  - Two-for-one
  - Senior citizen
  - Frequent flier

  – Weekend travel
  – Advanced booking
  – Package vacations
- Entertain at home.
- Curb lottery, casino gambling, and betting.
- Monitor cable and satellite expenses.
- Go to matinees or use afternoon discounts at movies.

Gifts
- Shop for a good buy.
- Avoid last-minute shopping.
- Buy off season (purchasing warm-weather clothing and items in the winter months).
- Allocate specific amounts for your charitable gifts.
  – Use checks for proof of contribution.
  – Consider gifts of appreciated property which offer added tax benefits.
  – Consider gifts of life insurance.
  – Give unwanted items to charity, get receipts for taxes.

Debts
- Consider a home-equity loan to get deductible interest.
- Pay off credit cards.
- Cut off credit term insurance.
- Watch actual percentage rate (APR).
- Always check finance charges.
- Keep track of grace periods on credit cards.
- Monitor annual fees on credit cards.
- Keep loan term less than the useful life of the purchase.
- Set specific payoff schedule.
- Consider accelerating payments.

Other
- Eliminate cigarettes.
- Reduce hair salon costs (maybe it's time for a new, less expensive hairstyle).
- Buy appliances off season.
- Be aware of service contracts.

- Buy pet food in bulk.
- Shop education expenses.
  - Set up education savings account.
  - Investigate financial-aid opportunities in advance.
  - Apply for all available loans, scholarships, and grants.
- Monitor bank fees; compare financial institutions.

YOUR BOOK OF DREAMS

Many people incorrectly believe that money is the factor that separates successful people from unsuccessful people. However, I believe that a financial plan (in most instances) is the factor that separates successful people from unsuccessful people. In my career as a financial planner, I've observed that individuals with a financial plan usually achieve their goals. Harvey Golub (Chairman of American Express) writes in his introduction to *Money Matters: Your IDS Guide to Financial Planning:* "By having a plan in place you have a much better chance of reaching your goal and coming out ahead—rather than always trying to catch up with your day-to-day expenses." Mr. Golub goes on to say that "achieving your financial dreams can be a reality if you plan now."

Before moving forward to consider the advantages of home ownership, let's see how a financial plan can help you increase your net worth to $200,000. After completing your written financial plan you will have in place your net worth goal, your strategies to achieve your net worth goal, and your specific timetable to achieve your net worth goal.

I believe that financial planning makes all things possible. Furthermore, I believe that a financial plan is your family's book of dreams. It is an outline of your financial dreams and the steps you are going to take to secure those dreams. In the African American community, it is not unusual to see dream books in people's homes, corner stores, and lottery outlets. Nevertheless, the only dream books I ever see help dreams materialize are financial plans.

INVEST IN A HOME

. . . I will walk within my house with a perfect heart.
—Psalms 101:2

There is something about owning a home that makes people feel secure. Maybe it has to do with the idea that you have control over what can and cannot happen in this space. Maybe it is the sense that you are making an investment in your own real property, rather than paying rent to a landlord. Or maybe it is the sense of planting roots in a community. I don't know what it is about home ownership that can stir a person's soul, but I know that many more African Americans wished they could enjoy both the emotional and economic benefits of owning their own residence.

The emotional benefits of home ownership cannot be measured in economic terms. Sheryl Hilliard-Tucker, editor of *Your Company,* a division of *Money* magazine, shared the story of how her in-laws did not purchase their first home until they were in their midfifties. Even then, they didn't believe that they could afford to buy a home. After Sheryl and her husband reviewed the couple's financial situation, they learned that the Tuckers not only had excellent credit but also had more than enough money stashed away for a down payment.

With the emotional support of their children, the older couple soon found and purchased their first home. According to Sheryl, "It was amazing to see the change in attitude when my in-laws became homeowners. They were proud of their sense of accomplishment and new home. Suddenly, they began taking an interest in the neighborhood and even decided that it was time for them to vote. As renters, they didn't believe that they had a right to vote—so they did not vote. What is amazing is that this didn't happen ten years ago, this happened in 1994."

With the support of their children, this older couple was able to become homeowners. Buying a home for the first time can be a challenging experience. There is the down payment to secure, the seller to haggle with, the realtor to work with, the mortgage to find, the closing to complete, and the children and family members to please. It is a tremendous undertaking. It is the biggest financial commitment most families will ever make. In this chapter we will review the basic steps you will need to take in order to purchase your first home.

Let's first review how owning a home can increase your net worth. Historically, the value of real estate appreciates over time. If you select a home carefully and maintain that home, over time you should be able to sell it for more than you paid. Appreciation, coupled with the tax deductibility of mortgage payments, makes home ownership an effective way to increase a family's net worth.

Like many people, I sometimes wish that I had not sold my first home. It was a small two-bedroom row house that I purchased from the city of Wilmington, Delaware. I was also able to get a mortgage from the city and used the money to rehabilitate the house. My mortgage was $200 per month, and the property was worth about $10,000. When I relocated to the Midwest in the mid-1970s, I sold the unit. Twenty years later I found out that small houses in the predominantly African American neighborhood were worth more than $70,000. This is a classic example of how home ownership can increase your family's net worth. If I hadn't invested in other real estate over the years, I would have been at a disadvantage. I believe that if I had the chance to do it all over again, I would have kept that first house just a little longer.

Home ownership can help many African American households increase their net worth. In the plan to increase your net worth to $200,000, about $50,000 to $75,000 of this total may come from the equity you build up in your home over the years. Let's consider for a moment all the money you can pay to rent a home. For example, if your rent equals $500 per month you're paying $6,000 a year. In ten years you will have invested $60,000 in your landlord's real estate. There is no question that your financial well-being might be better served if you had invested that $60,000 in your own property.

The primary issue is whether to invest in your own home or invest in someone else's. Most financial planners will tell you that it is best to own your own home. After seven years it does not make good economic sense to rent.

Now let's suppose that ten years later you want to send your child to college, retire, or buy a business. Can you ask your landlord for a loan or to return some of your rental payments? No. However, if you owned your home, you could use a portion of the equity to finance your endeavor. If you decide to sell your home, you can make money (capital gains, which are profits taken by selling capital assets for more than they cost) but once you leave a rental unit, you take nothing but your belongings.

One of the things I want to impress on you is that smart money always tries to get a better return. When renting, you are not giving your housing dollars a chance to work hard for you. Those dollars don't appreciate nor do they receive any tax benefits. The bottom line is that with home ownership your money works for you and in renting it does not. Hence, home ownership is the smart money move to make with your housing dollars.

Most of America's wealth is tied up in real estate. However, a 1990 report by the U.S. Bureau of the Census states that "More whites realize the dream of owning a home than African Americans. Forty-two percent (42%) of the African American households own their homes, and fifty-six percent (56%) rent; by contrast, sixty-seven percent (67%) of whites own their own homes." Refer to Chart 8, "Home Ownership in the United States" to see who owns and who rents in America.

CHART 8: HOME OWNERSHIP IN THE UNITED STATES

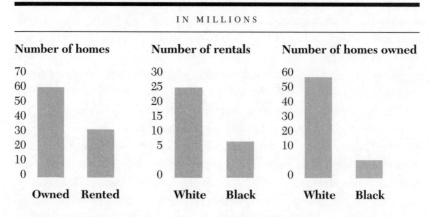

Homeowners include the owners of co-ops and condos. Rental figures do not include the 0.6 million people who have no cash rental agreements.

Reprinted by permission of Black Enterprise magazine.

Other studies have shown that America is still segregated; "redlining" or mortgage discrimination is still alive and well. African Americans are segregated to some degree in all of the thirty major cities with the highest African American population. Furthermore, in her book, *Don't Believe the Hype,* Farai Chideya noted: "In 1989 the Department of Housing and Urban Development (HUD) did a study using 'testers' (individuals who posed as house and apartment seekers)." The study found that whites received a much more favorable treatment:

1. Forty-five percent of the time, rental housing was more available to whites.
2. Thirty-four percent of the time, the white testers found it easier to find a home to buy.
3. Forty-six percent of the time, white individuals got more help in financing the home they wanted to buy.
4. Seventeen percent of the time, white applicants were offered lower rates and better terms on their loans.

The government is cracking down on housing discrimination and racially motivated mortgage lending practices. Unfortunately, it is very difficult to monitor people's attitudes. Many studies have confirmed that many white Americans do not want to live in neighborhoods where more than 25 percent of the residents are African American.

Luckily, African Americans have not let these barriers keep them from pursuing their dreams of owning a home. Our Chart 9, "To Own or Not To Own," indicates that African Americans are willing to take any steps necessary to become homeowners. This chart also shows the differences of opinion African Americans have about the equal access to home ownership. They know the important role home ownership plays in helping a family not only increase its net worth but also maximize the return on its housing money.

Because it is better to buy than rent, no one should let racial barriers deter him or her from buying a home. When house hunting, bear in mind that there are many great neighborhoods to invest in. Second, remember that there are many banks, mortgage companies, and savings and loans willing to give you a mortgage. African American savings and loan institutions have historically provided money to help African American families buy their first homes. In our *Resource Guide* you will find a listing of these institutions.

CHART 9: TO OWN OR NOT TO OWN

**What Price for Home Ownership? Survey Participants Were
Willing to Make These Sacrifices in Order to Own a Home**

	Blacks	Whites	Hispanics
Taking a second job	71%	53%	62%
Placing child in day care	51%	32%	38%
Living farther from work	46%	62%	50%
Tying up savings	37%	41%	44%
Incurring heavy debt	17%	17%	20%

**Barriers to Home Ownership. Survey Participants Faced These
Barriers When Trying to Buy a Home**

	Blacks	Whites	Hispanics
Down payment/ closing costs	66%	47%	59%
Monthly income	59%	39%	54%
Job security	38%	25%	46%
Credit	37%	21%	36%
Discrimination/ social barriers	21%	6%	13%

Reprinted by permission of Black Enterprise *magazine.*

In addition, many governmental and private organizations will help you secure your first home. Many cities have housing departments that sell lots and vacant or abandoned housing units. The Department of Housing and Urban Development (HUD) has local and regional housing counseling centers that will help you determine how much house your family can afford. Furthermore, the national credit counseling centers can also help you clear up credit problems, review your budget, and qualify for a mortgage.

Buying a home is one of the most important ways to boost your wealth. A well-chosen home should appreciate and provide you with a place to live and raise your family. It is a key part of any strategy to increase net worth and an investment that is well worth the time and trouble.

You can deduct the interest on your mortgage payment, as well as local property taxes. In addition, as you pay down your mortgage, you can watch your equity accumulate.

Nevertheless you should remember that maintaining a house can be costly. Most new homeowners will factor in their mortgage payments, insurance premiums, and taxes when researching costs. They know there are one-time expenses involved in buying a house, such as moving, and closing costs, attorney's fees, or mortgage points to pay.

In addition, the ongoing expenses of running a house—the painting, upkeep, repairs, and the like—are often a surprise. In some sections of the country, for instance, new homeowners are expected to buy their own major appliances. If you have not budgeted properly, a wonderful move into a new dream house could turn into a disaster when you find that there is no refrigerator or washing machine.

However, the most daunting obstacle facing many families who are attempting to buy a first home is accumulating the down payment. The good news is that you may not have to accumulate nearly as much as you thought. Thanks to Fannie Mae, you can purchase a home with only a three percent down payment. You'll find out more about that in the section of the this chapter on "Types of Mortgages." Now let's look at ways one can secure a down payment.

Five Ways to Acquire the Down Payment on Your House

1. Earmark a special savings account. You can establish a special savings account for your down payment. To help establish this account, you can use your income tax refund.

2. Earmark your annual bonus. If you know that you will get a bonus at work, save this money in your special house account.

3. Use the cash value of your life insurance program. If you already have a life insurance policy that you can cash in, you might do so. In Chapter 5, we will explain why cash value insurance might not be the best type of insurance for you.

4. Use your tax sheltered funds. If you have a 401(k) plan, Tax Shelter Annuity (TSA), Individual Retirement Account (IRA), or a profit-sharing or stock-ownership plan at your place of employment, consider using these funds for a down payment. Funds such as 401(k) plans and TSAs have special loan privileges for purchasing a house. But you must be careful when using retirement accounts. All have tax penalties for early withdrawals. If you take the money out before age sixty-two, you will be subject to a tax penalty. Consult your financial planner before making this move to see how it will affect your overall plans.

5. Secure gifts from your friends and family. In the past, banks were leery of prospective borrowers who showed up with large amounts of money for a down payment when they had relatively low-paying jobs. This situation was a problem for immigrants from the Caribbean and the Far East, where family members pooled their money to buy homes. However, the rules have loosened considerably, and lenders are willing to accommodate customers who can show that they are putting up some of their own money or that the money is a gift. Bankers want to insure that the borrower is not overextended with another loan.

A friend of mine, used a creative method to acquire the down payment for her first home.

In 1988, my friend accepted her current position and relocated to Missouri. Because she saw this as a long-term move, she also made the decision to invest in a home, and made an offer on a condo in a new development. The asking price was $60,000. She had nowhere near the required deposit and closing costs for the deal, but she did have an extensive collection of art work.

Immediately she had her art collection appraised by a licensed appraiser, took the appraisal, and insured the art for its value—in excess of $60,000.

Then my friend called her mortgage company and inquired about alternative financing. They gave her all the usual options—gifts from parents and so forth—but she raised the option of using her art as collateral for the full loan because she did not have the required down payment and closing costs. They took her offer, she paid the closing costs, and the condo was hers.

When time came to sell the condo last year and purchase a house, the art helped with the sale. The buyer offered her full price on the condo—if she would leave a couple of her paintings!

TYPES OF HOUSING

There are three major types of housing you can buy: the traditional single-family house, the condominium, and the cooperative. Each has its advantages and drawbacks.

SINGLE-FAMILY HOME

For many of us this is the ideal home that we dream about. When you buy a single-family home you will own the home and the land on which it sits. You can borrow against it or sell it when you wish. You are responsible for all costs associated with the house, such as taxes, maintenance, and insurance.

CONDOMINIUM

A condominium unit is one that you own in a multifamily development. It can be an apartment, townhouse, or a stand-alone home. You own the unit you buy, but in addition to the mortgage you pay a monthly maintenance fee to the condominium. Because it is a form of joint ownership, all the owners are responsible if a unit owner in the condominium fails to make monthly payments. There may also be rules in the condominium that govern everything from when you may play a musical instrument to what color drapes or blinds you can put on your windows.

COOPERATIVE

Unlike a single family home or a condominium, when you buy a co-op home, you do not own the property you live in. You are buying shares of stock in a corporation that gives you the right to live in a particular unit. (Cooperatives are usually an apartment building.) In addition to your mortgage, you must also pay a monthly maintenance fee and you are subject to the rules of the cooperative. Because you do not own the actual living space, but only shares of the corporation, mortgage loans for cooperatives are slightly more expensive than for condominiums or single-family homes. Cooperatives are not as popular as condominiums, but they do make up a big part of the housing stock in large cities.

HOW TO CHOOSE A HOME

Property acquired for use as your personal residence obviously has to meet a variety of standards. It should be a good value, be well constructed and well designed, and have appreciation potential. For a personal residence, hire a qualified professional to inspect the premises; you should know exactly what you are getting. The most significant part of buying a house as a personal residence is the "fit" to your lifestyle. Does the property have enough bedrooms, bathrooms, and storage space?

How about proximity to shopping or work? How are the schools? When asked about investing money, the actor Will Rogers once said, "I'm buying real estate; they aren't making any more of it. . . ." Remember that you and your family are unique, as is every single piece of property in the world. Try to fit the two together.

FINDING A GOOD DEAL

We can get a "good deal" in property through a variety of means:

- Inflation
- Below-market purchase
- Selective improvements

In other words, we get a good deal by buying well, making the property increase in value (i.e., improving it), or waiting out the actual effects of inflation. Many of us remember the California real estate market of the 1970s with houses appreciating at 15 percent a year. People became millionaires just by buying and selling houses! However, many experts predict the days of giant gains in real estate are over. In fact, some commentators believe that the baby boomers are moving their way through the market now and that the next generation is insufficient in size and income to purchase the housing units built for boomers. This theory is borne out to some degree on the east coast, where the real estate market is in the doldrums as we go into the late 1990s.

There is an old axiom: *The only person who always gets what he wants in a deal is the seller.* This is true: Sellers don't sell unless they get the desired price or terms. Our strategy in buying is to find a seller who will accept less than something is worth. Look for people in a hurry to sell or who are unaware of all facts or market conditions. Taking the time to analyze your potential home could convince the seller to take a lower price.

LOCATION

Question: What are the three most important things in real estate? Answer: LOCATION, LOCATION, LOCATION. You need to check on the following:

1. General Appearance

What is the general appearance of the house, the block or neighborhood, the community, and the surrounding communities?

2. Demographics

Demographics are the statistics of the community. Family income, family size, the number of new businesses, the number of bankruptcies, school enrollments, and so on.

3. Total Community

Try to get a feel for the total community—its outlook, its people, and its wealth. Consider the following:

- **Growth**

  Are there new commercial structures going up, or are there boarded-up buildings? New schools or school closings?

- **Unemployment**

  Try to determine the local unemployment rate. Real estate values tend to tie in to unemployment rates.

- **Income**

  What is the per capita income?

- **Average resident?**

  What is the average resident like? Is he the kind of person you want as a tenant? A neighbor? A prospective buyer?

- **Number of businesses**

  Is there only one business or industry in the area? Reliance on one employer can be devastating to real estate values if the employer pulls out.

  Analyzing these factors will give you a community profile. This profile will determine whether you want to meet the seller's price.

4. Competition

How much competition is there for whatever type of property you are buying?

DETERMINE THE CONDITION

The condition of the property is one of the most important factors in determining the value of the property. The ideal situation would be to find a great house that is undervalued. This, unfortunately, rarely happens, so you must look for reasons why the seller's price and your buying price are different. For example, while the seller thinks the property is a great deal, you must remind them that the property needs $15,000 worth of repairs.

An objective way to determine the condition of a residence is to have the house inspected. Always get a professional inspection on any property you are fully prepared to buy. However, you can do your own inspection by looking at the structure carefully. Use the following checklist.

1. Design
What is the overall design of the property? Is the style and size consistent with the neighborhood?

2. Layout
What is the layout of the house (floorplan)? Is it convenient, or is the bathroom on the other side of the kitchen?

3. Potential problems
Are there any obvious structural problems? Can you see major items the need repairs? Look at the following:

- **Roofs**
  Does the ridgeline (top edge) sag?
- **Wood Siding**
  Is it straight, or warped? Need paint?
- **Paint Blister**
  Is the paint bubbling?
- **Nail Pops**
  A nail pop is when the head of the nail protrudes from the wood siding or wall. It is also an indication of excess moisture in the wood.

4. Overall appearance
What is the overall appearance of the property? Is it messy, with an unkept lawn, and junk everywhere?

5. Kitchen
The kitchen is one of the most important selling points of a house. Look carefully at the kitchen with the eye of who will use it.

- **a. Size**
  Generally, the bigger the better. Kitchens are one of the most-used rooms in the house.
- **b. Work layout**
  The distance between the sink, stove, and refrigerator should be points of a triangle so the user does not have to walk fifteen feet to the refrigerator.
- **c. Cabinet space**
  Look for lots of cabinets, with good organization.

6. Bathroom

Look at the fixtures: old or new? Look for leaks in the plumbing. Run the water: Does rust come out? Is the pressure good?

7. Foundation

Check the foundation thoroughly. Look out for:

- **Dry rot**

  When the wood is soft and crumbly, without any exterior signs of moisture.
- **Termite shields**

  In humid climates, a metal termite shield should be installed. Look for telltale termite signs: small piles of sawdust near pinholes.

8. Drainage

Check the property's drainage. Feel the soil near the house: wet, soggy?

9. Roof

Look at the roofline and drain troughs.

- **a. Number**

  Look at the edge of the roof: how many layers do you see? Three is the suggested maximum number of recoverings for asphalt or fiberglass.
- **b. Bubbles**

  Roof bubbles indicate water in the underlying boards.
- **c. Age**

  Determine the age of the roof, if possible.

10. Basement

You are looking to avert an expensive waterproofing job on the basement. Scaling, or liming, is a white foamy-looking coating on cement walls that usually indicates water or moisture in the basement. Other surefire signs:

- **a. Water damage**

  Look for damage to items in the basement—furniture, the water heater, and the furnace. Cardboard cartons will show sign of moisture.
- **b. Dampness**

  Overall dampness in the basement is indicated by humidity on overhead pipes. A dripping sound usually indicates some groundwater or seepage.

11. Walls

Look for buckles, waves, foundation shift cracks, and ceiling wet spots.

12. Plumbing

Check the pressure at all taps. Look for drips and drainage problems under all sinks. The material of pipes is also important:

a. Iron or copper

Iron pipe will scale and eventually close up. It is heavy and not preferred. Copper does not corrode, provides an integrated sealed system, and will last longer.

b. Check taps

Poor pressure is an indication of an obstruction or excessive scaling.

13. Electrical

Check the overall appearance of the wiring, going into the basement. Take a switch plate off and look at the wiring: old or new? Paper insulation or plastic?

a. Fuse box

Are there wires or conduits running into the box? Are the fuses old? Are the wire runs labeled?

b. Number of outlets

Check rooms for sufficient outlets.

c. Breakers or fuses

In general, breakers (circuit breakers) are preferred over fuses. Breakers provide more safety at less operational cost, and are simpler to reset.

14. Heating System

Get copies of the last year's heating bills (get both the gas and electric bills). Also check:

a. Type

Is this a gas-forced air (preferred), gas gravity (expensive to operate), oil-forced air (smelly and expensive), electric (usually more expensive to operate), boiler (cheaper, depending on the kind, but very expensive to repair).

b. Age

Check the age of the furnace.

c. Condition

Is the furnace clean, is the area around it clean?

15. Insulation

Check the ceiling for insulation and the basement at the joists.

Your goal is to buy a house in decent condition for a good price and not pay for any unknown defects. If you find a defect, price out the repair, decide if the place is still worth having or how much to knock off your offer. Then, if you and the seller can't agree on terms, you can walk away knowing you made a fair offer.

WAYS TO PURCHASE A HOME

There are four ways to buy a house. *Paying cash* is the simplest and in many ways the best. Buying your dream home without a mortgage will save you thousands of dollars in the long term, because you are not paying for the use of someone else's money. Depending on the interest rate on your mortgage, over the life of a thirty-year mortgage, you can easily end up paying more than double the cost of the house itself. Unfortunately, paying cash is an option closed to most of us.

If you are lucky, you may find an owner who will allow you to *assume the mortgage.* That means that after you make a down payment, you simply keep paying the existing mortgage. Assumable mortgages are hard to find because most lenders insert clauses in their mortgages that require mortgage holders to pay the balance in full when the property is sold.

Finding an assumable mortgage can be a great bargain, however, since many of them were written when mortgage rates were low. The drawback, however, is that sellers know this. They will often raise their price because they know they are sitting on a very inexpensive mortgage.

At times the seller will finance the purchase in what is called a *purchase money mortgage* or a *land contract.* In some areas of the country these types of loans are fairly common. The difference between them is simple. In a purchase money mortgage you hold the title to your house. In a land contract you do not hold title to the property. The title reverts to you only when you have fully paid off the mortgage.

Some sellers want to hold the mortgage themselves, because they want a steady stream of income or do not need a lump sum to buy another house. However, seller financing can be a warning signal if it is the only kind of financing available to buy a house. It can mean that lending institutions have so little faith in a neighborhood that they are unwilling to make a mortgage. The lenders may believe that homes will not appreciate and that you will not be able to get your money back when you sell the house. That isn't always the case, but consider the fact that if institutional lenders aren't willing to invest in a neighborhood, maybe you shouldn't invest there either.

While you should always have an attorney execute the purchase of your home, it is even more important to have legal advice with the land contract, which can be a relatively complicated transaction. There may be provisions that restrict the length of the contract, which means that you would have to refinance the house after a certain period of time, usually three to five years.

You will also have to make sure that the deed is in escrow, that is, held by a third party, so that when the terms of the contract are met and you are ready to take the title, you do not have to worry about whether the seller or lender is bankrupt, dead, or otherwise difficult to locate. Your attorney will also help you decide how to handle taxes and insurance or the intricacies of buying under an existing land contract.

Most likely, however, you will borrow the money for your house from a commercial bank, a mortgage banker, a thrift, or a credit union. You'll usually find your mortgage either through the broker who helps you find your house or through the lending institution. Many lenders will now precertify or prequalify your loan, meaning that you will be able to shop for a house knowing exactly how much you will be able to borrow. I recommend doing this. Not every lender offers prequalification, but as the competition for making mortgages becomes fiercer, more lenders are offering this service. They will lock in an interest rate for your mortgage, tell you how much they will lend you, and give you a date by which you must complete the transaction.

You can also purchase your house the old-fashioned way: Find the house first and the mortgage later. Many of us follow that path and there is nothing wrong with it, if you know what to expect. So let's go through the home-purchase process step-by-step, assuming you have already found the house you want.

OFFER STRATEGIES

NEGOTIATING YOUR PRICE

DO YOUR HOMEWORK.
Do your homework on value early in the process. Is the price comparable to others, has it met the market, cost, and income tests? Are we hitting at the right price, or are we too high? Recent house sales are frequently listed in the local newspaper. Home sales are also recorded in county court houses.

Sellers usually price their property at a price higher whan that they really desire. Why? Because they have selling costs, broker's commissions, and so on. Also, usually sellers would like to get more than they really are looking for; that's business, isn't it? Depending on the market, a good offer strategy is to undercut the seller's asking price.

NORMAL MARKET
In a normal market homes sell within thirty to ninety days but not to the first or second lookers. In a normal market, your first-round offer should be 10 to 15 percent under asking price. This is because in a normal market, sellers tend to price about 10 to 15 percent over their perception of actual value.

HOT MARKET
In a hot market properties are gobbled up quickly. Smart buyers avoid hot markets, trying instead to be on the selling end. In a hot market, time is king. If you find a good deal and want it, you will usually have to offer fast and at the asking price. Many people are under the misconception that sellers have to take the first offer that comes in. This is untrue. A seller may consider many offers. To get your offer through in a hot market, when many offers are being considered, yours must be on the money.

An interesting strategy for getting the seller's attention in a hot market is to offer over the listed price. Your offer will certainly stand out. Remember, though, that you must be sure that the seller has mispriced the property because you are willing to give even more than the seller is asking.

DISTRESSED SELLER

The distressed seller is the prize of the clever real estate buyer. "Distressed" means the seller has to sell, because of their employment situation, divorce, bankruptcy, death in the family, or other pressing situation. A distressed seller will usually accept offers substantially below market value. A rule of thumb with distress sales is to make an initial offer, usually cash, at 25 to 40 percent under the asking price. Depending on the conditions and the reason for the distress, you can sometimes make the deal.

Finding Distressed Sellers Finding the prize requires some detective work. Real estate agents may assist you in locating distressed sellers, but agents are not really good sources. First, if it's a great deal, the real estate agent may grab it first. Second, if the seller has to deal with the agent, the seller has to pay a commission. Here are some avenues for hunting the distressed seller.

- **Foreclosures**
Check banks, mortgage companies, and other financial institutions for foreclosures. When a bank forecloses on a property, it is eager to get the property off its books. Since the bank has only the amount of the loan plus foreclosure costs invested in the property, it will usually sell it at below market price. Sometimes, the deal also includes financing. Contact the foreclosure department of the mortgage lending branch of local banks.

- **Estates**
Estates are public record. If you are familiar with an area, check periodically at the probate court for a record of properties being sold through estates. People sometimes die without a will or close heirs. In that case, the property is usually sold either by public sale or by auction.

- **Tax Sales**
Properties are also foreclosed through failure to pay property or income taxes. In these cases, a buyer can purchase property at auction for the back taxes.

- **Long Markets**
When property has been on the market a long time, the sellers will usually fall into one of two categories: They are holding out for their

price, no matter how long it takes, or they are ready to deal because they haven't gotten any offers. The second category is ripe for the low-ball offer.

• Transfers

Many large corporations help their employees relocate and sometimes buy the home of a displaced employee. Local companies may be another source of potential good buys.

• HUD/FHA Foreclosures

The federal government periodically sells houses it has repossessed on federal loans. Sometimes, these properties are significantly underpriced. However, their condition may be poor. To find a real deal, always inspect the property first.

GET COMPARABLES

Ask a helpful real estate person or use a multiple listing book to get comparable home and selling prices in the neighborhood. Compare these prices to the listing price. What are other similar properties selling for? How far over or under market is the property?

Now we know how to make an offer, negotiate earnest money, negotiate the price of the home in hot and cold real estate markets, and how to find distressed real estate property. Now let us see what other steps you need to make to secure your dream home.

SUBJECT-TO-FINANCING CLAUSE

If you are obtaining financing, make sure your offer contains a "subject to the obtaining of mortgage" clause. This clause is standard in most purchase offers. Set a reasonable time frame for applying for the mortgage. You don't want to lose your earnest money (see below) if the financing falls through.

When you put in the subject-to-financing clause, make sure you give yourself some room to work. Make it subject to a 5 percent-down mortgage or a 10 percent-down mortgage. You can always make a larger down payment if you desire. Some realtors suggest that you use the subject-to-mortgage clause as a "safety valve" to get out of a deal. If you drag your feet or do not cooperate with the lender, the bank will probably reject the mortgage. You can then get out of the deal and get your earnest money back.

SUBJECT-TO-INSPECTION CLAUSE

Always have the purchase conditioned on the completion of a satisfactory inspection. Too often, properties have significant defects that go unnoticed by the buyer. These defects can cost thousands of dollars in repairs, and can compromise the value of the offer.

ADVICE-OF-COUNSEL CLAUSE

Put a "subject-to-advice-of-counsel" clause in all offers. Set a reasonable time limit for notice. This clause is the way for a buyer to escape an offer that was rashly made or if the buyer rapidly finds a better deal. The subject-to-council clause is an excellent mechanism to back out of deals that lose their appeal after the emotions of the moment wear off.

WEAKNESS LIST

The weakness list is a list of the things you don't like about the property. It's too small, it's in a bad neighborhood, it's too far from businesses, it's too close to the highway. Try to highlight every negative. As a buyer, you should point out every little thing that is objectionable as a reason not to pay what the sellers are asking. Remember that sellers usually ask more than their desired price for the property, and your weakness list is a tool to justify a price reduction.

The weakness list is your justification for a lower price. Your attitude should be: The place is okay, but here is why it isn't worth what you say it is.

EARNEST MONEY

Earnest money is the deposit used to "seal" the offer. Earnest money is required under contract law to provide adequate consideration for the deal. The issue of earnest money becomes important to the seller since it shows the buyer's sincerity and financial strength. From the buyer's standpoint, earnest money funds part of the deal, but also ties up your funds for a period of time in an escrow account.

Earnest money shows financial strength and buyer commitment. Consider a purchase of an $80,000 house. If the buyer puts a $500 deposit down, it says that the buyer can walk away and lose only $500. In addition, at the crucial time of making the offer, a small deposit raises doubts in the seller's mind. Earnest money of 4 to 5 percent of the offered price (that translates to $3,200 to $4,000 for an $80,000 offer) is an indication that the buyer is serious.

One solution is the two-parts earnest money approach: Use $500 as the offer's earnest deposit, with the clause, "Upon acceptance, buyer will immediately deposit an additional $2,500 with the broker." This keeps more of your funds out of the broker's escrow account and still provides the advantages of making large earnest money deposits.

If you use a check for earnest money, you have a record of the transaction. Perhaps you can post date the check so the funds remain in your account longer.

Sometimes, a seller or broker will take a promissory note instead of a check for the earnest money deposit. This ties up none of your funds and still allows you to tie up the property. See if the seller will accept a note as a deposit.

DON'T LOSE YOUR COOL

Purchasing a home is a commercial transaction. If a buyer counters with the original selling price, this means that she or he doesn't want to negotiate. Remember, you have the money, and there are plenty of other properties. Don't lose your cool and say "take or leave it." Explain your desire to have the property, show why you think its value is less than the listed price, and submit your offer. If the seller rejects your final offer, talk with your feet by walking away.

SEVEN TIPS ON WORKING WITH THE SELLER'S BROKER

When buying a home listed with a real estate broker, you should always remember this important rule: The broker works for the seller, not the buyer. Here are seven tips that will help you negotiate with a seller's broker.

1. Keep your best offer to yourself.

Don't say how high or low you will go. You are dealing with an agent of the seller who has a responsibility to the seller. If you say to the broker, "Well, let's see if they take X," you are basically telling the seller you will go as high as that price. You don't want to tip your hand on what you will or will not do. Brokers are very keen on picking up signals from the buyer. They will ask what you think, how you like the property, what you would do with x, y, or z.

2. Make sure that the broker knows you are motivated.
Make sure the broker understands that you are an interested buyer and that it is in the interest of the broker to help you get together with the seller.

3. Remind the broker that you have the money.
The golden rule to some is, "He who has the gold makes the rules." Although some sellers feel they play the most important part in the deal, remember who has the money. Make sure the broker understands this, too. Politely point out that the deal requires a buyer.

4. Be honest.
Don't misrepresent yourself. Don't make claims for things that aren't true, for example, having a larger down payment or pre-approved mortgage limit. Such tactics tend to backfire.

5. Be patient.
Real estate deals are big business. Don't expect everything to happen at once. Be patient with brokers; their pay is based on the deal, too. If things are moving slowly, an occasional call doesn't hurt.

6. Watch out for generalizations.
Beware of the "the roof is like new". Remember to get the seller's representations in writing. Oral representations, or what the seller says, are not legally binding. The law allows so-called 'salesman's puff,' which are claims of the great value of property.

7. Be firm, considerate, and businesslike.
You want real estate to help increase your net worth. Be firm in your convictions. If the broker says, "They will never take this offer," firmly tell the broker it is his or her job to submit your offer or you will submit it yourself. Don't make unreasonable demands on the broker and try not to waste their time. Try to get your inspections and post offer viewings done at one time. Lastly, be professional; you may buy more properties in the future, so make friends and maintain a credible business reputation. It will pay off.

THREE NEGOTIATING TIPS

1. Round One—Find weaknesses, fix your offer, say nothing to the broker until you make your offer.
Guard your hand and say nothing about price until you make the offer. You have then made a formal statement about your opinion of the house's value.

2. Round Two—Save some ammo for the second round.
Many offers are countered. Save a weakness or two for the second round, your counter counteroffer. Again, keep your maximum buying price to yourself.

3. Round Three—As a smart buyer you should be low-balling the price.
The economy is slow and you may need the money. You will need money for costly repairs. The neighborhood school is not very good, and you will need money to send your kids to private schools. The taxes are too high. Make a list to share with the real estate agent for offering a lower price. After agreeing on the offering price you are only halfway through the process. Now you must secure a mortgage for your new home.

SECURING A MORTGAGE

In 1992, the Federal Reserve Bank of Boston completed a massive survey of mortgage applicants by race that showed, in essence, that African American borrowers are turned down for mortgages at a greater rate than white borrowers and that when all factors were considered, racism appeared to be a significant reason why. Even today, there are bankers and lenders who disagree with the way the federal study was conducted and its conclusions.

But for you, the news is good. That study, as well as general realization on the part of many bankers and the federal government that increasing home ownership is good both for individuals and for neighborhoods, has prompted bankers to loosen up a little bit. Specifically, it means that many banks and mortgage companies are now making mortgages that require smaller down payments, as long as borrowers meet certain qualifications.

The Federal National Mortgage Association (Fannie Mae) is an organization that has taken the lead in making more mortgages available. Fannie Mae buys mortgages from banks thus allowing banks to use the money they make selling the mortgage to make even more mortgages, thereby increasing the rate of home ownership around the country. When Fannie Mae, which is the largest mortgage maker in the country, lays down the law about what types of mortgages it will buy, bankers all over the country listen.

In order to boost home ownership, especially among minority borrowers, Fannie Mae has told participating banks that it will buy mortgages where the borrowers have put down as little as 3 or 5 percent, instead of the typical 29 percent. Though loans with down payments this low are still relatively new, lenders say that people who hold them don't default in much greater numbers than those with any other type of mortgage.

You will have to work to find these loans. They are available through the banks and lenders, not directly from Fannie Mae, and may not be widely advertised; you will have to ask your real estate broker or banker about them. You can also call Fannie Mae at a toll-free number for the names of the banks in your part of the country that make these loans. Fannie Mae will also send you a *free* booklet on home ownership.

These 3- or 5-percent-down mortgages are available only to prospective homeowners who earn 115 percent of the median family income in their particular region. There are some exceptions for high-cost cities such as San Francisco or New York, but these mortgages are clearly aimed at moderate-income home buyers who, depending on what area of the country they live in may have household incomes of roughly $40,000 a year.

Even without Fannie Mae prodding lenders to make mortgages more affordable, there are still reasons why buying a home is easier than you may think. In 1994, interest rates climbed sharply, making home loans more expensive. As a result, mortgage lenders all over the country were scrambling for clients.

They began making mortgages available to people whose credit records were less than perfect. While these loans will be more expensive than conventional mortgages, the difference is that two or three years ago, mortgages to consumers with "bruised credit," as bankers call it, would not have been available at all.

Banks are simplifying the way borrowers can get information about mortgages by installing consumer hotlines and sending their officers out to see you, instead of having you come into bank.

Banks are also offering mortgages in a variety of maturities and payment terms. Instead of a thirty-year-fixed mortgage, you can shop for mortgages that are fifteen years long, paid twice a month, or with interest rates that adjust after one, three, or five years.

Lenders are keenly aware of government pressure to avoid prejudicial lending, commonly known as redlining. The federal law explicitly states that lenders must make credit available in the communities in which they operate and cannot take deposits in African American neighborhoods without making loans available. In a recent case in Maryland, a bank was punished for not making loans in neighboring, largely African American Washington, D.C., even though it did not have a branch there.

As a result of this pressure, bank officers are more likely now than ever before to take a second look at a mortgage application that was once rejected. It means that banks may offer some basic forms of financial counseling to loan applicants. It means, in short, that banks are more inclined to look for a way to give you a mortgage than they are to look for a reason to turn you down.

The following chart shows the approximate gross income ratios banks require to give a mortgage. For example, if your income is $4,000 per month and rates are 10 percent, you could qualify for a $113,951 mortgage.

CHART 10: MAXIMUM MORTGAGE AMOUNT
30 Year

Monthly Gross Income	Current Mortgage Rates				
	8.0%	9.0%	10.0%	11.0%	12.0%
2000	68,142	62,141	56,975	52,503	48,609
2500	85,177	77,676	71,219	65,629	60,761
3000	102,213	93,211	85,463	78,755	72,914
3500	119,248	108,747	99,707	91,881	85,066
4000	136,283	124,282	113,951	105,006	97,218
4500	153,319	139,817	128,195	118,132	109,371
5000	170,354	155,352	142,439	131,258	121,523

When going for the preliminary visit to the banker, it is important to demonstrate your ability to repay the mortgage loan. The essence here is to be businesslike and organized.

Dress like the banker: wear a suit, look professional, shine your shoes, look neat. Bankers like to feel comfortable with the people they loan thousands of dollars to. Well-dressed professionals feel comfortable around other well-dressed professionals.

Thank the banker for his or her time. Tell the banker how much you need, how you intend to repay the loan, what you are buying, and other pertinent details.

Have your facts on the property ready. Keep a file with the purchase agreement, maybe a picture of the property, your homework on the property, etc. Leave a copy of the documents with the banker and how much money you want to borrow.

These steps will help you negotiate the best mortgage deal.

1. Relate any new information or favorable aspects of the property as an investment to the banker or broker.
2. State your request completely.
3. Add incentives. Explain what you will do to make the deal happen, such as pay points or legal fees.
4. Use any personal pull (deposits) tactfully, especially if you are a long-term customer with the bank.
5. Refer to other, better terms from other lenders.
6. Summarize the request and points in your favor clearly and accurately.
7. Thank the officer for her or his time and effort on your behalf.

WRITTEN APPLICATION

After the preliminary visit, you will usually pay a fee and make a written application.

Banks and lending institutions compete for mortgage dollars. Always shop the rates, either by reading the local newspaper or by calling various banks. You don't want to be paying multiple application fees without a reason. Many realtors know the best banks or mortgage brokers for your particular needs.

When you make written application, you will fill out a personal financial statement (a listing of assets and liabilities), sign verifications of deposits and employment, and agree to pay for a survey and appraisal of the property. The bank will also want a credit report. A great deal of this information can be found in your wealth-building financial plan.

HOW HOME OWNERSHIP CAN
INCREASE YOUR NET WORTH

Having reviewed the basic steps to buying a home, let's consider again how you can use your home ownership to increase your net worth. Let's assume that the home you purchase appreciates in value at least 3 percent a year (the rate of inflation). At this rate, your home value will increase by 15 percent in five years and 30 percent in ten years. Therefore, if you purchase a $50,000 home with a $5,000 down payment and a $45,000 mortgage in five years the home will be valued at $57,500 and in ten years at $65,000.

During this five- to ten-year period, you have reduced the amount of your mortgage (which is tax deductible). So let's see what the result would be in ten years if you decided to sell the property for a new one.

Sale Price	$65,000	(fair market value)
Mortgage	40,000	(payoff)
Balance	$25,000	(equity)

This will give you enough money to meet a 15 to 20 percent down payment on a $100,000 home and have money for closing costs. Now you'll repeat the cycle of the 3 percent added value, only on a $100,000 home. In five years, at 3 percent, it will be worth $115,000. In ten years, $130,000.

Your aim is to be prepared to sell your first home in seven to ten years. This will give you enough time to pay down your mortgage and experience some appreciation in the value of your property allowing you to pay off other bills and increase your family's income. This strategy may allow you to double the amount you pay for your second home. For example, if your first home cost $50,000, then your second home should be in the range of $100,000.

The major difference in buying your second home is that you should not have to worry about the down payment because it will come from the equity you built up in your first home. While your first down payment might have come from savings, tax returns, or friends, the second down payment will come from your existing equity.

Due to the greater cost, you will probably see more appreciation in the value of your second home than you saw in your first home. This is good, because in another ten to fifteen years you may want to use this equity for your retirement.

As you can see, owning a home is a great way to maximize the return on the dollars your family spends on housing. It is also a great way to help increase your family's net worth. Any way you look at it, owning a home, a condominium, or a co-op is a smart money move!

INVEST IN THE STOCK MARKET

A feast is made for laughter, and wine maketh
merry; but money answereth all things.
> —Ecclesiastes 10:19

Some people may wonder why a book written to help African American households increase their net worth has a chapter on investing in the stock market. These skeptics would probably say that hardworking families earning $20,000 to $50,000 annually should not be encouraged to invest in the stock market. To these naysayers I have but one reply, "Nonsense!"

Every year, millions of Americans increase their wealth substantially because they own stocks and securities. In the May 1, 1995, issue of Newsweek magazine, a story entitled "A Rising Tide Lifts the Yachts" explained how various investments help to widen the wealth gap between rich and poor Americans. The article pointed out that "The United States leads the industrialized world in its inequality of incomes."

Sharing the results of a study by economist Edward Wolff of New York University, the article stated: "The wealth of the richest 1% of U.S. households climbed from 20% of all stocks, bonds, savings accounts, home equity and other private assets in the mid-1970's to 35.7% in 1989. The haves have more now than at any time since 1929."

I don't remember reading in the U.S. Constitution that only affluent Americans should own appreciating assets. Furthermore, unless we begin to help the average American, including the African American, household, invest wisely in such assets, we will always have a vast amount of appreciating assets controlled by a small number of well-to-do Americans.

While it appears that diversity and affirmative action are no longer in vogue, we must note that neither were ever in vogue in America's financial community. In this vast sector of our economy, the term diversification has often been viewed as a prudent way to allocate financial assets. Diversity in the financial world has rarely been associated with inviting new investors from various cultures to increase their ownership of stocks and bonds.

Hence, we can understand why a Bureau of Census report states that while the average white household owns $3,420 in stock mutual funds, the average African American households owns $115 in these investments. Furthermore, while the average white household shows interest earnings of $7,308 a year, African American households interest earnings are only $872 annually. The lack of diversity among owners of financial assets becomes more alarming when you realize that the average investor in the stock market invests $20,000.

Given such economic facts, we can understand why the American investment community has given little attention to marketing to African American investors, hiring African American financial professionals, or supporting the development of African American investment companies, money managers, and publicly traded companies.

Most of the major financial and investment companies have long taken the stand that it is a waste of time to market to African American investors. Therefore, most of their advertising dollars target the affluent market, inviting its members to share the fruits of the American dream and corporate dividends while ignoring the rest of America, particularly those consumers or would be investors who earn less than $50,000 annually.

This strategy is sad because these companies are ignoring the majority of Americans and the underutilized financial resources of ethnic communities—like the $325 billion income pool of African Americans.

It also reinforces the notion that the stock market and its wealth building opportunities are the exclusive domain of the rich. The reality is that the stock market is for all investors who, according to Benjamin Graham, "expect a reasonable return on their investments without being exposed to much risk." Mr. Graham, who many consider the father of modern-day stock analyses, once stated that "An investor is one who after careful analyses expects an investment operation to promise safety of principal and an adequate return."

When referring to the investor, Mr. Graham gives no preferential treatment to anyone concerning race, gender, or age, nor should he. If there is one thing we know about financial investments (such as stocks and bonds), it is that they are void of prejudice. These investments perform their stated task regardless of their owner's gender, race, or age.

Nevertheless, it appears that the only time Wall Street wants to recognize dissimilarities is when the financial market experiences a turn for the worst. Then all of a sudden, we hear about "a black day on Wall Street" or "Black Monday." Perhaps in the future Wall Street professionals and journalists will stop using such injurious terms to define a correction or downturn in the financial market—such statements are just politically incorrect, especially given the fact that the African American community has so little invested in the stock market and has virtually nothing to do with its day-to-day function. Currently, there are only four African American–owned mutual fund companies, six African American–owned publicly traded companies, and less than a handful of African American–owned brokerage houses and money management firms with more than $1 billion under management.

WHY AFRICAN AMERICANS SHOULD INVEST IN STOCKS

There are numerous reasons why we have not routinely invested in the stock market. As a financial planner, I learned three of the chief reasons:

1. African Americans did not feel that they had enough money to invest.
2. African Americans were not aware of their investment options.
3. African Americans were too busy trying to survive to think about investing in the stock market.

While all of the reasons are valid, none justifies losing the wealth-building benefits of one of the world's greatest wealth-building tools—shares in growing companies. In many ways owning stocks in a growing company offers the same type of rewards as being an entrepreneur. The basic difference is that instead of running the business, you are an investor in the business. Nevertheless, as an investor you share the company's fortunes—good or bad.

One man I know in Detroit has spent most of his adult life as an investor. He says that he would rather let his money work for him than work for his money.

"I started out investing pennies here and there, and it kept adding up. Before I knew it, I was giving myself more than I was spending.

Investments are where the money is. We're talking about an area that supplies all the money for industry and also for the federal government. It's a tool that is necessary to general wealth. I started out investing in stocks; Chrysler is one that I've always had. Later on, I bought oil stocks, stocks in Asian companies, now I buy mainly telecommunications companies."

Eventually, his fortune grew to $300,000 in real estate and more than half a million in cash. My friend says that luck has nothing to do with it. He says, a financially successful person has money on his mind—all the time.

Chart 11, "Twenty Years of Investment Performance," illustrates that over the long term stocks are the best place to invest your money. The average return is 12 percent compounded annually. This return is better than any other investment option, and it helps preserve the purchasing power of your earnings.

Chart 12, "Reduction of Risk Over Time," illustrates that the best way to reduce your risk in the stock market is to invest for a period of ten years or more. It appears that the longer you invest in the market, the greater your chances to earn a profit of 12 percent compounded annually.

Given African Americans' small ownership of stock investments, few of our households will ever fully benefit from this high return, especially since many African American investors like to invest in sure things rather than stocks of companies. However, evidence of their preference for low-risk investments can be found in the fact that they earn $800 annually in interest.

Many African American households try to avoid investment risk by investing their money in "sure things" like bank certificates of deposits (CDs), fixed retirement accounts, and life insurance cash values. Unbeknownst to these investors, the money they deposit at these financial institutions is ultimately invested into the stock market. Most banks, pension plans, and insurance companies invest a large portion of their assets in the stock market. They do so to earn a 12 percent return. These shrewd financial organizations then credit the sure-thing savings account with 4 percent annual interest and keep the additional interest (8 percent) as profit.

CHART 11: TWENTY YEARS OF INVESTMENT PERFORMANCE, 1973–1993

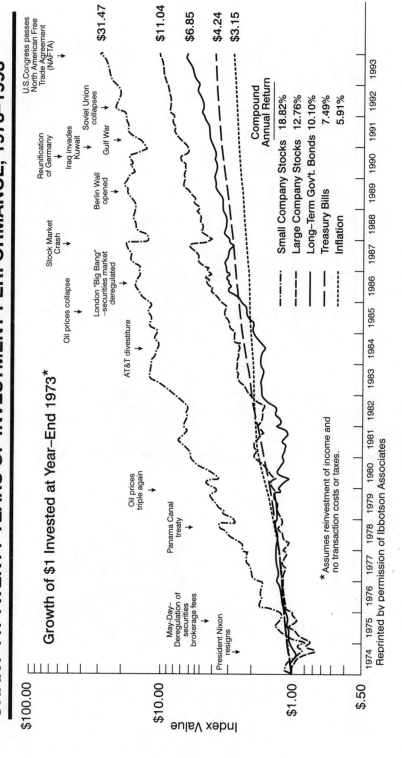

Growth of $1 Invested at Year–End 1973*

President Nixon resigns

May–Day– Deregulation of securities brokerage fees

Panama Canal treaty

Oil prices triple again

AT&T divestiture

Oil prices collapse

London "Big Bang" –securities market deregulated

Stock Market Crash

Berlin Wall opened

Reunification of Germany

Iraq invades Kuwait

Gulf War

Soviet Union collapses

U.S.Congress passes North American Free Trade Agreement (NAFTA)

$31.47

$11.04

$6.85

$4.24

$3.15

	Compound Annual Return
Small Company Stocks	18.82%
Large Company Stocks	12.76%
Long–Term Govt. Bonds	10.10%
Treasury Bills	7.49%
Inflation	5.91%

* Assumes reinvestment of income and no transaction costs or taxes.

Index Value

$100.00

$10.00

$1.00

$.50

1974 1975 1976 1977 1978 1979 1980 1981 1982 1983 1984 1985 1986 1987 1988 1989 1990 1991 1992 1993

Reprinted by permission of Ibbotson Associates

CHART 12: REDUCTION OF RISK OVER TIME, 1926–1993

Each bar shows the range of compound average
annual returns for the specified holding periods

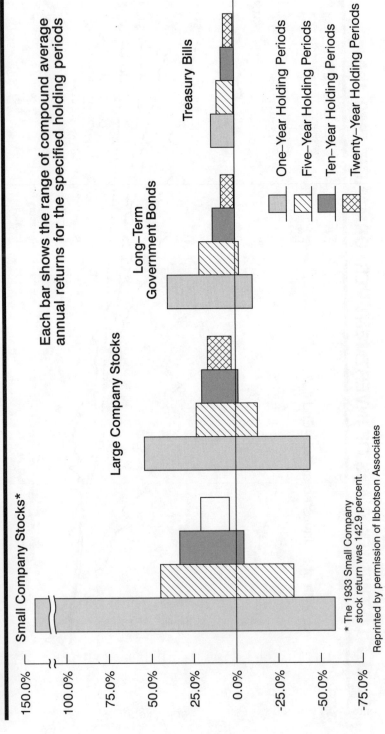

Small Company Stocks*

Large Company Stocks

Long–Term
Government Bonds

Treasury Bills

One–Year Holding Periods

Five–Year Holding Periods

Ten–Year Holding Periods

Twenty–Year Holding Periods

150.0%

100.0%

75.0%

50.0%

25.0%

0.0%

-25.0%

-50.0%

-75.0%

* The 1933 Small Company
stock return was 142.9 percent.

Reprinted by permission of Ibbotson Associates

Now, let's take a closer look at the safe investments. We'll assume that you've placed $5,000 into a savings account at your bank, which earns 2 percent interest. After a twelve-month period, your investment's value will be $5,100. Now, we must subtract at least 20 percent for taxes (the lowest tax bracket is 20 percent); therefore, your after-tax return is $5,080.

In addition we must adjust for inflation or the cost of living expense, that is, the annual increase in the price of certain goods and services. These goods and services are vital to living: food, housing, gasoline, transportation, etc. Chart 13, "Impact of Inflation," shows that over the last ten years the inflation rate in the United States has averaged 3.5 percent. After making an inflation adjustment, your $5,000 investment is valued at $4,903. That's right, your safe investment lost almost $100 of its purchasing power. A major point is that all investments are subject to inflation risk—including the sure thing.

Ten years from now your safe $5,000 investment might buy only $3,500 worth of food. Why? Because in ten years inflation will reduce your investment by 30 percent (approximately 3 percent annually for the next ten years).

It is now easy for you to understand why many financial planners believe that you should always try to maximize the return on your investment. By doing so, you have a greater chance of making more money, and more importantly, of protecting your future earning power. Historically, the stock market has been one of the best investments to increase wealth and protect your income from inflation.

Theodore J. Miller drives this point home in his book *Invest Your Way to Wealth*. Regarding stock ownership, Mr. Miller writes that "If it's wealth you want, look to the stock market. No other investment available to intelligent amateurs with average resources, average willingness to take risks and limited time to spend on active management delivers as well as stocks over the long run. Not real estate. Not bonds. And certainly not savings accounts. . . . Stocks aren't the only things that belong in your investment portfolio, but they are the most important."

In this chapter you will learn how to earn 10 to 12 percent on your investment. Furthermore, you will learn how to substantially increase your net worth by investing only a few dollars a month in the stock market.

You will also learn how investing 10 percent of your income ($2,000 to $4,000) a year can help you increase your net worth to $200,000 in ten years. You will be doing this without exposing your initial principal to enormous risk and without using any complicated investments.

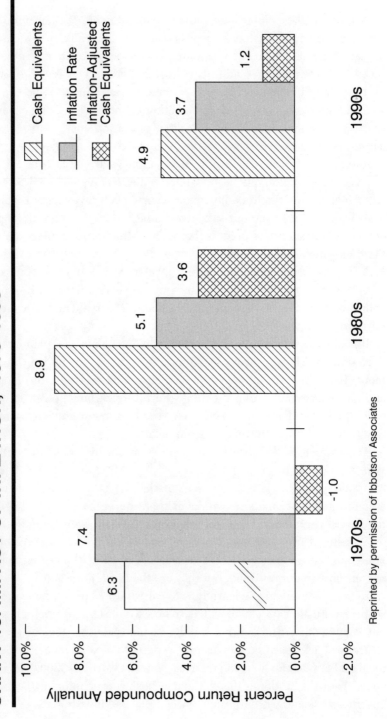

CHART 13: IMPACT OF INFLATION, 1970–1993

Legend:
- Cash Equivalents
- Inflation Rate
- Inflation-Adjusted Cash Equivalents

1970s
- 6.3
- 7.4
- -1.0

1980s
- 8.9
- 5.1
- 3.6

1990s
- 4.9
- 3.7
- 1.2

Percent Return Compounded Annually

Y-axis: 10.0%, 8.0%, 6.0%, 4.0%, 2.0%, 0.0%, -2.0%

Reprinted by permission of Ibbotson Associates

I know it sounds almost impossible, but it is not. You will be primarily using mutual funds, a proven method of wealth accumulation that people have been using for more than seventy-two years. According to the Investment Company Institute, the first mutual fund was created in 1924. Today, there are approximately 5,000 mutual funds in more than twenty categories. You are going to see how to take $25 a week and build a small fortune. But first, let's find out more about financial investments and their ability to increase your net worth.

VARIOUS TYPES OF INVESTMENTS

Before you invest, you must understand your investment goal; then select the type of investment that matches your goal. Of course, no one investment can help you reach all of your financial goals. Ultimately, your financial portfolio will have several investments. Each investment will help you meet a particular financial goal. For example, if you want to accumulate an emergency fund, you probably want an investment that is safe, liquid, and easily accessible. A savings account at the credit union might meet this need.

If you have a long-term goal, you might choose a stock mutual fund. These funds tend to do well in the long run. If on the other hand you were striving for retirement income, you might choose a bond mutual fund. These funds can generate income to supplement your retirement income. Later in this chapter we will create a model portfolio that will guide you in reaching your financial goal. For now, let's review the three basic types of investments.

CASH INVESTMENTS
The money market is the market for short-term liquid investments such as short-term savings accounts, bank certificates (CDs), and treasury bills. Cash investments satisfy the liquidity and safety needs of a portfolio. If you need safety of principal, cash is the investment for you. Cash and other money market investments assure you that the cash you put in will be there later.

INCOME INVESTMENTS
Income investments include government notes and bonds, income mutual funds, bond funds, municipal bonds, corporate bonds, annuities, preferred stocks, government housing funds, and long-term certificates. The

term of income investments is usually longer than one year. This means that most income investments tend to be interest-rate sensitive. In the short run, their value will fluctuate with interest rates, but as they near maturity, they will yield the original rate. Income investments are suited for matching investment goals with similar time lines, like retirement, or purchasing a specific asset. If you plan to purchase a house in five years, a five-year CD is a suitable income investment. Income investments traditionally yield one or more percentage points above money investments.

EQUITY INVESTMENTS

Equity investments represent an ownership interest. By owning stock, you expect a higher return than someone with an income investment because you are taking the additional risk of ownership. In the long run, the rewards of owning companies will be greater than the rewards of loaning corporations money. In the long run, equity investments usually outperform debt investments by five to six percentage points. However, equity investments are both interest-rate and market sensitive. This means that equity investments can have significant fluctuations in value. For this reason, equities are not suitable for short-term goals.

STOCK OWNERSHIP

Stocks are equity investments. This means that when you own stock in a corporation, you own part of that corporation. This type of ownership provides an investor with the possibility of dividends plus appreciation, or growth, of the share price. As the value of the corporation increases or decreases, the value of the stock you own reflects the change.

Some African Americans who have never invested in the stock market wrongfully equate investing with gambling. But when you purchase a lottery ticket; put coins in a slot machine; make a bet at a race track, in a card game, or on your favorite sport team, you do not have any equity ownership. In other words, you do not own the lottery machine, the slot machine, the casino, the horse, the track, or the sport team.

Only a few gamblers are lucky enough to win, that is, earn a return on their bet. The odds are normally against the gambler ever winning any sizable amount of capital.

On the other hand, stock investors have not only their capital investment but also an asset that may increase in value. Additionally, they have a team of corporate officers always working for them.

Prudently investing in stocks and gambling have nothing in common. Of course, there are people who speculate in the stock market, but most speculators are professionals. The majority of investors are long-term investors, and normally they profit the most. The point is that investing in the stock market is not akin to gambling. Gambling is a game of chance, but stock market investing is a claim to corporate ownership.

KINDS OF STOCKS

People often ask me to explain the stock market. It is as its name implies, a market where investors can purchase shares of corporate stock. Only corporations can issue stocks. Partnerships, sole proprietorships, and limited partnerships cannot issue corporate stocks. Stocks are traded in three major stock markets: the New York Stock Exchange (NYSE), the American Stock Exchange (AMEX), and the National Association of Security Dealers Automated Quotation System (NASDAQ). Stocks sold on the exchanges are often referred to as listed stocks, while stocks traded on the NASDAQ are usually referred to as over the counter (OTC) stocks.

There are several different categories of common stock. These categories are usually based on the industry of a particular company.

Blue-chip stocks have a long history of paying dividends in good and bad times. These companies (Caterpillar, Alcoa, Jenny Craig, John Deere) are usually quite large and stable.

Cyclical stocks are affected by the business cycle. Automotive and retail stocks are good examples because in slow economic times consumers will not spend as much on items such as cars and clothing.

Defensive stocks are the opposite of cyclical stocks. Defensive stocks are not affected by the business cycle. Utilities are defensive stocks because even in bad times consumers still need electricity and heat.

Growth stocks represent companies that retain a large amount of earnings and reinvest them to fund company expansions.

Income stocks pay constant and high dividends. Utilities are income stocks because of their history of paying constant dividends.

Speculative stocks are the riskiest of all stocks. They usually are new companies with no proven track record or companies near bankruptcy.

DIRECT STOCK INVESTMENT

The industry has defined three major types of investors: small investors who invest a small amount of money in stocks; large investors who invest over $20,000 in the stock market; and institutional investors—mutual funds, pensions funds, banks, insurance companies, and other major financial institutions.

Many stock brokers do not want to deal with small investors, and they will not tell you about the investments that may be better suited for the small investor because these investment options offer the broker only a small commission, if any. Before we review these investments, let me share a few basic points.

- Consider direct stock investment as a way to learn more about the stock market and investing in companies. I believe that in order to learn about the stock market you must invest in it.
- Commit only a few dollars a month to direct stock investments, because while you will be looking for profit from your direct stock investment, your major interest is increasing your financial acumen.
- While building your portfolio of stocks, you should concentrate on financial wealth building using indirect investments—mutual funds.
- The experience you gain from your direct stock investments will help you become a better mutual fund investor.
- You may decide to invest only in mutual funds. This approach is acceptable; however, you will still need to understand direct stock investments.

FOUR DIRECT STOCK INVESTMENTS
FOR SMALL INVESTORS

The most commonly used direct stock investments suitable for small investors include company stock plans, dividend investment plans (DRIPs), personal retirement plans, and investment clubs. All of these investments allow small investors an opportunity to buy shares of major companies without investing a large sum of capital.

COMPANY STOCK PLANS

Company stock plans let employees buy stock on a weekly or quarterly basis. Employees can purchase one share at a time or have a certain amount of their salary purchase shares on a regular basis. Often employees can purchase their company stock without a charge.

There was a time when all major companies encouraged their employees to purchase company stock, and many companies gave stocks as an annual bonus to their employees. Today, however, such perks are often reserved for senior management. Nevertheless, employees may buy company stock on their own, and this is an excellent way to build a stock portfolio.

In the past, companies also fully funded an employee's pension plan. Unfortunately, many current employees may never receive this benefit because companies now either share pension funding with employees or make employees solely responsible for their pensions.

PERSONAL RETIREMENT PLANS

Personal retirement plans are primarily Individual Retirement Accounts (IRAs) and 401(k) retirement accounts. Most brokerage firms allow small investors to purchase shares of common stock with a relatively small investment for such plans. For example, brokers prefer to trade stocks in whole lots, that is, 100 shares. An IRA investment of only $500 to $2,000 may not be enough to purchase 100 shares, the brokerage firm will still allow you to purchase odd lots, that is, less than 100 shares of stock, for your IRA or other personal pension plans.

DIVIDEND REINVESTMENT PLANS

Almost 900 companies offer dividend reinvestment plans. DRIPs allow current shareholders to purchase stock directly from the company, bypassing brokers and commissions. Most DRIPs allow investors to reinvest their dividends at no charge and many DRIPs allow investors to send optional cash payments (OCP) to purchase additional shares of stocks.

According to Charles B. Carlson, author and financial planner, "Optional cash payments give small investors the ability to buy attractive blue-chip stocks when they otherwise might not be able to afford them." There are several ways that you can join a DRIP. You can contact the company directly, or you can contact the three organizations listed here.

The National Associations of Investors Corporation (NAIC) at (313) 543-0612

Moneypaper at (914) 381-5400

First Share at (800) 683-0743

All three of these organizations charge a small fee ($5 to $20 per share) to purchase one share of stock on your behalf. After you have purchased your first share, you can begin to send OCPs and build a portfolio of blue-chip companies.

In the *Resource Guide* you will find a list of companies that offer DRIP programs. At the present time there are seven publicly traded African American companies. Unfortunately, none of them offers a dividend reinvestment plan. Here is the list:

African American Publicly Traded Companies

1. United American Health Care
   City: Detroit
   Exchange: NYSE
   List Symbol: UAH
   Products/Services: Health Care Services

2. Caraco
   City: Detroit
   Exchange: NASDAQ
   List Symbol: CARQ
   Products/Services: Generic drug manufacturer and distributor

3. Granite Television
   City: New York
   Exchange: NASDAQ
   List Symbol: GBTVK
   Products/Services: Television Broadcasting

4. Black Entertainment Television
   City: Washington, D.C.
   Exchange: NYSE
   List Symbol: BTV
   Products/Services: Cable television network

5. Envirotest Systems Corp.
   City: Phoenix, AZ
   Exchange: NASDAQ

List Symbol: ENVI
Products/Services: Automobile emissions tester

6. Carver Federal Savings
   City: New York
   Exchange: NASDAQ
   List Symbol: CARV
   Products/Services: Savings and loans

7. Pyrocap International Corp.
   City: Woodbridge, VA
   Exchange: AMEX
   List Symbol: PYREC
   Products/Services: Manufacturers and markets fire suppressant compounds

INVESTMENT CLUBS

Investment clubs represent another way many small investors are investing in the stock market today. Over 200,000 Americans participate in investment clubs to enhance their knowledge about investing and increase their individual net worth. If you decide to form an investment club and it becomes profitable, your monetary rewards could be more than you ever thought possible. In the first year or two many clubs experience losses or minimal gains, but as members become more knowledgeable and cash deposits grow, many clubs see their gains increase exponentially.

In Chapter 9, "Wealth-Building Steps for African American Women," we discuss how to start an investment club. This chapter considers the investment philosophy that has helped many investment clubs become successful at selecting stocks.

THE NAIC PROVEN PHILOSOPHY

The National Association of Investors Corporation (NAIC) is the association that provides guidance to investment clubs. Over the years, NAIC has developed a very profitable investment approach. NAIC's four basic principles for successful stock market investing consistently aim at long-term capital appreciation. All investors can increase their stock market returns by following these four principles.

1. INVEST REGULARLY

It is virtually impossible to find anyone who has built a fortune over a lifetime by forecasting short-term movements in the stock market. In contrast, millions have profited from purchasing sound stocks regularly because the stock market has always increased in value over the long term. When you invest equal sums of money at regular intervals, such as monthly, semiannually, or annually, you are utilizing the technique of "dollar-cost averaging." This means that you buy more stock shares when the price of stock is lower and fewer shares when the price is higher.

Dollar-cost averaging is the primary tool small investors have to make money is the stock market. The system levels off the peaks and valleys of the share prices and works best if practiced over the full business cycle—at least five years. Regular investing enables the investor to make money even when the market is down. It also frees the investor from trying to compete with professional investors at market timing.

The following table shows the advantages of dollar-cost averaging in fluctuating markets.

CHART 14: FLUCTUATING MARKET

Monthly Investment	Selling Price of Stock of Mutual Fund	Number of Shares Purchased
$50	4.0	12.50
50	2.5	20.00
50	1.5	33.33
50	1.0	50.00
50	2.0	25.00
50	4.0	12.50

Investment	$300.00
Total number of shares:	153.33
Final Price:	×4.00
Value of shares purchased:	**$613.32**

Even when investing larger lump sums, I recommend that you establish a systematic (monthly) investment program and not worry about whether the market is up or down. This reduces your cost per share without you having to know the right time to buy. While dollar-cost averaging has definite advantages, it cannot assure a profit or protect against loss in declining markets, therefore the investor should consider his or her ability to continue to invest for the long term.

2. REINVEST YOUR EARNINGS

Companies pay out their annual profits in the form of dividends that are similar to interest payments. Many investment clubs try to realize a 4 to 6 percent dividend yield from the companies they invest in. They often reinvest the earnings to produce a compound rate of return. In essence, they buy more shares of a company with that company's profits. These reinvested dividends along with appreciation in the value of the stock help investment clubs enjoy stock market success.

3. INVEST IN GROWTH COMPANIES

A company must attain growth over a period of years to warrant a growth designation. Many investment clubs invest only in companies with a five-year history that demonstrates stability and management capability. Management is the single most determining factor of growth. Many seasoned investors believe that growth is most reliable when produced by management, as opposed to industry growth, or universal product growth.

Investment clubs try to identify companies that have shown growth in the past and are positioned to continue growing in the future. To recognize growth-oriented companies, club members review annual reports to find out if a company has experienced a consistent growth in sales, a consistent growth in earnings, and a superior return on stockholders' equity.

4. DIVERSIFY TO REDUCE RISK

Investment clubs are advised to invest one fourth of their funds in major companies and one fourth in small companies. The remaining half of their portfolio is invested in midsize companies.

By following these guidelines, many investment clubs experience a rate of 8 to 10 percent in price appreciation. The appreciation coupled with dividends enables investment clubs to attain a 14 percent overall return. The goal of the investment club is to average 12 to 14 percent annually.

Investment club members understand that no stock will be purchased without a standard analysis and report on the company in question. Although they are not expected to become professional analysts, members are proficient in applying some important tests to assist the club in becoming successful in buying and selling stocks.

One analyst I know says an investment club is a group of people who pool their money to make profits, like the NAIC. This group invests all of its capital in the stock market. They use NAIC principles to determine what stocks to invest in, and the club uses the individual dues to make those investments. "We have a portfolio and things are going quite well," says one analyst who works for the Ford Motor Company. "We have not taken anything out, we left everything in, we reinvest our dividends and we just let our portfolio grow."

Starting an investment club is pretty simple. "The hardest thing about working in our club is getting people to actually study the stock," she says. "If you have a group who understand that they are supposed to study the stocks, become acquainted with the stock market and interested in becoming more educated, then things are much easier. But when you have to pull people together to study to force them to learn and all that stuff, it gets difficult."

People who are not interested in studying the stock market and really becoming involved should not join investment clubs. "If they're not people interested in studying or in attending classes or becoming knowledgeable in at least one of the NAIC tools, then they are not good candidates."

The great thing about the NAIC's principles for stock market success is that they help the small investors become informed investors. Informed investors research companies before they invest their money and understand why they invested in that particular company. Their research also helps them stay the course should the overall stock market decline or the economy experience a recession. Informed investors don't let market or economic conditions overshadow their investment decisions. Instead, they remember why they invested in a company, and when market and economic factors change, informed investors look at the initial reasons for their stock purchase and make a decision to hold or fold.

If the company is still doing well or as expected, then informed investors keep their investments. If, on the other hand, the company is not performing well, then informed investors may decide to trade their holding for a new one.

In this regard, informed investors are like experienced whisk card players. Experienced whisk players have a competitive edge on the novice players. Experienced players are more likely to win because they not only have a better understanding of the game but also remember which cards were played. They understand their opponents' strengths and weaknesses and can calculate the likelihood of their winning the game.

How can they do this? They do it because they not only enjoy the game and winning but also take the time to become informed card players rather than recreational card players. Investing time to become an informed investor can help you become a better stock investor in the same way.

I am reminded of this concept often by investment professionals who have appeared on *The Color of Money* television show. Peter Lynch, the former money manager of the Fidelity Magellan Fund, is considered one of the greatest stock pickers and money managers of our times.

When appearing on the show, Peter shared one of the major reasons for his success. "You must know what you're investing in. Never invest in any company that you can't explain with a crayon," he said. In other words, if you don't fully understand the business a company is in, then maybe you are investing in the wrong company.

Peter Lynch points out that being an informed investor is your best tool to achieving success with direct stock investments. For those who want to learn more about Peter's success as a stock picker, I highly recommend both of his books, *Beating the Street* and *One Up on Wall Street.*

Few people know that individuals are eligible to become members of the NAIC and take advantage of its investment advisory services. To join, call (313) 543-0612.

For additional information about direct stock market investing, you may also want to contact the American Association of Individual Investors (AAII) in Chicago, Illinois. This organization provides information to small investors who want to make their own stock market investments. It can be reached at (312) 280-0170. For an annual membership fee of $49, you receive a monthly newsletter, the *AAII Journal,* several annual stock market investment guides, and membership in a local AAII chapter.

MUTUAL FUNDS

Many people do not want to be bothered with all the work associated with researching, managing, and trading individual stocks. This type of individual would prefer to invest in a mutual fund. They offer many of the same benefits of direct stock investment but without a lot of the work. Of course you still have to select a mutual fund that has a good track record and matches your long-term goals. Nevertheless, the process is less time-consuming than selecting and managing individual stocks.

In fact, next to performance, convenience is probably the major reasons that many Americans choose to use mutual funds to invest indirectly in the stock market. (Other ways that Americans invest indirectly in the stock market are through pension funds, variable life insurance policies, and variable annuities.) Mutual funds are the most popular investment today for indirect investment in the stock market. In fact, mutual funds are generally the recommended vehicle for investment amounts less than $25,000. Let's see why investors like mutual funds so much and why mutual funds are an ideal investment for small investors.

When investors use mutual funds, they pool their money with other investors to buy a large portfolio of stocks or bonds. In general, mutual funds offer an investor the following benefits: diversification, professional management, liquidity, and convenience.

All mutual funds offer diversification. Most mutual funds take the pooled resources of their investors and purchase stocks from several hundred various companies. Diversification helps protect the value of the portfolio. To diversify simply means to own many investments instead of a few. An individual can diversify by purchasing shares of stock, money market instruments, and bonds. You could then diversify by purchasing stocks in several different industries, or even by purchasing several stocks in the same industry. By purchasing many different securities, mutual funds reduce the risks of owning individual securities. If one security declines in value, the total fund is only slightly affected.

There are several rules concerning diversification. Some investment advisors think that if an investor owns ten different stocks, then that investor's portfolio is well diversified. Other investment advisors think that the magic number should be forty or fifty different companies. In either case, building a diversified portfolio can be very costly in terms of research time and commissions. Today many investors like the benefits of owning a mutual fund, and they often buy more than one mutual fund, again to add further diversification to their investment portfolios.

Mutual funds offer professional management and administration at nominal fees. Managing stock investments can be a complex issue. Mutual funds provide the management without the high costs of buying separate equity investments. You give up a small percentage of your investment to pay the mutual fund for this service.

Another benefit of investing in mutual funds is liquidity. Many investors like knowing that they have access to their funds. The mutual fund will redeem your shares for the net asset value on the day requested. Mutual funds are readily redeemable either by the fund (open-end funds) or on the open market (closed-end funds).

The biggest benefit of mutual funds is convenience. Many funds have low minimum-investment requirements and will allow investors to open an account with only a small payment. Additionally, mutual funds offer systematic investment plans with bank authorization, investment prospec-tuses, annual reports, transfer services, and accurate record keeping. Some will even let you invest without paying a front-end sales charge.

There is a variety of mutual funds, and investors can match their in-vestment goals with the correct type of mutual fund. The Investment Company Institute classifies mutual funds in twenty-two broad cate-gories according to their basic investment objectives; check the *Resource Guide* for a complete listing of the types of mutual funds. Primarily, mu-tual funds are similar to stock and bond investments and fall into the cat-egories of cash, growth, income, or a combination of growth and income.

Chart 15, "Group Performance," lists the general categories and their returns over the last five years. We will primarily limit our discussion to three types of funds that can help us reach our goal of $250,000 in ten years: the balanced fund the growth and income fund and the interna-tional stock fund.

CHART 15: GROUP PERFORMANCE
Comparing mutual funds by investment objective

You can use this table to compare the performance of a mutual fund against other funds with the same investment objective. The table, compiled by the Morningstar research firm, includes the investment objective and its abbreviation; the average year-to-date for each objective group; the best 3-year annualized return in each group; the average 3-year performance; and worst 3-year performance in each group.

	RETURNS			
Investment objective	Avg YTD	Best 3-yr	Avg 3-yr	Wrst 3-yr
DOMESTIC SPECIALIZED STOCK FUNDS				
Utilities (SU)	-0.3	15.0	10.9	3.4
Technology (ST)	-1.3	61.0	26.7	-8.3
Precious Metals (SP)	-3.4	35.8	1.8	-20.5
Natural Resources (SN)	0.0	22.4	10.2	-1.0
Financial (SF)	-0.9	26.1	21.4	13.7
Health (SH)	-1.8	22.0	14.4	7.0
Unaligned (S)	0.4	47.5	10.3	-1.3

Investment objective	Avg YTD	Best 3-yr	Avg 3-yr	Wrst 3-yr
DOMESTIC GENERAL STOCK FUNDS				
Small Company (SC)	-0.4	32.5	15.2	-0.4
Equity-Income (EI)	-0.5	20.6	14.6	5.4
Growth and Income (GI)	-0.7	24.2	16.9	-9.2
Growth (G)	-0.7	43.1	17.5	-4.4
Aggressive Growth (AG)	-0.6	45.4	17.4	-23.5
INTERNATIONAL STOCK FUNDS				
Pacific Stock (WP)	-0.9	11.1	-1.4	-24.6
Europe Stock (WE)	-1.3	18.8	11.5	3.6
Foreign Stock (WF)	-0.7	19.9	-0.3	-29.6
World Stock (WW)	-0.8	25.4	6.9	-6.9
HYBRID FUNDS				
Convertible Bond (CV)	-0.4	16.2	11.4	5.2
Income (I)	-0.2	18.1	10.5	3.0
Balanced (B)	-0.6	18.3	13.6	1.9
Asset Allocation (AA)	-0.8	30.8	12.3	-4.8
INTERNATIONAL BOND FUNDS				
Short-Term Income (SW)	-0.3	9.2	2.9	-2.0
World Bond (WB)	-0.3	19.7	10.0	-8.8
CORPORATE BOND FUNDS				
High Quality (CQ)	-0.4	15.5	8.6	2.7
General (CG)	-0.5	21.6	10.1	2.7
High Yield (CY)	0.2	15.4	9.7	4.9
GOVERNMENT BOND FUNDS				
Adj-Rate Mortgage (GA)	-0.1	12.5	4.4	-1.1
Treasury (GT)	-0.6	32.3	11.2	2.4
Mortgage (GM)	-0.4	21.3	9.6	3.2
General (GG)	-0.5	21.9	9.1	2.6
MUNICIPAL BOND FUNDS				
Single State (MS)	-1.3	13.0	8.7	4.5
National (MN)	-1.1	12.7	8.1	1.5

Reprinted by permission of The Detroit News *and* Morningstar Research.

The balanced fund, or growth and income type of fund, generally has a three-part investment objective: (1) to conserve the investor's initial principal, (2) to pay current income, and (3) to promote long-term growth of both principal and income. Balanced funds also have a port-folio mix of bonds, preferred stocks, and common stocks.

As you can see from Chart 15, the average balanced fund has returned 13.6 percent annually, and the growth and income return has been 16.9 percent during the same period. The balanced fund offers growth oppor-tunities without exposing your assets to much market fluctuation. This is a conservative move; perhaps as you become a more experienced investor, you will decide to become a more aggressive investor.

International stock funds invest in equity securities of companies lo-cated outside of the United States. To be categorized as international funds, two-thirds of their portfolios must be so invested at all times.

For added diversification, many financial advisors suggest that you in-vest some portion of your portfolio outside of the United States. Again from Chart 15 we can see that over the last five years the annual return on the average international stock fund has been 19.9 percent. Today, given the opportunities in other countries, many advisors suggest that in-vestors have at least a domestic mutual fund and an international mutual fund. Chart 16, "Mutual Fund Styles of Investing," shows the impact an international fund can have on your portfolio.

Later in this chapter, I will show you how these three types of mutual funds can help you reach your financial goal. Now, however, let's find out how to select a mutual fund, because even though you know the type of fund you need, you still need information that will help you select the right one.

SELECTING A MUTUAL FUND

Before investing in a mutual fund, you must identify the goal you want a mutual fund to help you achieve. Do you want to have an emergency fund? Will the funds be used to pay for college or retirement? Will you need the fund to provide extra income now or can you wait several years before using the income the fund generates? When selecting a mutual fund, as with selecting a stock, you always want to match the fund objec-tive with your investment goal.

For example, our primary goal is to build a net worth of $200,000 in ten years. Therefore, we selected mutual funds that offer the potential for capital appreciation. Our balanced fund, our growth and income fund, and our international equity fund fit this goal. We will be investing a small

CHART 16: MUTUAL FUND STYLES OF INVESTING, 1975–1993

Growth of $1 Invested at Year–End 1975*

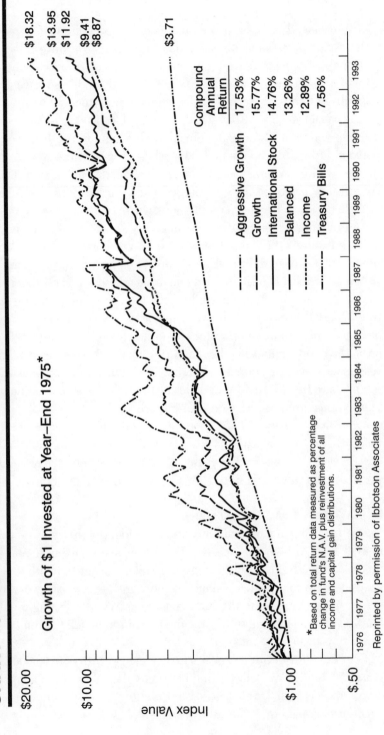

	Compound Annual Return
Aggressive Growth	17.53%
Growth	15.77%
International Stock	14.76%
Balanced	13.26%
Income	12.89%
Treasury Bills	7.56%

$18.32
$13.95
$11.92
$9.41
$8.87
$3.71

*Based on total return data measured as percentage change in fund's N.A.V. plus reinvestment of all income and capital gain distributions.

Reprinted by permission of Ibbotson Associates

Index Value

amount of money on a regular basis (dollar-cost averaging), and we will also try to find a no-load or low-load fund. Load is the word mutual funds use to refer to a sales charge. All mutual funds are in business to make money, and they do so in many ways. Some take out a sales charge when you invest; others take out a sales charge when you redeem your shares. You can pay your fee before or after investing. If you want the fund, you will have to pay the sales charge. Your choice may depend on which way you like to eat your salad—before or after a meal.

Many advisors advocate buying no-sales-charge and low-sales-charge funds whenever possible. Personally, if the fund makes money for me, I don't worry about the sales charge. I don't want to do the work myself, and therefore I am willing to pay someone else to do the work. However, I don't want to be overcharged for the services.

In addition, mutual funds charge some form of annual management fee. As a rule I try to avoid stock funds with annual expense ratios greater than 1.5 percent. You should also avoid funds that have total expense ratios greater than 5 percent. You can find sales-charge information in the fund prospectus and its annual report.

To help you get started in building your mutual fund portfolio, Chart 17, "Funds That Let You Start Small," lists sixty-seven mutual funds that welcome small investors. Of the nine mutual funds that are managed by African Americans, three welcome small investors with systematic payment plans. While the fund offers this service, investors must request it when completing their application. Here are nine mutual funds managed by African Americans:

1. The Dreyfuss Third Century Fund is managed by NCM Capital, whose CEO is Maceo Sloan. Call (919) 688-0620 for more information.

2. The Acacia Fund is managed by NCM Capital, whose CEO is Maceo Sloan. Call (919) 688-0620 for more information.

3. The Ariel Appreciation Fund is a growth-oriented socially responsible fund managed by John Rodgers and Eric McKissack. Call (800) 292-0140 to get a prospectus.

4. The Ariel Growth Fund is a growth fund managed by John Rodgers, but it is currently closed to investors.

5. The Calvert New Africa Fund is an international fund that primarily invests in African-based companies. The Calvert New Africa

Fund is managed by Justin Becket and Clifford Mpare of New Africa Advisors. Call (800) 368-2748 for a prospectus.

6. The Calvert Capital Accumulation Fund is a long-term capital appreciation fund that invests in the stocks of small- to medium-size companies. One unique feature of this fund is that it has a pool of several emerging portfolio managers: Three African American men, one Hispanic American, one Hispanic female, and three Caucasian women. For more information about the fund, call (800) 368-2748.

Brown Capital Management offers three no-load funds for investors with $10,000 or more to invest ($2,000 for IRA and Keogh plans). These mutual funds are:

7. The Brown Capital Management Equity Fund, which seeks capital appreciation.

8. The Brown Capital Management Balanced Fund, whose objective is a combination of capital appreciation and income.

9. The Brown Capital Management Small Company Fund, whose objective is capital appreciation in companies with operating revenues of $250 million or less. To learn more about the family of Brown Capital Management Mutual Funds call (800) 525-FUND.

OPENING A MUTUAL FUND ACCOUNT
To review a mutual fund, call the fund's toll-free number and request a prospectus and an annual report. It's wise to review two or three mutual funds in a particular category.

The prospectus is the best tool to help you select a mutual fund. The prospectus provides information pertaining to a particular fund's portfolio, investment objectives, manager, sales charges, expenses, past performance, number of shares issued and yields.

When reviewing the prospectus and annual report, here are some important questions you want answered:

* What is the objective of the fund?
* What are the sales charges (loads) ?
* Are there telephone exchange privileges? (Can you change your investment by phone?)

- Are there free dividend reinvestments? (Can you reinvest your dividends without charge?)
- Is the fund a member of a family of funds?
- What is the minimum initial investment?
- What is the fund's past performance? (Look at one, three, five, and ten year returns.)
- How long must you stay in the fund to avoid a back-end sales charge?
- What is the minimum IRA or retirement plan investment?
- Does the fund have a systematic bank withdrawal (i.e., automatic investment) plan?

If you have questions after reading the prospectus and annual report, call the fund and ask an account service person to answer your questions. If necessary, the service person can also recommend a local financial planner, broker, or registered representative who can review the prospectus with you. Again, your primary goal is to make sure that the mutual fund's investment objective matches your investment goal.

Once you have decided that the mutual fund is right for you, fill out the application form and mail it along with your initial investment. I highly recommend making regular investments directly from your payroll, credit union account, or bank checking account.

Several magazines and newspapers annually rate the best mutual funds. Some of the more popular ones are *Money* magazine, *Kiplinger's Personal Finance, Barron's,* and the *Wall Street Journal.*

To find out about African American–managed mutual funds, you can consult *Black Enterprise* magazine, a monthly business magazine for Black Americans, and *The Color of Money Journal,* a quarterly personal finance magazine for people of color. For a subscription call (800) 257-4707. You can also call the trade association of emerging (minority) money managers: The National Association of Security Professionals (NASP) at (404) 521-1846.

These days, few young African Americans are concerned about increasing their net worth. This is a shame, because youth favors small investors. It gives them more time to invest in the stock market. People with more time can build great fortunes by investing small amounts of money. It is encouraging to see that some young African Americans are taking control of their financial future in a positive way.

CHART 17: FUNDS THAT LET YOU START SMALL

The following are among the no-load funds, or fund families that sell no-load funds, that either have minimum initial investments of $500 or less or allow investors to open an account with a reduced minimum investment of $500 or less if they make regular contributions through an automatic investment plan. Single-state tax-free funds are not included.

Fund or Family	Normal Minimum Investment	Automatic Plan Minimum Investment	Phone Number For Prospectus
AARP	$500	$50	800-322-2282
Amana	100	100	800-728-8762
American Pension Investor	500	100	800-544-6060
America's Utility	1,000	20	800-487-3863
Anthem	1,000	50	800-273-3936
Armstrong Associates	250	—	214-720-9101
Babson	500–2,500	100	800-422-2766
Baron Asset	2,000	500	800-992-2766
BayFunds	2,500	500	800-229-3863
Berger	250	250	800-333-1001
Brundage Story & Rose	1,000	50	800-545-0103
Bull & Bear	1,000	100	800-847-4200
Capstone	200–10,000	25	800-262-6631
Charter Capital Blue Chip Growth	50	—	414-257-1842
Dreman	1,000	100	800-533-1608
Eclipse Financial Asset	1,000	50	800-872-2710
Evergreen Foundation	500	500	800-235-0064
Evergreen Real Estate	100	100	800-235-0064
Fasciano	1,000	50	800-848-6050
Fidelity Retirement Growth	500	100	800-544-8888
First Omaha	500	100	800-662-4203
Founders	1,000	50	800-525-2440
Freemont	2,000	50	800-548-4539
Gabelli	1,000–25,000	100	800-422-3554
Galaxy	2,500	50	800-628-0414
General Securities	500	50	800-939-9990
Green Century Balanced	2,000	100	800-934-7336
Guinness Flight Investment	5,000	100	800-915-6565
Harbor	2,000	500	800-422-1050
Heartland	1,000	50	800-432-7856
Hercules	250	100	800-584-1317
Invesco°	1,000	50	800-525-8085
Janus	1,000	50	800-525-8983
Leeb Personal Finance	2,500	50	800-545-0103
Legg Mason Global Governments	1,000	50	800-822-5544
Lexington	1,000	500	800-526-0056
Merriman	1,000	50	800-423-4893

Fund or Family	Normal Minimum Investment	Automatic Plan Minimum Investment	Phone Number For Prospectus
MSB	$50	$—	212-551-1920
Neuberger & Berman	1,000–2,000	50	800-877-9700
Nicholas†	500	500	414-272-6133
Northern	2,500	250	800-595-9111
ORI Growth	2,000	100	800-407-7298
Pauze U.S. Govt. Total Return Bond	1,000	100	800-327-7170
Pax World	250	250	800-767-1729
Portico	1,000	50	800-982-8909
Preferred	1,000	50	800-662-4769
T. Rowe Price#	2,500	50	800-638-5660
Primary	500–2,500	50	800-443-6544
Prudential	1,000	50	800-225-1852
Rembrandt	2,000	50	800-443-4725
Safeco	1,000	100	800-426-6730
Schafer Value	2,000	500	800-343-0481
Scudder	1,000	100	800-225-2470
Sentry	500	200	800-533-7827
Stagecoach	1,000	100	800-222-8222
Strong	250–2,500	50	800-368-1030
Twentieth Century°°	250–2,500	50–250	800-345-2021
UMB	1,000	100	800-422-2766
United Services	1,000	100	800-873-8637
USAA††	1,000	100	800-382-8722
Value Line	1,000	40	800-223-0818
Vanguard STAR	500	500	800-662-7447
Vista	2,500	250	800-648-4782
WPG##	2,500	50	800-223-3332
Wright EquiFunds	1,000	50	800-888-9471
Yacktman	2,500	500	800-525-8258

°Excluding Invesco Small Company. †Nicholas and Nicholas Income only. #Excluding Summit funds.
°°Excluding International Emerging Growth fund and all fixed-income funds. ††Cornerstone and Income Stock only. ##Excluding Growth and Quantitative funds.—No automatic investment plan.

Reprinted by permission of Kiplinger's Personal Finance magazine

A friend of mine in Colorado is a testament to that. She said that she watched money fly out of the window that she should have been spending elsewhere or saving.

Those habits continued until her parents bought her a $22.50 ticket to a financial planning workshop run by a Denver financial planner. At that point, she changed her attitude about money.

Now a program director at a Denver-area YMCA, she began to do

*the simple things she learned in the workshop. Instead of going out for
lunch every day, she started brown bagging; instead of shopping regularly, she finds clearance sales to avoid paying full price; instead of
seeing movies at prime time, she goes to bargain-price twilight shows.*

"Basically, my goal is just to live comfortably," she said. "If something happened to my job, I'd be able to make it through without
debt." Once she reaches her objective of a $1,500 balance in her
money market fund, she will begin to invest in stock funds for more lu-
crative growth.

She says that making the moves she has made is an easy thing to do;
it only involves being in the right mind-set.

"I think really the main thing is it doesn't matter how much money
you make, as long as you have a lot of stability, instead of living from
paycheck to paycheck."

SAMPLE SMALL INVESTOR MUTUAL PORTFOLIO

Let's see how we can use the information on mutual funds to reach our
goal of $200,000. To illustrate this, suppose you decided to save ten per-
cent of your family's annual salaries of $40,000, or $4,000 a year. Because
you are a first-time investor, you are conservative when choosing a mutual
fund. After reviewing your goals, you decide to make monthly payments
into your credit union and to dollar-cost-average monthly into two mutual
funds: one growth and income fund and one international fund.

The credit union can help you build an emergency fund of $5,000, or
two months of living expenses. Also to reduce your taxes and save for retirement you decide to try to maximize the investments in your company's 401K retirement plan. We also assume that your spouse wants to
join an investment club with ten other African Americans. Here is your
monthly allocation. By the way, I will refer to you and your spouse as
Mr. and Mrs. Money.

CHART 18: MONTHLY ALLOCATION OF $333: YEARS 1 AND 2

Goal	Investment	Amount
1. Emergency fund	Credit union	$166
2. Mr. Money's 401(k)	Balanced fund	$61
3. Mrs. Money's IRA	International fund	$61
4. College education	Investment club	$25
Total:		**$333**

MONTHLY ALLOCATION OF $333: YEARS 3 TO 5

Goal	Investment	Amount
1. Home down payment	Credit union	$166
2. Mr. Money's 401(k)	Balanced fund	$61
3. Mrs. Money's IRA	International fund	$61
4. College education	Investment club	$25
Total:		**$333**

MONTHLY ALLOCATION OF $333: YEARS 6 TO 8

Goal	Investment	Amount
1. Car/business down payment	Credit union	$100
2. Mr. Money's 401(k)	Balance fund	$61
3. Mrs. Money's IRA	International fund	$61
4. Education	Investment club	$25
5. Education fund	Balanced fund	$66
Total:		**$333**

MONTHLY ALLOCATION OF $333: YEARS 9 AND 10

Goal	Investment	Amount
1. Business fund	Credit union	$100
2. Mr. Money's 401(k)	Balanced fund	$61
3. Mrs. Money's IRA	International fund	$61
4. Education	Investment club	$25
5. Education fund	Balanced fund	$66
Total:		**$333**

INVEST, MY CHILD, INVEST

It is amazing what you can achieve using the credit union, a growth and income fund (balanced fund), an international stock mutual fund, and an IRA. In our illustration, let's assume you adjusted your credit union allocation to meet certain short-term goals, like your emergency fund, a car down payment, a new home down payment, and a business equity fund.

We also positioned your 401(k) investment into a balanced mutual fund to have both stocks and bonds in your small portfolio. This was a conservative investment choice, but it was designated as an additional resource for college education and a new home down payment. In selecting this invest-

ment mix we anticipate an average return of 4 percent on the credit union
account, 10 percent on the balanced fund, 12 percent on the international
fund, and 15 percent with the investment club. Assuming that your investments perform as in the past, you would receive an average of 10 percent
return on your total investment. At this rate your household's investment
would accumulate in the following manner:

CHART 19: INVESTMENT RESULTS IF
FUTURE PERFORMANCE EQUALS PAST PERFORMANCE

Year One	Investment	Value
1. Emergency fund	Credit union	$2,100
2. Mr. Money's 401(k)	Balanced fund	$ 805
3. Mrs. Money's IRA	International fund	$ 819
4. College education	Investment club	$ 345
Total		
Year One:		$4,069
Year Two:		$9,230
Year Five:		$26,835
Year Ten:		$70,054
Year Fifteen:		$139,659
Year Twenty:		$251,757

You can see that now your family is on their way to reaching its
$250,000 net worth goal. In our final chapter we will total the accumu-
lated assets to see if you have reached your net worth goal.

An encouraging note about this hypothetical projection is that your
family has accumulated over $100,000 in cash without increasing its
monthly investments. Imagine your net worth if you consistently increase
your savings as you receive annual bonuses and raises or if you make a
point of reinvesting a portion of your annual tax refund. Our imaginary
family did not increase its investments as its income increased; however,
that pattern does not mean that you should not increase your investments.
When you make a conscious effort to find extra money to invest in stock
funds, you can literally turn chump change into big bucks.

You're probably saying that your household doesn't have $333 a
month or $4,000 a year to save and invest. In Chapter 2, "Establish a
Wealth-Building Plan," we reviewed ways to find extra money to invest.
Once you've identified ways to cut back on your current living expenses,
you still may not have $300 a month to save, that's okay. Remember, your

first goal is to save ten percent of your income, but you can start saving as much as you can every month. As you begin to see your financial assets grow, you will find more money to invest. Using the same three investments and receiving the same returns, $100 and $200 would grow in the following manner:

CHART 20: MONTHLY ALLOCATION OF $100: YEARS 1 TO 10

Goal	Investment	Value
1. Emergency fund	Credit union	$25
2. Mr. Money's 401(k)	Balanced fund	$25
3. Mr. Money's IRA	International fund	$25
4. College education	Investment club	$25
Total:		
Year one:		$1,320
Year five:		$8,058
Year ten:		$21,037
Year fifteen:		$41,939
Year twenty:		$75,603

MONTHLY ALLOCATION OF $200: YEARS 1 TO 10

Goal	Investment	Value
1. Emergency fund	Credit union	$75
2. Mr. Money's 401(k)	Balanced fund	50
3. Mrs. Money's IRA	International fund	50
4. College education	Investment club	25
Total:		
Year one:		$2,640
Year five:		$16,117
Year ten:		$42,074
Year fifteen:		$83,879
Year twenty:		$151,206

Even $100 a month or $25 a week will grow into a substantial amount when invested in mutual funds.

I recommend credit unions, balanced mutual funds, and international funds, coupled with a personal retirement account, as the primary types of investments to help African American families reach their goal of accumulating $200,000. Of course, there are many other options, and as your investments grow and your knowledge of investing increases, you may decide to try them.

Last year at a seminar in Portsmith, Virginia, an African American gentleman in the audience shared his belief in mutual funds. He said that his friend started saving $25 a month in mutual funds over twenty-five years ago. Today his friend's account is valued at more than $1 million.

African Americans who invest in the stock market have numerous responsibilities. Our culture and the larger culture in which we live force us to defend our decision to invest in stocks. Every time you tell someone about your investments, be prepared to defend yourself. I wish I could change society's attitude toward the African American investor. Unfortunately, I cannot, but I can share several tips that may make your investment experience more comfortable.

First, be aware that if you are the first stock investor in your family, you may be viewed as teacher, role model, and financial provider to other family members. In all likelihood, when other family members need monetary advice and financial help, they may turn to you. To prepare yourself for these situations become an informed investor, read as much as you can about stocks, businesses, and mutual funds, establish an emergency fund to help others, and be willing to share the benefits of dollar-cost averaging in stock mutual funds.

Secondly, African American investors will have to deal with non–African American financial advisors who will dismiss you as a small investor wanting to waste their time. If faced with such behavior calmly explain to them why your business is valuable. Emphasize that:

- You plan to make regular monthly investments over the next ten years in the total range of $12,000 to $40,000.
- You are establishing a systematic investment plan with their firm.
- You plan to tell your employers, co-workers, family members, and friends about the investment, if impressed by the firm and the fund's performance.
- You understand that you will be buying ownership in various companies.
- You will not be calling them every time the stock market or the economy has a slump. In fact, you are looking forward to several down cycles because they will help you purchase more shares of mutual funds at a reduced rate.
- You will be reviewing your investments twice a year.

- You plan, if possible, to place your investments inside of your personal pension plans. While explaining this, ask for a prospectus and have the advisor begin processing your application.

Thirdly, as an African American investor you will be expected to understand the basic concepts of socially responsible investing, that is, not investing in companies that have a history of endangering nature, have discriminatory hiring practices, or manufacture alcohol or fire arms. In recent times the socially responsible investment community has given a broader definition to this term by making sure that socially conscious investors have more choices when attempting to do the right thing. For example, with the abolishment of apartheid in South Africa, it is now socially responsible to invest in this emerging market through direct investments, open-end mutual funds or through closed-end mutual funds.

Chart 21, "Returns for Social Conscience Funds" lists some socially responsible mutual funds. Most of these funds test potential investments against social screens, in addition to matching them to their other investment objectives.

CHART 21: RETURNS FOR SOCIAL CONSCIENCE FUNDS

STOCK FUNDS	TOTAL RETURNS, ANNUALIZED ENDED MARCH 31, 1992		
	1 year	3 years	5 years
Calvert-Ariel Appreciation	10.9%	na	na
Calvert-Ariel Growth	12.7%	9.5%	13.7%
Calvert Social Investment Equity	7.9%	11.9%	na
Calvert Soc. Investment Managed Growth	8.6%	10.5%	7.7%
Dreyfus Third Century	9.0%	15.0%	11.2%
New Alternatives	6.9%	10.7%	8.1%
Parnassus	29.2%	9.4%	6.9%
Pax World	10.5%	16.6%	10.7%
Righttime Social Awareness	4.5%	na	na
Average Stock Fund	**12.5%**	**12.5%**	**8.4%**
BOND FUNDS	1 year	3 years	5 years
Calvert Social Investment Fund	10.7%	11.0%	na
Average Bond Fund	**10.4%**	**10.4%**	**8.0%**

Source: Morningstar, Inc.

As an African American investor, I have found that the general market's definition of being socially responsible is often too confining. Many of the current politically correct investments do not include matters that I am deeply concerned with. Here are some of the questions a company I invest in or do business with must answer. Unfortunately, since there are no companies that monitor these social screens as an African American investor, I must ask these questions myself.

- How many people of color are employed by the investment company, financial planning company, and brokerage firm that are courting my business?
- How many minority money managers do these companies have?
- Are any African American investment companies managing a portion of the company's pension fund?
- How many minorities are on the board of directors?
- Are these companies working with other minority companies?
- Do the firms support African American charities?
- Does the company invest in or utilize any other African American publicly traded company?

During the last three years several people have advocated a variety of ways to increase the wealth of African Americans. Some people have proposed that African Americans stop attending multi-million dollar conventions in white hotels. According to them, the funds could be better used for building African American hotels and convention centers.

Others have proposed that African Americans do business only with African American entrepreneurs or within the confines of the African American community. A third proposal encourages African Americans to simply raise their economic lot by pulling up their bootstraps. Although these proposals have merit, they are not realistic because they will not help increase the wealth of African Americans. These proposals are similar in nature to Marcus Garvey's "Back to Africa" movement— emotionally inspiring but rationally impractical.

On the other hand, increasing the number of African American investors holds enormous promise for increasing the wealth of African Americans. Unfortunately, there are no influential African American leaders strongly advocating this option.

Nevertheless, if more African American families invested 10 percent of their incomes on a regular basis, then we would have a viable strategy for economic empowerment. Such a strategy would financially empower individual households, and in so doing, improve the collective economic condition of African Americans for many generations.

When faced with making an important decision, I always ask myself: Will the decision I make today matter one hundred years from now? If it will not matter in one hundred years, then there is no need for me to be anxious about my decision. On the other hand, if the decision I make today will have a lasting impact, then I should consider the consequences carefully.

The financial decisions I make today can impact the lives of people living 100 years from now. The monetary decisions I make today can affect the lives of my descendants living in the year 2096.

If I invest wisely, the estate I leave behind could benefit not only my children, but my grandchildren, and great-grandchildren. Furthermore, if I can teach my children, by example, the importance of investing in the stock market, I could start a new family tradition—one that could be passed along to future generations.

I owe it, therefore, to myself and to the generations that will come after me to invest my resources wisely and to teach my children how to do the same. When the day comes and they ask me for financial guidance, I want to look them straight in the eye and say, "Invest, my child, invest." I will share with them the information I have learned about investing in the stock market. By doing these things, I will live a fuller life; I will also help my descendants to live fuller lives in a sublime place they will one day call home—Abundance!

FIVE

INSURE YOUR FINANCIAL FUTURE

To every thing there is a season,
and a time to every purpose under the heaven: a
time to be born, and a time to die . . .
                                    —Ecclesiastes 3:1–2

Best-selling author Robert Fulghum once said in an interview that "one cannot truly appreciate living until one can understand the process of dying." It sometimes seems as if by understanding the finality of death we are more appreciative of life.

Nevertheless, many African Americans dislike talking about death or anything associated with death. Hence, many African American families rarely have a frank discussion about life insurance, wills, or other estate-planning matters—causing needless emotional and economic pains after they've died.

It is not only prudent but necessary for African American households to discuss what to do after a family member passes away. For example: How will creditors be paid after a breadwinner dies? Will the breadwinner's children be able to attend college? Who will take care of the breadwinner's parents? Who will inherit the deceased's assets? How much money will the deceased's survivors need? Getting your financial house in order while you are alive and well will lessen the likelihood of a probate court stepping in and answering these questions for you after your passing. Unfortunately, if you leave it unattended, you will not have a say in how the probate judge distributes your assets, provides for your family, or puts your financial affairs in order.

Many Americans are under the impression that their financial responsibilities expire when they do, but this is not so. Someone, usually a family member, must get the deceased's financial affairs in order. That means the family member must arrange the funeral, pay any unpaid bills, collect and review important documents, meet with lawyers and probate judges, dispose of property, and make arrangements for the care of children or elderly parents.

Many African American families have painfully endured this probate process, which may be understandable if a loved one was taken away suddenly. However, enduring such stress needlessly, only because people are uncomfortable talking about the financial responsibilities that accompany death, is foolishness. Furthermore, it is a self-imposed gag order that many African American households have lived with for too long. The time has come to begin to discuss openly the need and ways we can protect our dreams—even when faced with death.

INSURING YOUR FINANCIAL FUTURE

I like to refer to this process as insuring your financial future, which involves choosing to live a healthy lifestyle, buying life insurance, and preparing a will. The significance of insuring your financial future becomes clear when you realize that African Americans have a shorter life span than white Americans.

Having a shorter life span means that on average African Americans also have less time to earn money, provide for their families, and increase their net worth. If African American men and women were on an equal playing field with their white counterparts, they would add six more years of compound interest, six more years of earned or social security income, and six more years of appreciation to their homes and businesses. Adding six years to any portfolio represents a significant amount of additional wealth-building opportunity, and this is especially true for African Americans who must rely on the time value of money to help their small amount of regular savings grow into larger pools of investment capital.

Many factors have contributed to the shorter life span of African Americans, including crime, limited access to health care, high-risk diets, poor exercise habits, poverty, discrimination, and the overall lack of awareness as to the secrets of longevity. Whatever the causes, the results are the same: a shorter life span means a shorter time period for African Americans to increase their household's wealth.

Thus, while African American households need all the extra time they can get to build their family assets, they are also the households with the least amount of time to do so. What makes matters worse is the fact that in some instances African Americans can take steps to increase their own life span, but have chosen not to do so. The authors of *The Black Man's Guide to Good Health,* put it plainly, "In the grand scheme of things, life is a relatively short journey. Sometimes we get so busy trying to earn a living that we forget to take proper care of our health. Proper care of our bodies, however, can improve the quality of our everyday living and give us more time to earn a living and to do those things we enjoy most."

The authors conclude that "By putting a little effort toward prevention now, (African Americans) can save themselves from endless suffering later." In addition, this suffering can also be measured not only by the physical pain endured, but in the dollars lost. For a moment, let's put aside the economic consequences of passing away and consider the pain thousands of African American households face as they deal with these realities:

- Owing largely to death from violence, there are only eighty-five African American men for every one hundred African American women in the twenty-five to forty-four age group.
- African Americans are two-and-a-half times more likely to die from alcohol-induced causes than whites and twice as likely to die from drug-induced causes.
- The African American infant mortality rate is twice as high as that of whites.
- African American heart patients get less advanced treatment than white patients.
- African Americans who go into cardiac arrest are half as likely as whites to survive once they are admitted to a hospital.
- African Americans are more likely to suffer a kidney failure, but less likely to get a transplant.
- Sixty percent of the total African American population in the United States live in communities with one or more uncontrolled toxic waste sites.
- In 1989, Americans making less than $9,000 a year were at least three times more likely to die early than people making $25,000 or more a year.
- In 1985, the U.S. Department of Health and Human Services re-

SMART MONEY MOVES FOR AFRICAN AMERICANS

ported that more than 60,000 minority Americans die each year from preventable diseases.

- African American men have the highest cancer rates in the nation.
- African American women have a cancer rate that is higher than that of white women.
- Lung cancer, which kills 140,000 Americans each year, is the most preventable form of cancer. Ninety percent of lung cancer deaths are caused by smoking. Eleven percent of African Americans are heavy smokers.
- African American women are two and a half times more likely than white women to die from cervical cancer. This form of cancer is highly preventable if caught early.
- African Americans are only 12 percent of the population, but account for 30 percent of people with AIDS.
- Fifty-four percent of children under age thirteen with AIDS are African Americans.
- African Americans are twice as likely to die from adult-onset diabetes than whites are.
- Heart disease is the leading killer in the nation. African American men have the highest incidence of heart disease; the rate for African American women is much higher than the rate for white women.
- African Americans are thirty-three percent more likely than whites to have high blood pressure, which can lead to kidney disease, stroke, heart failure, and blindness.
- African Americans' eating patterns are still influenced by the foods available during slavery—pigs' feet, chitterlings, and other high-fat and high-cholesterol products.
- African Americans are more likely to be murdered than whites. The African American male homicide rate, seventy-one deaths per 100,000 African American men, is seven times the white male homicide rate.

African American's hope for a longer life expectancy lies in the fact that many of these life-threatening patterns are within our control. As more African Americans choose healthier lifestyles, we will drastically improve our life expectancy. Chart 22, "A Heartfelt Warning," has some helpful hints from the editors of *Black Enterprise* magazine. This chart provides useful information about what African Americans can do to reduce their rate of heart disease.

CHART 22: A HEARTFELT WARNING

To evaluate your risk factors, have regular checkups. To reduce those risk factors:
- Restrict the amounts and kinds of fat and cholesterol in your diet
- Stop smoking
- Control high blood pressure
- Exercise regularly
- Lose weight
- Take your medicine

I encourage your friends and family to join you in a healthful way of life:
- Share healthy cooking tips with your friends and neighbors.
- Suggest that your church, synagogue, mosque, or community group hold a blood pressure screening.
- Find partners to exercise with three or four times a week.

Take action in your community and at work:
- Urge that grocery stores and restaurants that you patronize offer a wider choice of healthful foods.
- Insist on a no-smoking section in restaurants and other public places.
- Ask for more healthful choices in your company's vending machine or cafeteria.
- Request a no-smoking policy if there isn't one.
- Start a fitness walking club or aerobic exercise class.

Reprinted by permission of Black Enterprise *magazine*

Chart 22 suggests the importance of African American households taking a stand for good health; viewing good health as an economic tool may help many African American households take this important stand. Again we turn to the authors of *The Black Man's Guide to Good Health:* "When we learned about our rights as citizens of America during the civil rights movement, we became empowered to make changes. Now it's time for us to become empowered again. This time, we must make changes that have to do with one of the most important issues ever—saving our own lives."

UNDERSTANDING LIFE INSURANCE

It is not uncommon in the African American community to attend a funeral and hear people whispering, "I hope he had insurance." I have attended several funerals where family members have been called upon to donate money to help defray the cost of the funeral expenses. Many African Americans do not own a life insurance policy. The absence of insurance is not limited to less affluent African American households, however. Many middle-class African American's do not have life insurance either.

Everyone knows that life insurance is a misnomer in the sense that it cannot replace a person's life. What life insurance can do is replace a substantial part of the insured's income. Hence, life insurance becomes income protection to replace the future earnings that may be lost because of the untimely death of an individual.

According to Alan Lavine, author of *Your Life Insurance Options,* "Eight out of ten American families have some life insurance coverage." According to the American Council of Life Insurance, a trade group in Washington, D.C., the average family has $115,000 in insurance coverage. In 1992, consumers took out $156 billion in insurance coverage. Despite all that protection, the National Insurance Consumers Organization, in Alexandria, Virginia, reports that, "Twenty percent (20%) of all policies are dropped after two years and almost 50 percent (50%) of all policies were cashed out after ten years."

Additionally, the American Council of Life Insurance reported that in 1989 the average size policy for each insured person was $35,000 and that most insurance was purchased by men to protect the income needs of their families. (1) African Americans own $17 billion in personal insurance and pensions according to *Black Enterprise* magazine. (2) When you average this figure out per household, African Americans really come up short. (3) The average married couple owns $78,700 of insurance, while African Americans own approximately $545 of life insurance.

While it is true that many white families view life insurance as income protection, many African American households still view life insurance simply as a way to pay for funeral or burial expenses. This may account for the small amount of life insurance African American families own and be the reason that African Americans view insurance as a death-related product as opposed to a life-enriching tool that can help the deceased's family.

For many years white insurance companies would not sell life insurance to African Americans. Norman Dacey documents in his book, *What's Wrong With Your Life Insurance,* that "As recently as the early part of the twentieth century, (White Insurance) company rate books unabashedly warned *'Negroes and Indians* need not apply' for coverage."

In response to such discrimination, African American churches and fraternal organizations started their own burial societies. Many of these organizations later emerged as African American insurance companies. Although there are approximately fifty African American insurance companies today (see the *Resource Guide* for listing), their annual premium sales and assets pale in comparison to those of larger white insurance companies whose assets alone are $1.6 trillion dollars.

In the beginning African American insurance companies marketed high-cost industrial policies to African American consumers. Norman F. Dacey described how industrial policies worked: "The peculiar names *industrial, debit,* and *home service* are used to identify a class of insurance that was meant to be sold to people with very low income. These are the policies that were once sold for a premium of as little as five or ten cents a week. There was a time two or three generations ago, when a $250 insurance policy would pay the funeral bills. Industrial insurance provided the $250." Insurance policies were serviced by insurance agents who visited the insured's home to collect the premium every week—usually on payday before the money was spent. Today, people can still buy these policies; however, the payments are monthly and the insured amounts are written in $1,000 increments. Fortunately for many consumers, industrial policies are falling out of favor. According to the Life Insurance Fact Book, in 1986 there were only $42 million industrial policies in force and $305,000 sold that year. Today, many African American insurance companies still service industrial policies.

Because African Americans continue to buy life insurance to pay for burial expenses, many African American families are underinsured. In trying to ensure that family members are buried with dignity, African Americans fail to make sure that the family can replace the income of the deceased family member.

According to Norman F. Dacey, "Most families have two estates—an 'acquired estate' and a 'potential estate.' The 'acquired estate' is represented by the tangible property currently owned, whereas the 'potential estate' is represented by the future earning power of the breadwinner." All African American households must have life insurance protection that will protect the "potential estate" of that household. When I discuss the concept of insuring your financial future, I am referring to using insurance to protect the unacquired earnings of a deceased individual.

Given the cost of industrial insurance, it is easy to understand why many African American families believe that they cannot afford more than a few thousand dollars of life insurance. Likewise, many African American families are persuaded to buy whole-life insurance or universal-whole-life insurance rather than term insurance. Both are similar to industrial insurance in that they are high-cost insurance plans that offer very little insurance protection.

Another name for these types of insurance is "cash value life insurance." The name refers to the so-called saving or cash value accumulation within the life insurance policy. In essence, these policies combine a saving plan with a term insurance policy. There have been several excellent books written about the fallacies, abuses, and problems associated with cash value insurance policies. I have already referred to one of them, *What's Wrong with Your Life Insurance* by Norman F. Dacey, so I won't delve into all the reasons that cash value plans will not work in your wealth-building program.

I recommend purchasing *annual-decreasing-term-to-age-sixty-five* insurance or *level-term-to-age-sixty-five* insurance. This type of insurance policy:

- Provides the maximum protection.
- Is less expensive.
- Is a simple, understandable life insurance program.

All life insurance premiums are based on mortality tables. Historical data help insurance companies predict the average life span of any given group of people of a certain age, income, and state of health. On the basis of this information, life insurance companies can establish their mortality rates, or cost, per $1,000 of insurance for a particular age group. When you buy term insurance, you are paying for your natural mortality rate only. When you buy a cash value policy, you pay for your natural mortality rate, plus you add money that is placed into a savings or investment side fund within the policy. Because term insurance lets you pay for your natural mortality rate, many financial planning professionals refer to term insurance as buying pure protection.

When buying term insurance, you should understand that every year your cost will match your increased mortality rate. Additionally, at age sixty-five you will find yourself with only a small amount of life insurance protection or no insurance protection at all. This will not be an issue for you if you have taken the advice in this book and invested a small portion of your earning every month. At age sixty-five you should be self-insured, meaning you have enough liquid assets to pay for your funeral with enough left over to help your heirs.

Another reason that I suggest term insurance is because of its affordability. In addition to needing money to bury our loved ones, many African Americans need money to provide for our children and money to pay for the family car or home. When you total these expenditures, it is easy to see how a $5,000 or $10,000 whole-life insurance plan won't be enough. In fact, most financial planning professionals suggest that a family insurance policy be at least five times the breadwinner's income. Therefore, a household in which each spouse earns $20,000 needs $200,000 in insurance protection. The payment on $200,000 of whole-life or any cash value insurance is expensive compared to payments on $200,000 on term insurance, which is affordable to most households. Here is an example: A non-smoking male at age forty-three can buy a $100,000 whole-life policy for $1,700 a year. The same person can purchase a $100,000 universal-life policy for $1,200 a year or a $100,000 annual-renewable-term policy for $252 a year. It is not uncommon for cash value life insurance to cost ten times more than term insurance for the same protection.

Chart 23, "Salary x Five Approach," shows how you can calculate your family's insurance needs using the five-times earning formula. Chart 24, "Assumed Annual Investments," compares the cost of term insurance to cash value insurance. Charts 25, "Term Insurance Example," and 26, "Whole Life Insurance," show how much you will spend if you buy a renewable-term, whole-life, or universal-life policy.

A third reason for buying term insurance is that it is an easy-to-understand policy. Don't invest in anything that you don't understand

and can't explain to a friend in five minutes. This advice is relevant whether you are talking about a business venture, a new mutual fund, or life insurance. Many fast-talking insurance agents will try to convince you that you can understand all the bells and whistles associated with a cash value insurance plan. In reality, cash value insurance plans are so convoluted that even many insurance professionals don't understand the product they are selling. Insurance agents make the biggest commissions on cash value policies and the least commission on term insurance. Which would you try to sell? There is a saying in the insurance business, "If you sell term insurance you can't eat, but when you sell whole life insurance you can't sleep."

In any case, you don't need bells or whistles when you buy insurance, you need income protection. You need to protect your financial future, which might be in jeopardy if you passed away prematurely. Term insurance can provide the basic income protection you need—it is simple to understand and it offers maximum protection at a reasonable price.

By using term insurance you will be able to protect your family and still have money to save for your long-term investment goals. When you stop allowing an insurance company to invest for you and start investing the extra money yourself, you will get a better return on your dollar than the insurance company's cash value. Also, you have complete control and access to your funds whenever you need them.

CHART 23: THE "SALARY X FIVE" APPROACH

	AMOUNT OF INSURANCE
Income	5×
$25,000	$125,000
35,000	175,000
45,000	225,000
55,000	275,000
65,000	325,000
75,000	375,000
95,000	475,000
105,000	525,000

Reprinted by permission of Educational Technologies Inc.

CHART 24: ILLUSTRATION OF ASSUMED ANNUAL INVESTMENTS OF $1,648 IN SHARES OF WINDSOR FUND. 25-YEAR PERIOD

Assuming that an initial investment of $1,648 was made on December 31, 1962, and a similar sum was invested on December 31 of each year thereafter, the table below shows the accumulated investment and accumulated value over an elapsed period of twenty-five years. All income dividends and capital gains distributions were reinvested. Windsor Fund has no sales charge.

| Year Ending Dec. 31 | WINDSOR FUND | | | | UNIVERSAL LIFE | |
	Cumulative Annual Investment	Fund Value at End of Year	Death Benefit of Decreasing Term Insurance	Total Estate Value	Cash Value*	Estate Value and Death Benefit
1962	1,648	—	100,000	100,000	—	100,000
1963	3,296	3,505	97,800	101,305	1,724	100,000
1964	4,944	5,641	94,200	99,841	3,590	100,000
1965	6,592	8,932	90,600	99,532	5,610	100,000
1966	8,240	10,285	87,000	97,285	7,798	100,000
1967	9,888	15,173	83,400	98,573	10,166	100,000
1968	11,536	20,067	79,900	99,967	13,179	100,000
1969	13,184	20,956	76,200	97,156	16,193	100,000
1970	14,832	23,935	72,700	96,635	19,206	100,000
1971	16,480	27,271	69,100	96,371	22,220	100,000
1972	18,128	31,813	65,500	97,313	25,234	100,000
1973	19,776	25,501	61,900	87,401	29,702	100,000
1974	21,424	22,864	58,300	81,164	34,170	100,000

| | WINDSOR FUND | | | | UNIVERSAL LIFE | |
Year Ending Dec. 31	Cumulative Annual Investment	Fund Value at End of Year	Death Benefit of Decreasing Term Insurance	Total Estate Value	Cash Value*	Estate Value and Death Benefit
1975	23,072	36,971	54,800	91,771	38,639	100,000
1976	24,720	55,778	51,100	106,878	43,107	100,000
1977	26,368	57,974	47,600	105,574	47,576	100,000
1978	28,016	64,704	43,900	108,604	54,304	100,000
1979	29,664	80,994	40,400	121,344	61,032	100,000
1980	31,312	100,900	36,800	137,700	67,760	100,000
1981	32,960	119,458	33,200	152,658	74,488	100,000
1982	34,608	147,050	29,600	176,650	81,216	105,580
1983	36,256	192,902	26,000	218,902	91,500	117,120
1984	37,904	232,115	22,400	254,515	101,784	128,247
1985	39,552	298,816	18,800	317,616	112,069	138,965
1986	41,200	361,045	15,200	376,245	122,353	149,270
1987	41,200	365,486	-0-	365,486	132,638	159,165

*Based on nonguaranteed current interest and nonguaranteed current mortality charges.

Although the illustration reflects the long-term rise of securities prices, it should be noted that ten weeks before the end of the period covered, the leading market index suffered the sharpest loss in its history. That decline, too, was reflected in the results shown here. Such a program of investment does not assure a profit or protect against loss in declining markets. No adjustment has been made for any income taxes payable on dividends or distributions.

Reprinted by permission of Simon and Schuster.

ILLUSTRATION OF ASSUMED ANNUAL INVESTMENTS OF $1,648 IN SHARES OF FIDELITY MAGELLAN FUND
25-YEAR PERIOD

Assuming that an initial investment of $1,648 was made on May 2, 1963, and a similar sum was invested on each December 31 thereafter, the table below shows the accumulated investment and accumulated value over an elapsed period of 24¾ years. All income dividends and capital gains distributions were reinvested at net asset value. Fidelity Magellan Fund's 3% sales charge is reflected in the figures shown.

| Year Ending Dec. 31 | FIDELITY MAGELLAN FUND | | | | UNIVERSAL LIFE | |
	Cumulative Annual Investment	Fund Value at End of Year	Death Benefit of Decreasing Term Insurance	Total Estate Value	Cash Value°	Estate Value and Death Benefit
1962	1,648	—	100,000	101,648	—	100,000
1963	3,296	3,740	97,800	101,540	1,724	100,000
1964	4,944	6,063	94,200	100,263	3,590	100,000
1965	6,592	14,693	90,600	105,293	5,610	100,000
1966	8,240	17,503	87,000	104,503	7,798	100,000
1967	9,888	37,278	83,400	120,678	10,166	100,000
1968	11,536	54,106	79,900	134,006	13,179	100,000
1969	13,184	46,321	76,200	122,521	16,193	100,000
1970	14,832	40,641	72,700	113,341	19,206	100,000
1971	16,480	56,499	69,100	125,599	22,220	100,000
1972	18,128	75,101	65,500	140,601	25,234	100,000
1973	19,776	45,054	61,900	106,954	29,702	100,000

	FIDELITY MAGELLAN FUND				UNIVERSAL LIFE	
Year Ending Dec. 31	Cumulative Annual Investment	Fund Value at End of Year	Death Benefit of Decreasing Term Insurance	Total Estate Value	Cash Value*	Estate Value and Death Benefit
1974	21,424	33,834	58,300	92,134	34,170	100,000
1975	23,072	50,464	54,800	105,264	38,639	100,000
1976	24,720	71,102	51,100	122,202	43,107	100,000
1977	26,368	82,975	47,600	130,575	47,576	100,000
1978	28,016	110,878	43,900	154,778	54,304	100,000
1979	29,664	169,814	40,400	210,214	61,032	100,000
1980	31,312	290,119	36,800	326,919	67,760	100,000
1981	32,960	339,434	33,200	372,634	74,488	100,000
1982	34,608	504,169	29,600	533,769	81,216	105,580
1983	36,256	700,322	26,000	726,322	91,500	117,120
1984	37,904	716,177	22,400	738,577	101,784	128,247
1985	39,552	1,026,442	18,800	1,045,242	112,069	138,965
1986	41,200	1,271,761	15,200	1,286,961	122,353	149,270
1987	41,200	1,286,084	-0-	1,286,084	132,638	159,165

*Based on nonguaranteed current interest and nonguaranteed current mortality charges.

Although the illustration reflects the long-term rise of securities prices, it should be noted that ten weeks before the end of the period covered, the leading market index suffered the sharpest loss in its history. That decline, too, was reflected in the results shown here. Such a program of investment does not assure a profit or protect against loss in declining markets. No adjustment has been made for any income taxes payable on dividends or distributions.

Reprinted by permission of Simon and Schuster.

CHART 25: TERM INSURANCE EXAMPLE

The A+ Insurance Company
Insured: J.J. Doe   November 1, 1991
Agent: Smith

Male, age 35, Nonsmoker Term
Waiver of Premium Benefit

$100,000 Annually Renewable Term, renewable to age 100 and
convertible to age 65. Reentry to age 70.
First-year premium $130

PREMIUM PAYMENT SCHEDULE

Year	Age	Premium	Guaranteed Maximum
1	35	$130	
2	36	142	
3	37	158	
4	38	173	
5	39	186	
	total	789	
6	40	202	
7	41	217	513
8	42	236	541
9	43	252	573
10	44	276	607
	total	1,972	3,225
11	45	165	642
12	46	204	675
13	47	235	709
14	48	255	752
15	49	275	809
	total	3,106	6,812
16	50	338	887
17	51	401	990
18	52	465	1,114
19	53	539	1,255
20	54	645	1,409
	total	5,495	12,467

Reprinted by permission of John Wiley and Sons, Inc.

CHART 26: WHOLE LIFE INSURANCE

Year	Annual Premium	Projected Year-End Dividends	Guaranteed Cash Value	PUAs Cash Value	Total Cash Value	PUAs Death Value	Total Death Benefit
1	1,710	280	254	280	534	1,013	102,013
2	1,710	291	1,956	597	2,553	2,086	102,068
3	1,710	362	3,699	1,016	4,715	3,422	103,422
4	1,710	434	5,485	1,545	7,030	5,023	105,023
5	1,710	508	7,353	2,197	9,550	6,894	106,894
6	1,710	585	9,265	2,986	12,251	9,045	109,045
7	1,710	666	11,243	3,927	15,170	11,487	111,487
8	1,710	751	13,282	5,038	18,320	14,232	114,232
9	1,710	842	13,648	6,338	19,986	17,300	117,300
10	0	937	15,369	5,822	21,191	15,359	115,359
11	0	1,035	17,132	5,374	22,506	13,709	113,709
12	0	1,136	18,238	5,001	23,939	12,342	112,342
13	0	1,244	20,769	4,731	25,500	11,299	111,299
14	0	1,352	22,639	4,551	27,190	10,526	110,556
15	0	1,459	24,534	4,467	29,001	10,008	110,008
16	0	1,511	26,468	4,485	30,953	9,732	102,739
17	0	1,679	28,439	4,626	33,065	2,742	109,742
18	0	1,793	30,428	4,890	35,318	9,900	109,990

WHOLE LIFE INSURANCE

Year	Annual Premium	Projected Year-End Dividends	Guaranteed Cash Value	PUAs Cash Value	Total Cash Value	PUAs Death Value	Total Death Benefit
19	0	1,902	32,436	5,284	37,720	10,479	110,479
20	0	2,032	34,454	5,824	40,278	11,219	111,219

AGE

			TOTAL PREMIUMS				
60	15,390	1,679	28,439	4,626	33,065	9,742	109,742
65	15,390	2,221	39,541	7,411	45,952	13,497	113,497
70	15,390	2,976	48,774	14,957	63,731	23,962	123,962
95	15,390	5,807	87,374	199,359	286,733	219,718	312,718

SUMMARY OF PREMIUMS

$100,000 Whole Life	1,710.00	145.35
Total Premium	1,710.00	145.35

Norman Dacey compared buying a universal-life policy with buying a term policy and investing money in a mutual fund. As you can see for yourself in Charts 25 and 26, the mutual funds helped his net worth grow ten times more than the universal-life policy did. These illustrations also help you understand how you can financially insure your future by buying term to sixty-five life insurance and saving as much as you can in a mutual fund account.

A word of advice. If you do not have the intestinal fortitude to buy term insurance and invest the money on your own, then you may be better served buying a universal-life insurance plan. These plans will at least let you invest a portion of your savings in a variety of mutual funds. However, universal-life policies are very expensive and have many hidden costs. Nevertheless, if you can't buy term and invest the rest on your own, then this may be your best alternative.

In addition to term insurance there are several other pure insurance products that can help you insure your financial future. Disability insurance can pay up to 60 percent of your income if you are sick, disabled, and unable to work. Depending on the type of policy you purchase, if you are permanently disabled, you could be assured an income for your lifetime or until age sixty-five. Most disability policies are pure protection policies and, therefore, do not have a cash fund that will increase your premium payments. Not as apparent but just as beneficial to insuring a family's potential estate are company-sponsored insurance plans, family insurance riders, waiver of premiums, disability insurance riders, and mortgage insurance.

Notice I did not include consumer credit insurance policies. These policies are basically a way for car salespeople or appliance dealers to increase their sales by selling you a life insurance policy that pays off the loan on these items should you die. A large term-insurance policy will also enable your family to pay off a car loan or other consumer loan; therefore, you do not need such insurance.

Several other issues associated with life insurance are common in the African American community. These issues include the following:

- **Turning life insurance policies over to funeral directors.** This practice was started when life insurance proceeds were primarily used to pay for burial costs. However, today, a good portion of a family's future net worth may be tied up in an insurance policy. Therefore, the policy shouldn't be handled by anyone who is not part of the immediate family.

- **Teenage parents. If a young person in your household has a child, make sure that person has at least $100,000 of term insurance.** Many teenage girls are having babies, and the risk of the child becoming fatherless is very high. It is, therefore, important that *both* teenage parents have life insurance to help defray the cost of raising the child should something happen to one of the young parents.

- **Always choose a Triple A–rated insurance company.** You can request free ratings on any insurance company from Standard and Poor's at (212) 208-1527, Moody's at (212) 553-0377, or Duff and Phelps at (312) 368-3657. Also a list of A rated companies from AM Best is provided in the *Resource Guide*.

- **Get three referrals from people you trust when looking for a reputable insurance agent.** Interview all three and evaluate them on the following points:
  – Does the person listen to you?
  – Does the person respond to your questions and explain things to you?
  – Does the person respond to your calls right away?
  – Are all of your questions answered or are you given a sales pitch?
  – Does the agent review your financial situation before making recommendations?
  – Does the agent explain all the fees, charges, and commissions?
  – Does the agent show you realistic illustrations or examples?

- **Avoid being persuaded that a mutual insurance company is better than a stock company.** Both sell life insurance for a profit, and the so-called dividends that mutual companies share with their policyholders are not investment dividends but a creation that the insurance companies refer to as "insurance dividends." In reality, insurance dividends are nothing more than a return of your excess premium payment. If you really want to share in the profits of an insurance company, you must do what other investors do: buy the insurance company stock.

- **Remember, insurance companies are the world's largest financial institutions, with assets over $1.6 trillion.** They got that way by using other people's money. The majority of insurance policyholders never file a death claim or receive a cash payment. If you decide that you are tired of your insurance company, don't just stop sending your payments. Write a letter and request the return of any unused premiums and non-collected cash value.

• **Place your insurance papers and will in a safe, centrally located place where your family can get to it in case of an emergency.**

INSURING YOUR DREAMS

Because African Americans try to avoid discussing death-related financial matters, many of our households do not have a written will. Wills are a necessary part of insuring your financial future; they are important for no other reason than to let people know how to distribute your insurance proceeds. When people leave an estate without a will, the courts and state distribute the estate.

I believe that everyone needs a will regardless of the size of the estate. A will is a legal document that tells your family how to divide your money and possessions. Wills specify who is to inherit what. Wills are fairly easy and inexpensive to write, and you can find a do-it-yourself guide at any bookstore or have a lawyer prepare one. Either is legally binding.

Now, let's see how you could insure your family's future. Again, I will refer to you and your spouse as Mr. and Mrs. Money. We will assume that Mr. and Mrs. Money decided to cash in their old whole-life policy, which primarily insured Mr. Money. The old policy had a $50,000 death benefit and cost the family $1,000 a year. It also had a $10,000 rider for Mrs. Money and $5,000 riders on their two children.

After realizing the benefits of term insurance, the Money family shopped around and found the You Bet Your Life Insurance Company. From this triple A–rated insurance company, the Money family bought a $100,000 level-term-to-sixty-five policy on Mr. Money and $100,000 annual-reducing-term policy on Mrs. Money. This family also purchased a rider for $3,000 on each child. Their new annual premiums will be $600.

Making these smart insurance moves will save your family $400 a year in life insurance premiums. That means you will have an additional $400 a year ($33 a month) for your long-term goal.

It is always a good feeling to find additional dream capital (money you can use to secure your dreams), but in this case, it is also comforting to know that even death cannot impede your family's journey to abundance.

ENTREPRENEURSHIP: THE ULTIMATE SMART MONEY MOVE

All hard work brings a profit, but mere talk leads only to poverty.
                                                    —Proverbs 14:23

"My friend in New York is making *real* money," I overheard a successful entrepreneur in his own right, tell a mutual friend at a reception. I had to find out how someone as wealthy as this man would define financial success or "real money." So I asked him, "What's *real* money to you?" He replied, "When you can take home $1 million a year—that's real money, and that is what my friend in New York who has a tire wholesale business is doing. And I am very proud of him."

Today, there is only one occupation that can offer the average African American the ability to earn what this man refers to as "real money." This occupation is business ownership. In spite of the enormous wealth-creating potential of owning a business, historically only a few African Americans have pursued this occupation. As a result, in our population of 33 million, there are only 424,165 African American businesses. This represents almost 1.2 percent of the African American population. By comparison, white Americans have approximately 12,481,730 businesses; entrepreneurs represent approximately 5.9 percent in their population. The small number of African Americans engaged in entrepreneurial activities is hard to understand given the fact that African American entrepreneurs earn on average twice as much as employed African Americans. The 1992 U.S. Census data illustrate that while the median African American family income was $21,550, the average earnings for an African American business was over $50,000—and $189,000 for our white counterparts. In addition, minority-owned small businesses accounted for 9 percent of all U.S. firms and almost 4 percent of their gross receipts. Combined, the total earning of minority businesses was more than $78 billion. While this sum represents only a small percentage of the United States gross domestic receipt of $1.9 trillion, it still shows that owning your own business is an enormous wealth-creating opportunity.

These facts suggest there is room for more African Americans to join the ranks of the successful entrepreneurs. These facts also suggest why I believe entrepreneurship is the ultimate smart money move for African Americans.

But becoming a business owner is not for everyone. I will show you what it takes to become a successful entrepreneur, as well as why the African American community needs to produce more business owners. Even if you have already decided that you don't want to own your own business, you should still read this chapter. Learning about what makes a successful business will help you in selecting stocks suitable for your investment portfolio. This information may also help you understand why your current employer makes certain decisions. Besides, who knows, one day you may change your mind, or it may be changed for you. With corporate downsizing, fewer job prospects, or an unexpected opportunity, you may find yourself in the ranks of the self-employed.

One such situation happened to me. I was minding my own business—literally—when I got a call from a stranger who asked if I ever considered publishing an African American business publication. The call came from the associate publisher of Corporate Detroit *magazine. He asked me to meet him and his publisher for lunch. Intrigued, I went and was offered the opportunity to be the publisher of a new magazine for Detroit's affluent African American community.*

The supplement was entitled Corporate Colors, *and its acceptance in the community exceeded everyone's expectation. Readers and advertisers alike adored the new business publication. Nevertheless, the parent company, Business Journal Publishing and its core magazines* Corporate Detroit, Corporate Cleveland, *and* Corporate San Diego *were in dire financial trouble. After several attempts to refinance the troubled organizations, Business Journal Publishing decided to cut its losses and sell the assets of the corporation eight months after I joined the organization.*

Upon hearing that the Detroit magazine was up for sale, I started to

call my friends to tell them that one of the nation's top business maga-
zines was on the selling block. At first, I didn't consider buying it my-
self because I was too busy producing The Color of Money *television*
series. Besides, I thought that whoever bought the magazine would
ask me to stay and continue publishing the successful Corporate Colors *supplement.*

I eventually contacted Marilyn French Hubbard, director of training
and organizational development for Health Alliance Plan and a long-
time friend who had written a business column for the magazine. After
telling her the reason for the call, she said, "Well, Kelvin, why don't you
buy it?" Only Hubbard could make the inconceivable sound obvious.
Somehow Marilyn's words jarred me to consider the possibility of buy-
ing and running a magazine company and publishing a magazine
whose 35,000 readers were mostly white. In less than an hour I decided
that maybe I should pursue it. So I got on the phone and talked to Bill
Dorn who owned Business Journal Publishing at the time. Bill told me
he had one offer but that he wasn't satisfied with it. If I made a better
offer, he would sell the magazine and all of its assets to me.

I asked him for one week to come up with an offer. He agreed and I
was off and running. I had worked on several business deals before so
I knew that the first thing I had to do was to review the financial con-
dition of the business and then formulate a business plan to make the
magazine profitable. Since most of my money was already tied up in
the television program, I also had to find an investor or bank willing
to finance the deal.

I worked around the clock and finally outbid the other interested
buyer. Two months later my new partner, Dr. Margaret L. Betts, and
I made magazine history when we successfully completed a leverage
buyout of Corporate Detroit *magazine. It became one of the first*
major regional business-to-business publications to be owned by an
African American investment group.

Although my financial commitment at the time was less than
$50,000, after the buyout was completed I found myself owning 50
percent of a fifteen-year-old publishing company with three well-
respected magazines, Corporate Detroit, Corporate Colors, *and* Michigan Business.

Our new company did not have to assume any of Business Journal
Publishing's debt. Instead, we assumed all operating expenses and the
cost of its sixteen-member work force. A year after assuming the

CEO's duties of the magazine, I have taken very little income from the operation. Nevertheless, my interest in the magazine has increased my net worth substantially, and the value of the publishing business is still growing.

Now, I am not taking home that million-dollar income my friend spoke about earlier. However, if I decided to sell my interest today, I would receive more than $1 million. This additional wealth was generated in less time than it took me to write this book, and my experience helps to illustrate how most African Americans can increase their wealth by deciding to become entrepreneurs. Furthermore, this small piece of magazine trivia helps you to understand that you never know when a good business opportunity will come along. So the best thing you can do is to be prepared for it when it arrives. Now let's find out if you have what it takes to become a successful entrepreneur.

WHAT IS AN ENTREPRENEUR?

Given the fact that the word "entrepreneur" evokes so many images, I thought that it would be good to define how I use the term. Jeffry A. Timmons offers us a complete definition of entrepreneurship in his insightful book, *The Entrepreneurial Mind.* There he writes, "Entrepreneurship is the ability to create and build something from practically nothing. It is initiating, doing, achieving, and building an enterprise or organization, rather than just watching, analyzing or describing one. It is the knack for sensing an opportunity where others see chaos, contradiction and confusion. It is the ability to build a founding team to complement your own skills and talents. It is the know-how to find, marshal and control resources (often owned by others) and to make sure you don't run out of money when you need it most. Finally, it is a willingness to take calculated risks, both personal and financial, and then do everything possible to get the odds in your favor."

Mr. Timmons also notes that "While anyone can try to start a business, relatively few can grow one to beyond $1 million in sales. According to government data, only about 1 in 30 businesses had annual sales of over $1 million." This observation may explain why few African American businesses have annual sales over $1 million.

Mr. Timmons also suggests the right size a business needs to be in order to become successful. The businesses with the most likelihood of experiencing long-term success have a minimum of ten employees and sales over $500,000. Mr. Timmons's research also points out that "survival odds, and prosperity—namely significant job creation—improve even further once the $1 million in sales level is attained." This is why we must encourage existing African American entrepreneurs and future African American entrepreneurs to establish million-dollar operations.

THIRTEEN MYTHS ABOUT ENTREPRENEURSHIP

Folklore and stereotypes about entrepreneurs are remarkably durable, even in these informed and sophisticated times. Take, for instance, the following examples of myths and realities about entrepreneurship; twelve were compiled by Mr. Timmons, and I added the last one.

Myth 1: Entrepreneurs are born, not made.

Reality: There is increasing evidence that successful entrepreneurs emerge from a combination of work experience, study, and development of appropriate skills. While there are no doubt attributes that you either have or you don't, possessing them does not necessarily an entrepreneur make, and other skills of equal importance can, in fact, be acquired through understanding, hard work and patience.

Myth 2: Anyone can start a business. It's a matter of luck and guts. All you need is a new idea; then go for it.

Reality: If you want to launch and grow a high-potential venture you must get the odds in your favor. You cannot think and act like an inventor, or a promoter, or even a manager; you must think and act like an entrepreneur.

Myth 3: Entrepreneurs are gamblers. They roll the dice and take the consequences.

Reality: Successful entrepreneurs are very careful to calculate the risks they take. They get others to share risk with them, thereby lowering their personal exposure. When they find they can avoid or minimize risks they do so.

Myth 4: You are better off as an independent: one entrepreneur, owning the whole show yourself.

Reality: It is extremely difficult to grow a venture beyond $1 million in profitable sales working single-handedly. Ventures that succeed usually have multiple founders. Besides, one hundred percent of nothing is nothing.

Myth 5: Being an entrepreneur is the only way you can really be your own boss and completely independent.

Reality: Entrepreneurs are far from independent, and have many masters and constituencies to serve and juggle partners, investors, customers, suppliers, creditors, employees, spouse, family and social and community obligations.

Myth 6: Entrepreneurs work longer and harder than managers in big companies.

Reality: According to a recent survey of Harvard Business School alumni, a spectrum of "hours per week worked" shows that the self-employed actually work more *and* less than their corporate counterparts. If you can make money for a large company, chances are you can do it for your own company.

Myth 7: Entrepreneurs face greater stress and more pressures and thus pay a higher price for their role than any others.

Reality: Being an entrepreneur is stressful and demanding. But there is no evidence that it is any more stressful than other demanding professional roles, such as a partner in a large accounting or law firm, or head of a large corporation or government agency.

Compared to managers in the Harvard study, nearly three times as many entrepreneurs said they did not plan to retire ever; almost three fourths said they would be entrepreneurs again if they had to do it all over. Most entrepreneurs enjoy what they do; they reported more fun than drudgery; they thrived on the flexibility and innovative aspects of their jobs. Other studies also show that entrepreneurs report very high job satisfaction.

Myth 8: Starting your own company is a risky, hazardous proposition which often ends in failure.

Reality: Success, rather than failure, is more common among higher potential ventures because they are driven by talented and experienced founders in pursuit of attractive opportunities, who are able to attract both the right people and necessary financial and other resources to make the venture work.

Myth 9: Money makes the difference. If you have enough working capital you will succeed.

Reality: Money is the least important ingredient in new venture success. If the other pieces and talents are there, the money will follow.

Money is not a prime motivator, either. Entrepreneurs thrive on
the "thrill of the chase." Time and again, even after they have made
a few million dollars, they still work long hours and launch more
companies.

Myth 10: Start-ups are for the young and energetic.
Reality: While these qualities may help, it appears that age is no bar-
rier to a start-up, and can have advantages, such as well-developed
networks of contacts. One study showed that one fifth of the
founders were over forty when they embarked on their entrepreneurial career, the majority were in their thirties, and just over one-
quarter did so by the time they were twenty-five. Further, numerous
examples exist of start-ups whose founders were over sixty.

**Myth 11: Entrepreneurs are motivated solely by the quest for
the almighty dollar; they want to make money so they can
spend it.**
Reality: Growth-minded entrepreneurs are more driven by building
the enterprise and realizing long-term capital gains than by instant
gratification through high salaries and perks. A sense of personal
achievement and accomplishment, feeling in control of their own
destinies, and realizing their vision and dreams are also powerful
motivators. Money is viewed as a tool and a way of keeping score.

**Myth 12: Entrepreneurs seek power and control over others
so they can feel in charge.**
Reality: While many entrepreneurs are driven this way, most successful growth-minded entrepreneurs are just the opposite. They
are driven by the quest for responsibility, achievement and results,
rather than power. They thrive on a sense of accomplishment from
outperforming the competition, rather than on a personal need for
power expressed by dominating and controlling others. They gain
control by their results.

**Myth 13: African Americans do not have what it takes to be
successful entrepreneurs.**
Reality: Of course this is totally unfounded; nevertheless, there are
many African Americans and others who believe this myth to be true.
Let me just say that given their drive to make it in face of incredible
odds, I believe that African Americans are well suited for entrepreneurship. To support my belief, let me suggest that you take notice of

these successful African American entrepreneurs: Reginald F. Lewis (TLC Beatrice International Holdings, Inc.); John H. Johnson (Johnson Publishing Company Inc.); Earl Graves (Earl G. Graves LTD.); Dave Bing (The Bing Group); Bill Picard (Regal Plastics); Percy Sutton (Inner City Broadcasting); Robert Johnson (Black Entertainment Television); Dr. Julius Combs (United American Healthcare); Oprah Winfrey (Harpo Productions); Whoopi Goldberg (Whoopi Goldberg Ltd.); Maceo Sloan (NCM Capital Inc.); Madame C.J. Walker, Mrs. George Johnson (Johnson Products); and Don Barden (Barden Communications, Inc.). You can find more listed in our African American Entrepreneur Hall of Fame at the end of this chapter.

Having defined what an entrepreneur is and some of the myths surrounding this notable occupation, let's move on to some of the basic information you will need to know if you decide to become a business owner.

STARTING A BUSINESS

It is unlikely that your first attempt at business ownership will result in the creation of a Beatrice International, Johnson Publishing, or Maxima Corporation. All three represent some of African Americans' largest and most successful business enterprises. More than likely, your first or second business venture will have less than $1 million in annual sales. The United States government categorizes such companies as small businesses. Do not let this title fool you! Small businesses mean big business for the owner and for the country.

According to recent polls, most of the new jobs created in this country are created by small businesses. Additionally, small businesses create huge income and net worth potential for their owners. As with my purchase of *Corporate Detroit,* thousands of people increase their net worth substantially by owning a small business.

There are several ways to define *small business.* One way to define a small business is to look at how many people it employs. The government uses a range of fifty to one hundred employees to separate small businesses from larger businesses. If your business has less than fifty employees, it is a small business.

The financial industry typically uses asset size to define the size of a business. Banks, savings and loans, credit unions, brokerage houses, and the like are the organizations that mainly use this definition. They use the amount of deposits (under $1 million is small) to measure the size of the business.

The most frequently used definition is annual sales. If the business has sales of $500,000 or less, many experts define it as a small business.

THE RIGHT TIME TO START A BUSINESS

When is the right time to begin your own business? Many potential business owners ponder this question and often get caught up in it for too long, as the time never seems to be quite right. They say they'll take the plunge when they save more money, when the children graduate from school, after the mortgage is paid off, or when they retire. Although each of these is a very good reason not to quit your job to start your new business, they are not reasons to postpone starting the process. Starting any venture requires planning, saving, and researching. Waiting to begin this process could be detrimental to your success. If the feeling is right, then the time is right. As they say at Nike—Just do it.

If owning a business is what you want, and you know that's what you want, then begin your planning today. Set your timetable and start the process. If done properly, it could be the most rewarding experience of your life.

SUCCESS AND FAILURE

Let's not make light of the fact that proper planning is extremely important. The statistics concerning the failure rate of small businesses in this country are staggering. The U.S. Department of Commerce reports that in 1985, 80 percent of the business start-ups were closed by year end. In 1987, 80 percent of the survivor's doors were shut by the end of 1990.

With this information in hand, I contend that the primary difference between success and failure is proper preparation. A very large percentage of the new businesses failed within the first two years. The problems are in the early stages of business operation, which should have been addressed in the planning stage. Here are some of the reasons that many small businesses fail in the first two years of operation:

1. Lack of research.
2. Improper marketing.
3. Improper management.
4. Lack of capital.
5. Lack of technology.

Early-stage planning should include each of these areas, but, some of the research should be done by professionals. We will discuss this later in the chapter.

EFFECTS OF CORPORATE DOWNSIZING

In the 1960s, 1970s, and a large portion of the 1980s, American companies led a charmed existence. We were the manufacturing Mecca of the world. Our profits and personal incomes were fat and healthy, but our investment in industry was inadequate. By the mid-1980s, we found that the fat was gone and it was time to start living lean. Corporate downsizing is a result of three decades of spending as opposed to saving.

Small business has taken over as the number-one employer of the American work force. Many Fortune 500 companies now routinely farm out (i.e., outsource) processes they once did themselves, usually hiring small businesses to do the work. So, owning your own business will not only be good for you, but for your community and your country. Before you start planning for it, though, be honest. Do you have what it takes?

SMALL BUSINESS MANAGEMENT

TWO TYPES OF BUSINESS OWNERS

There are basically two types of business owners: the technical expert and the entrepreneur. The technical expert is the individual who has spent much of his or her life in a particular discipline and is considered an expert in that field. These individuals, at some point in their career, decide to apply their expertise to building a business of their own. Entrepreneurs, on the other hand, have no measurable expertise in the discipline for which they decide to start a business. They feel their knowledge of the market climate and general business operation is enough to make them successful. Both types of business owners can be successful in their respective endeavors. However, each must be careful not to fall prey to the pitfalls that have historically made success elusive.

The pitfall of the entrepreneur is that he or she will not have a clear understanding of the product, the technology, or the process that creates the product. (Thus, their customers will be unhappy and their businesses will fail.)

The pitfall of the technical expert, on the other hand, are in the area of business management. Although this individual has a vast knowledge of the processes that directly create the product, he or she may not be adequately versed in the many other aspects of operating a business. Accounting, marketing, corporate structuring, sales, and human resources are areas that typically present problems to the technical expert.

CONSULTING PROFESSIONALS AND HIRING PROFICIENT STAFF

To make up for their shortcomings, both the entrepreneur and the technical expert should consult with a number of professionals, including lawyers, accountants, marketing specialists, management specialists, human resources specialists, and administrative specialists.

The alternative to retaining professionals is to hire staff to perform some of the tasks for your business. As the business owner, you should make an analytical assessment to ascertain whether hiring staff or retaining professionals, or a mix of both, is financially feasible for you and your company. Your original plan should address how you will handle these areas of your business. (We will discuss the importance of your business plan later in the chapter.)

GROUP START-UPS

Oftentimes, it may make sense to start your business with other individuals. Sometimes they will have the capital you need, or you each may be an expert in a different discipline, thereby cutting the cost of hiring staff or retaining outside professionals. However, if you decide to join forces with other individuals in your business endeavor, it is even more vital that you plan and schedule each and every move.

Different people naturally have different motivations, and when you are in business with someone, you have to check and recheck to see that everyone is moving in the same direction with the same ideas. Before you venture into business with other individuals, you should make thorough assessments of your potential partners' visions of what your business should be and make sure that they correlate with yours. If you are having problems with their visions of the business, you may have to look for other partners. For example, they may want to leave the business to their children, and you may want to take the business public.

CHOOSING YOUR PRODUCT

For the technical experts, this decision may already be made because they expect to start a business in their area of expertise. For the entrepreneur, however, who may not be an expert in a particular discipline, choosing a product is a very important decision. Some questions the entrepreneur should keep in mind when making this decision are as follows: Is the product in high demand? Is it possible for technology to make the product obsolete in the near future? What are the production costs? How is the competition providing this product or service? What is the average profit of other companies in the same business?

MARKETING TO YOUR CUSTOMER

Once you have chosen a product, it is time for you to understand your customer. Identifying your customer lets you know how to market to the customer. Not knowing who the customer is could eventually lead to spending time and money marketing to the wrong clientele. You must understand who will use your product most often. For example, if your product is upscale men's clothing, you need to understand who is buying this type of clothing, what their median income level is, what types of jobs they have, where they live, what type of cars they drive, what types of shoes they wear, and so on.

This type of information is called demographic information and can be found in the census section of your local library. Other information can be purchased from local market research firms that develop and sell demographic data.

CHOOSING A LOCATION
AND ADVERTISING VEHICLE

After you have identified your customer and researched the demographics, you must choose a location for your business. On the basis of your demographic information, your location should be convenient to your customers. Location is less important if you service commercial accounts because business customers are more cost driven than location driven. However, if your business caters to retail customers, your location is extremely important.

Choosing suitable advertising is very important for both commercial and retail businesses. Advertising is of course, another cost of doing business and should be analyzed carefully. Many advertising vehicles are available: word of mouth, fliers, direct mail, newspapers, magazines, billboards, shop windows, television, radio, etc. Good demographic information can help you select the best advertising vehicles to reach your customers.

CAPITALIZATION

Capitalizing your business is an issue that every potential business owner must address in the early stages of planning. For many businesses, however, this may not be the only time that capitalization becomes an issue. Lack of capital remains the number one cause of most small business failure. Fortunately, lack of capital, i.e., cash flow shortages, the inability to repay loans, shortage of inventory, inability to cover payroll, and overhead costs, is easy to detect.

Many failed-business owners mistakenly blame their company's problems on lack of capital when, in fact, the company may have a multitude of other problems that are causing a capital problem. This does not mean that there are not situations where lack of capital is legitimately a company's only problem, but lack of capital as the only problem usually signifies inadequate planning. To prevent this problem let's discuss various sources of start-up funding a new business owner can tap.

SAVINGS

Savings are the most popular way to fund business ventures. Many business owners use this source because they don't know of any other way to obtain cash. Savings can also be the least expensive source of capital, free from fees, interest, and issuing stock either now or at some time in the future. If you feel you have enough money saved to finance your endeavor and you decide to use savings as your source of capitalization, make sure you have a backup plan. Often the start-up process stalls because of mistakes or unforeseen situations that make it necessary to secure additional capital in order to continue the process.

BORROWING

The most traditional source for borrowing is your local bank. Banks are typically very conservative in their small business lending departments, and many will not even consider start-ups for at least three years. If your business has passed that threshold, banks are worth checking out. Banks may also consider small business start-up loans if you can offer substantial collateral, like your home.

The process of applying for a small business loan generally requires in-depth paperwork and a lot of time. Because of the failure rate of small businesses, the banker will typically want as much collateral as possible as well as a personal guarantee in order to complete the deal. A personal guarantee is a promissory note to personally repay the loan should the business fail.

The banker will analyze your plans with a trained, constructive, and critical eye. You must make sure that the information that you submit is correct and complete, for first impressions are extremely important. In your dealings with the bank, keep in mind the three primary issues that it will assess: *credit, collateral,* and *character.* These issues will be the basis by which they make their decision to approve or deny your loan request.

An asset-based loan is another borrowing vehicle that may be available to you. Asset-based loans are generally used with companies that have been in business for some specific period of time. This loan is one in which the loan is secured by a specific operational asset of the business, typically accounts receivable or machinery and equipment.

Another source of loans is the Minority Enterprise Small Business Industrial Centers (MESBIC). These are financial institutions set up by individual Fortune 500 companies. The idea is to promote the development of small business in the minority community in order to supply a specific Fortune 500 company, such as General Motors, Amoco Oil, and Ford Motors. You can find out about a MESBIC by calling the sponsoring company. There is also a national organization of MESBICs that can put you in touch with a sponsoring company near you. Check the *Resource Guide* for the number.

There are also many investment-based lending institutions that pool funds from several investors in order to make non-traditional high-risk loans to businesses. These organizations can be difficult to locate because they are usually classified as investment organizations rather than lending organizations. This type of borrowing is generally very expensive and should not be the first choice for capitalizing your business endeavor. This kind of loan should only be entertained if no other sources are available.

Many local governments participate in a variety of loan programs tailored to small business. Local and state governments have programs to encourage new businesses to locate in certain areas and create jobs. The federal government and the Small Business Administration also have several loan programs. You can ask your banker about these loans. Government loans usually have lower interest rates than any of the other borrowing vehicles we have discussed because governments want to promote the continued creation of small business in this country.

EQUITY PARTNERS

Another way to capitalize your business endeavor is to sell stock in your company. You must first, however, formulate your ideas and present them to your prospective stock buyers. At this stage of business capitalization, I would suggest that you present this information only to people you know and trust. You must be careful about sharing your ideas with others. You wouldn't be the first person to have someone else cash in on your idea.

There are two types of stock that you can sell: common stock and preferred stock. Common stock enables others to buy into your business and enables you to raise capital that does not have to be paid back. However, you lose some control of your business. Therefore, it is important not to sell too much common stock, or you could lose total control of your business. Just remember to retain at least 51 percent of the common stock for yourself.

On the other hand, you could sell preferred stock. Preferred stock is nonvoting stock, which means that the stock purchaser has no ownership in the business. You can sell as much preferred stock as possible without losing control. However, the preferred stockholder must be paid back. Preferred stockholders usually purchase stock with the understanding that they will be paid back at a premium at some point in the future. This type of stock is sometimes referred to as quasi-equity because it starts off as equity, but after a period of time, be it one year, five years, or ten years, it converts to debt.

VENTURE CAPITALISTS

Venture capitalists are investors who invest in selected companies or ideas for companies, Venture capital groups generally look for companies with ideas that are on the forefront of technology in any particular industry. The cost of this type of funding is typically paid to the venture capital group in the form of common stock or preferred stock, depending on the situation.

DOCUMENTATION AND ORGANIZATION

DESCRIPTION AND ORGANIZATIONAL CONCERNS
FOR NEW BUSINESSES

It is important, unless you are an attorney yourself, to retain a lawyer to handle your legal documentation and to advise you on legal matters. You will definitely need some assistance from your attorney and your CPA for certain items. For instance, what type of legal description do you want for your company? Your company could be a sole proprietorship, a partnership, a sub-S corporation, a C-corporation, and so on. It is important for you to understand the legal and tax implications of each legal description before you choose one for your business. Other documentation that require an attorney and/or CPA are DBA documents, tax partnership agreements, and purchase agreements. This decision will affect your business throughout its existence; it will also affect your tax bracket.

ORGANIZATION CHART

It is a good idea to create your ideal organizational structure chart showing how you want to structure your company and what positions will report to whom. This may seem premature, but it will help others to understand your plans. Understanding what positions need to be filled in your company and how much each employee will be paid makes it easier to plan your payroll and expense budgets.

WRITING A BUSINESS PLAN

This is the culmination of all that we have discussed in this chapter. Your business plan should cover many topics: a description of your business and its products or services; your location, who your customers will be, where you can find them; what you will charge for the businesses' products and services; what kind of advertising you will use and how much it will cost; who your competition is; your business strengths and weaknesses; who will manage your operation; what management skills and background they have; how much it will cost to start this business; what your personal investment will be; how you will raise additional capital (if applicable); what your projected earnings and expenses are; and what your projected net income will be. The business plan should be a comprehensive presentation of your business venture. Because of its importance you will need professional help in putting it together, or you will at least need to find a good business guide with a sample plan in your book store.

TRAITS OF SUCCESSFUL BUSINESSES

In addition to your business plan, many other factors will influence the odds of your succeeding or failing in your own business. For example, the magazine *Canadian Business* recently reported on a survey conducted by Thorne Riddell on almost 2,000 sole proprietorships started in 1978. In a follow-up survey in 1981, the study found, interestingly enough, that only 25 percent of the firms with male owners had survived, while 47 percent of the firms started by women were still in business. Keeping in mind that the Canadian economy is somewhat different from that of the United States, it is still worthwhile to note the four major factors that seemed to separate the winners from the losers in the Thorne Riddell study.

CHART 27

Factor	Successful Firms	Failures
Degree of Preparation	Spent 6 to 10 months to research and prepare for their ventures.	Spent less than four months to prepare for start-up.
Use of Advisers	90% utilized professional advisers such as lawyers and accountants in starting up.	Only 25% sought professional help at an early stage.
Business Education, Reading	Almost 70% had taken business-related courses before starting business and also regularly read business books and magazines.	Only 10% had attended business courses or now took time to read business material.
Expectations of Income	More than half said they started with modest expectations, typically about $12,000 a year (Canadian), and were prepared to be patient for signs of success.	36% said they fully expected to make barrels of money within 3 years. The anticipated level of annual earnings they most often quoted was $40,000 (Canadian).

Source: "Women: The Best Entrepreneurs," Jane T. Cook, in Canadian Business, *June 1982. Reproduced with permission.*

THE PROS AND CONS OF ENTREPRENEURSHIP

Now you know the basics of starting a business. However, before you rush out the door to get started, let's review several other important points, namely, the advantages and disadvantages of owning a business. Too often business failures can be directly attributed to entrepreneurs who go into business for the wrong reason. In fact, if you are considering going into business for any reason other than creating a financially successful organization, then you are going into business for the wrong reason. Review the pros and cons of business ownership to help decide if entrepreneurship is the right choice for you.

ADVANTAGES

- Being your own boss; not having to report to a manager or supervisor.
- Having the independence and power to make your own business decisions, for better or worse. For many entrepreneurs, this is one of the major payoffs of owning a businesses.
- Direct contact with customers, employees, suppliers, and others.
- The personal satisfaction and sense of achievement that come with being a success, plus the recognition that goes with success. For most successful entrepreneurs, money is not the real goal, but merely a way of keeping score in the game of business.
- The opportunity to be creative, to develop your own idea, product or service; the chance to make a living doing something you truly enjoy.
- Doing something that contributes to others, whether it be providing an excellent product or service, providing employment, or paying dividends to stockholders.

DISADVANTAGES

You may not have thought much about the downside, if you are like most people. Awareness of the potential disadvantages should not discourage you from your goal of going into business for yourself, if you have a strong commitment to that goal. However, forewarned is forearmed, and it will not be helpful for you to view the real world of business through rose-colored glasses.

- In many ways you are still not your own boss. Instead of having one boss, you will now have many—your customers, the government agencies to whom you must report, and, in some cases, your key suppliers.
- There is a large financial risk. The failure rate is high in new businesses, and you may lose not only your own money but also that of your friends and relatives who may have bankrolled you.
- The hours are long and hard. When you start your business, you will no longer be working a nine-to-five job. Count on working ten- to twelve- or even fifteen-hour days, often six or seven days a week.
- You will not have much spare time for family or a social life. You can forget about taking any long vacations for the next few years, since the business is unlikely to run without your presence for any great length of time.
- Your income will not be steady, unlike a salary. You may make more, or less, than you could working for someone else, but in either case your income will fluctuate up and down from month to month.
- The buck stops with you. If a problem arises, there is no boss to pass it along to. You are the boss now, and all the responsibility is yours. If anything goes wrong, the cost comes out of your pocket.
- You may be stuck for years doing work you do not like. Unlike an employee, you cannot simply quit and look for a better job. It may take you years to sell the business or find some other way to get out of it without a major financial loss if you should decide you don't like it.

Now, if you still feel that you have what it takes to be an entrepreneur—congratulations! You have thought about it more than many people do before making the leap into business ownership. To find out how you can improve your chances for entrepreneurial success, fill out the following questionnaire.

CHART 28: SELF-EVALUATION CHECKLIST FOR GOING INTO BUSINESS

Under each question, check the answer that says what you feel or comes closest to it. Be honest with yourself.

Are you a self-starter?
___ I do things on my own. Nobody has to tell me to get going.
___ If someone gets me started, I keep going all night.
___ Easy does it. I don't put myself out until I have to.

How do you feel about other people?
___ I like people. I can get along with just about anybody.
___ I have plenty of friends—I don't need anybody else.
___ Most people irritate me.

Can you lead others?
___ I can get most people to go along when I start something.
___ I can give orders if someone tells me what we should do.
___ I let someone else get things moving. Then I go along if I feel like it.

Can you take responsibility?
___ I like to take charge of things and see them through.
___ I'll take over if I have to, but I'd rather let someone else be responsible.
___ There's always some eager beaver around wanting to show how smart he is. I say let him.

How good an organizer are you?
___ I like to have a plan before I start. I'm usually the one to get things lined up when the group wants to do something.
___ I do all right unless things get too confused. Then I quit.
___ You get all set and then something comes along and presents too many problems. So I just take things as they come.

How good a worker are you?
___ I can keep going as long as I need to. I don't mind working hard for something I want.
___ I'll work hard for a while, but when I've had enough, that's it.
___ I can't see that hard work gets you anywhere.

Chart 28—Continued

Can you make decisions?

___ I can make up my mind in a hurry if I have to. It usually turns out okay, too.

___ I can if I have plenty of time. If I have to make up my mind fast, I think later I should decide the other way.

___ I don't like to be the one who has to decide things.

Can people trust what you say?

___ You bet they can. I don't say things I don't mean.

___ I try to be on the level most of the time, but sometimes I just say what's easiest.

___ Why bother if the other fellow doesn't know the difference.

Can you stick with it?

___ If I make up my mind to do something, I don't let anything stop me.

___ I usually finish what I start—if it goes well.

___ If it doesn't go right away, I quit. Why beat your brains out?

How good is your health?

___ I never run down!

___ I have enough energy for most things I want to do.

___ I run out of energy sooner than most of my friends seem to.

Now count the checks you made.

How many checks are there beside the first answer to each question?

_____

How many checks are there beside the second answer to each question?

_____

How many checks are there beside the third answer to each question?

_____

If most of your checks are beside the first question, you probably have what it takes to run a business. If not, you're likely to have more trouble than you can handle by yourself. Better find a partner who is strong on the points you're weak on. If many checks are beside the third answer, not even a good partner will be able to shore you up.

Source: "Checklist for Going into Business," Small Marketers Aids #71 (Washington, DC.: Small Business Administration, 1977 Revision)

THE $10,000 START-UP

As discussed earlier in the chapter, potential entrepreneurs find many reasons to deter them from starting their lifelong dream of owning their own business. One of the reasons is the lack of capital. Many potential business owners believe that without the help of outside financing it is impossible to start a business. However, the Small Business Administration (SBA) reports that 70 percent of all African American owned business start-up capital is funded from personal savings or by family and friends, as illustrated by Chart 29, "Small Businesses Get Shortchanged."

CHART 29: SMALL BUSINESSES GET SHORTCHANGED

KNOCKING ON BANK DOORS
Percent of small-business owners seeking bank loans within the last three years who have received financing

Black	White	Asian-American	Hispanic
62.4%	79.7%	72.1%	71.8%

BANK BIAS
Percent of small-business owners who encountered discrimination while seeking bank funds

59.2%	2.9%	18.4%	28.6%

FAMILY TIES
Percent of small-business owners who obtain financing from friends and/or family members

23.5%	16.2%	22.4%	12.7%

VENTURING OFF
Percent of small-business owners seeking financing from venture capitalists and/or investors

12.6%	7.8%	5.1%	7.0%

Reprinted by permission of Black Enterprise *magazine*

It is possible to start a business with an investment of $10,000 or less. In order to stay within a $10,000 budget, you must first understand the typical costs involved with starting a business. For illustrative purposes we will group businesses into four types: manufacturing, light manufacturing, retail, and service.

Manufacturing is probably the most costly to start. Manufacturers take raw materials and transform the raw materials into a finished product. The costs associated with this type of start-up include the following:

- Purchase of machinery and equipment.
- Purchase of raw material inventory.
- Acquisition of plant and office space.
- Purchase of office equipment and supplies.
- Hiring of capable and experienced staff.
- Technical research and development.
- Market research and development.
- Strategic plan development.

Light manufacturing also employs some type of process that results in a finished product, but does not require the use of heavy machinery or a technical staff. The costs associated with this type of start-up include the following:

- Purchase of light equipment.
- Purchase of materials.
- Acquisition of office and warehouse space.
- Purchase of office equipment and supplies.
- Hiring of staff.
- Market research and development.
- Strategic plan development.

Retail businesses purchase inventory and sell it to the consumer as is. Without the processing machinery and equipment to purchase, this start-up may prove to be less costly than the previous two. However, depending on the type of merchandise that is being sold, inventory costs can be substantial. The typical costs associated with this type of start-up include the following:

- Purchase of inventory.
- Acquisition of showcase space.
- Purchase of office equipment and supplies.

- Hiring of staff.
- Strategic and market plan development.

Service businesses can be the least costly because there is usually no inventory or processing. The fact that this group does not typically have to be concerned with the purchase of heavy equipment or inventory makes it very attractive to entrepreneurs trying to maintain a $10,000 budget. The typical costs associated with this type of start-up include the following:

- Acquisition of office space.
- Purchase of office/specialized equipment and supplies.
- Market plan development.
- Hiring of staff.
- Strategic plan development.

Because the service group tends to be labor intensive, that is, it thrives on the labor of individuals (as opposed to a capital intensive), the start-up costs can be extremely low in comparison to the other groups.

Here are some cost-cutting measures you can try. Not all of the following start-up cost-cutting ideas can be used in all of the groups, but many work for more than one group.

- Lease machinery and equipment whenever possible. Although you will not own the machinery or equipment, a leasing arrangement will obtain machinery at a fraction of the initial purchase cost.
- Outsource your manufacturing process to an established manufacturer of a similar product. This will alleviate the need to purchase machinery and equipment, plus you will not need as much plant space.
- Buy from a catalogue.
- Purchase inventory on a consignment basis.
- Avoid hiring staff; try to do as much on your own or ask family members to help.
- Start the business in your home.
- Don't quit your day job. If it is possible, start your business part-time. This strategy will alleviate the pressure of making money right away.

THE HOME-BASED START-UP

Many African Americans start their businesses at home. This approach captures many of our cost-cutting ideas. When you operate your business out of your home there is no office lease, family members make up your work force, it is usually a service business, no heavy machinery is required, and inventory is low.

To discuss the costs associated with a business start-up, I have chosen four of the most popular home-based businesses to analyze.

1. TRAVEL AGENCY

Home-based travel agencies have grown tremendously within the last five years. The typical start-up costs are as follows:

A.	On-line computer equipment and link	$5,000
B.	Office equipment and supplies	$900
C.	Printing: business cards/letterhead/flyers/brochures	$600
D.	Business/marketing plan development	$1,000
E.	Computer software	$500
F.	Working capital	$2,000
	TOTAL	$10,000

2. CUSTOM DRESSMAKING/SUIT MAKING

This business requires expertise in designing and tailoring, and you can work part-time. The typical start-up costs are as follows:

A.	Production and computer equipment/software	$3,000
B.	Materials and supplies	$1,000
C.	Display inventory: fabric/mannequins/signage	$750
D.	Printing: business cards/brochures/catalogues	$2,000
E.	Business/marketing plan development	$1,000
F.	Working capital	$2,250
	TOTAL	$10,000

Note: To keep inventory costs low, printing a catalogue as opposed to purchasing inventory can save the business a tremendous amount of capital during the start-up phase.

3. COMMERCIAL PRODUCT DISTRIBUTION

This business could distribute anything from commercial cleaning products to baked goods. The unique feature is that only enough product is ordered from the manufacturer to cover orders that you have in place. The ability to bill your inventory costs directly to your customers will reduce your costs significantly. By establishing purchasing terms with your manufacturer(s), you can give credit terms with your customers. It is important that your customers are creditworthy and have the ability to pay you on time. The typical start-up costs are as follows:

A.	Computer/office equipment	$3,000
B.	Computer software	$300
C.	Office supplies	$500
D.	Printing: business cards, brochures	$1,500
E.	Inventory stock	$2,700
F.	Capital funds	$2,000
TOTAL		$10,000

4. COMMERCIAL JANITORIAL SERVICE

Although this is a home-based business, much of the work is performed outside of the home after normal business hours. This allows the entrepreneur to sell the service during the day and have the staff perform the work after hours. The typical start-up costs are as follows:

A.	Computer equipment and software	$2,700
B.	Cleaning equipment and supplies	$1,250
C.	Two months lease payments on transportation	$1,500
D.	Printing: business cards/brochures	$1,500
E.	Marketing/business development	$1,000
F.	Two weeks staff salary	$2,050
TOTAL		$10,000

There are a few items that are constant in all of these examples: the proper computer equipment and software; the proper marketing vehicles such as business cards, brochures, catalogues, and marketing plan; and a business plan. In order to be competitive in your chosen field, you must have the correct technology, communication, and administrative tools.

JOIN THE DREAM TEAM AND INCREASE YOUR NET WORTH

Earlier in the chapter I discussed how starting or buying an existing business can have a positive effect on your net worth. I increased my net worth by purchasing a business, and I have watched other entrepreneurs do the same.

To buy an existing business, you must first identify a business with undervalued assets, which means that the assets of the business are not fully valued because of the economic climate, the inability of management to produce to the asset's capacity, the bad name that the business created because of unfair or bad business practices, or a number of other reasons. Once you have identified the business, whether it is for sale or not, you must next assess whether the operation can be turned around so that under your management the assets can increase in value. Unless you are part of the staff or the business is for sale, this may be difficult. If your assessment is positive—meaning you can increase the value of the assets of the business—make an offer. The offer should be equal to the market value of the assets in addition to any intangible worth the business may have. You should note, however, that the due diligence to assess the potential should be done by professionals—a CPA and an attorney.

If you are successful in turning the business in the right direction and increase the value of the company, your net worth will increase as well. Let's see how starting even a small business in your home can increase your net worth. Let's assume that you started a home-based business for $10,000. After two years, your gross sales were able to grow to $70,000 with a net profit of $50,000.

Due to the goodwill (reputation) of your business, the IRS would value your business operation equal to at least $100,000, or twice the net profit. So if you decided to sell your business to a neighbor, your asking price would be at least $100,000.

Unfortunately, many business owners never know the value of their business, because it's not assessed until after they pass away and the surviving family is given a large estate tax bill.

You can keep this from happening by having an insurance company or CPA give you a business valuation report. This computer report will give you an idea of the value of your business and the impact your business can have on your net worth.

The creation of a much larger African American business class is important and offers many wealth-building opportunities for both African American entrepreneurs as well as for the African American community for two reasons: Small businesses create jobs, and entrepreneurs play a number of important roles in the African American community. Here are positive contributions that African American entrepreneurs make to their communities.

1. Entrepreneurs are good role models.
2. Entrepreneurs depend less on government for their survival.
3. Entrepreneurs' incomes are higher than the income of average Americans.

4. Most African American entrepreneurs have strong Christian values.
5. Entrepreneurs support African American political candidates and causes.
6. Entrepreneurs create businesses that appreciate in value.
7. Entrepreneurs create wealth-producing enterprises that can be passed from one generation to the next.

Even though all of the roles the African American entrepreneurs play are significant, to me their most important role is acting as positive role models for African American youths. Today, thousands of African American youths, primarily males, die needlessly, and a disproportionate number are involved in America's illegal drug trade.

These young people need role models they can respect and emulate. I believe the most viable candidates for such positions are African American entrepreneurs. African American entrepreneurs have the lifestyle and income most young African Americans, including drug runners, envy. In addition, few African American entrepreneurs' successes are based upon athletic or musical talent.

Many of the super entertainers and sport figures that African American children admire are truly gifted individuals. There may never be another baseball player like Jackie Robinson, a boxer like Muhammad Ali, or a basketball player like Michael Jordan. Likewise, we may never witness another Mahalia Jackson, Oprah Winfrey, or James Earl Jones. But we know that there will be many, many African Americans who will enjoy business success, primarily because business success does not depend on the ability to entertain or to play sports. More of us have the entrepreneurial ability to enjoy the success of business stars like John H. Johnson, Earl Graves, Reginald Lewis, Madame C. J. Walker, or Terrie Williams.

Unfortunately, the media doesn't give the African American businessperson the same attention that it gives to our superstars. If it did, we would see more African American children practicing how to balance a ledger instead of practicing how to dunk a basketball. Consequently, we must highlight African American business leaders as role models, and we must encourage more young people to follow in their paths to financial glory. To help in this process I have assembled what I like to call the African American Entrepreneurs' Hall of Fame.

Here is a list of African American business pioneers. At times, they have risked everything to operate their own businesses. Contrary to popular belief, the African American entrepreneurial class is not a new occurrence. In the seventeenth and eighteenth centuries, free African Americans owned inns and construction companies; did tailoring, framing and catering; and owned many other small enterprises. By 1929, the National Black Business League, which was started by Booker T. Washington, estimated that there were "about 65,000 black-owned businesses in the United States." In this' Hall of Fame, we can only salute a few of the most successful African American entrepreneurs but we pay homage to them all.

In remembering them, let us assess what we can do today as potential African American entrepreneurs. These men and women had less to work with and more obstacles to jump than we do today. In spite of these challenges, they operated businesses that even by today's standards would be considered successful.

CHART 30: AFRICAN AMERICAN ENTREPRENEUR HALL OF FAME

Name	Life Span	Enterprise
1. Anthony Overton	1854–1946	Banker, Manufacturer
2. Jesse Binga	1865–1950	Banker, Financier
3. Maggie L. Walker	1867–1934	Banker, Organizer
4. John Jones	1816–1879	Businessman crusader
5. William Leidesdorff	1810–1848	Millionaire
6. Robert L. Vann	1887–1940	Pittsburgh Courier founder
7. A. G. Gaston	1892–(unknown)	Millionaire
8. Robert S. Abbott	1870–1940	Publisher, the Chicago Defender
9. Charles C. Spaulding	1874–1952	Founder of the North Carolina Mutual Life Insurance Company
10. Jan Ernest Matzeliger	1852–1889	Inventor, Businessman
11. Gilbert Faustina	1897–(unknown)	Cigar manufacturer
12. Horace Stephen Ferguson	1870–(unknown)	Restaurateur
13. John Henry Dickerson	1864–(unknown)	Capitalist
14. James Wormley	1820–1884	Hotel owner
15. Isaac Myers	1835–1891	Shipyard owner
16. John Henry Murphy	1840–1922	Founder of the Baltimore Afro-American Newspaper
17. Richard R. Wright, Sr.	1855–1945	Educator, Banker
18. John C. Asbury	1862–1932	Businessman
19. Grandville T. Woods	1856–1910	Inventor
20. Edward Booth	1810–1900	Gold miner
21. Madame C. J. Walker	1869–1919	Cosmetic manufacturer
22. Norbert Rilliex	1806–1894	Engineer, inventor
23. John Merrick	1859-1921	Businessman, one of the founders of the North Carolina Mutual Life Insurance Company

Name	Life Span	Enterprise
24. Mary McLeod Bethune	1875–1955	Educator, Founder of Bethune-Cookman College
25. Richard Henry Boyd	1843–1922	Minister, Publisher of the National Baptist Publishing Board
26. Annie Turnbo Malone	1869–1957	Entrepreneur, Pioneer in African American beauty culture
27. Sarah (Sara) Spencer Washington	1889–(unknown)	Entrepreneur, Philanthropist, Creator of Apex Beauty Colleges
28. Robert S. Abbott	1870–1940	Founder and Editor of the *Chicago Defender*
29. E. C. Berry	1854–(unknown)	Hotelkeeper
30. James C. Thomas	1864–(unknown)	Mortician
31. W. R. Pettiford	1847–(unknown)	Banker
32. Samuel Scottron	1843–(unknown)	Inventor, Manufacturer
33. William M. McDonald	1866–(unknown)	Business, Fraternal leader
34. Thomas Wellington Thurston, Jr.	1866–(unknown)	Silk manufacturer
35. James N. Shelton	1872–(unknown)	Mortician
36. Garrett Augusta Morgan	1879–(unknown)	Inventor, Manufacturer
37. John Mitchell, Jr.	1863–(unknown)	Banker, Publisher
38. William Harold King	1868–(unknown)	Editor, Publisher
39. Alonzo Franklin Herndon	1858–(unknown)	Capitalist, Founder Atlanta Mutual
40. Charles Andrew Griffin	1884–(unknown)	Regalia Manufacturer

THE DREAM TEAMS OF AFRICAN AMERICANS

African American entrepreneurs continue to represent most of the strengths of America—character, endurance, motivation, intelligence, ingenuity, and success. African American entrepreneurs represent Black America well on the front lines of corporate America and in manufacturing operations around the world. They are in our communities and in major cities. They are the individuals who live the American dream and help others live it. They are the men and women who challenge the American free-enterprise system to live up to its credo of "give me your tired, your poor, your huddled masses." African American entrepreneurs hold up the dream for other African Americans to see and say: I too want to have the dream like so many of the African American entrepreneurs. As the owners, keepers, and showers of the American dream, African American entrepreneurs collectively can be given the title of "African American dream team."

African Americans like to talk about their favorite sport teams, but there is no African American–owned professional sport franchise in America. The sport franchises that do exist avoid moving their teams into the inner-city and hire few African Americans, other than athletes, in their organizations.

So the only real teams we should boast about are our African American businesses. Their challenge is to survive and grow. Every day they must compete effectively to beat back the opposing team's social, political, and economic barriers.

We can find our teams in every major city. Their scores are the number of employees, sales, and stockholders they have. We should start committing their economic victories to memory. We should always remember what Reginald Lewis won with TLC Beatrice International, and what Madame C. J. Walker won with African American hair care.

Likewise, we should challenge our children to learn the economic coaches, players, and superstars who played on these African American business teams. These business teams inspired us in the past and they will play a much more important role in the future of African Americans. As dream makers and dream keepers, they will help African Americans find a way to the economic land of milk and honey.

SEVEN

SMART CREDIT MANAGEMENT MOVES

And ye shall know the truth, and the truth shall
make you free.
                    —John 8:36

Credit report companies want people to believe that individuals can be defined by their credit report, and unfortunately, many people believe this myth. In reality, a credit report is just a history of how a person repays loans.

A credit report may list your late payments, but it cannot explain your due date was on the fifth of the month but the finance company's computer recorded a late payment because it was programmed for the first of the month. Nor can a credit report explain a family's efforts to repay a loan after experiencing a hardship or employment interruption. As we begin our discussion of smart credit moves, remember a good, bad, or indifferent credit report cannot define or validate your humanity.

Historically, many African American families have been misled by finance companies. They have been misled to believe that a "little down" is a smart money move and that using credit is always the best way to buy consumer products. In addition, we have been led to believe that once our credit rating has been damaged, we are the lowest form of debtor on earth and that we have no right to ever *think* of buying something on credit again.

These myths have led to an untold number of family break-ups, caused unnecessary emotional stress, and created undeniable economic pain. As a result, many African Americans totally misuse or underutilize our greatest wealth building tool—debt capital.

Who is to blame for this fiscal brainwashing? We could point to many individuals and institutions. We could easily indict greedy carpetbaggers who took advantage of newly freed slaves and slaveholders who abused former slaves under the tenant-farmer and sharecropper system. This insidious abuse could be followed to the North with the low-down-payment plans, high-interest finance companies, and dishonest used car operations. Today, the practice of giving easy credit to families who are unprepared to handle credit is widespread. This behavior is practiced by credit card companies, mail-order houses, and rent-to-own operations.

These companies are so successful in enticing African Americans to use credit that the African American share of the national indebtedness far outpaces its percentage of the population. Overall, 68.5 percent of all minority families are in debt for mortgages, home equity loans, installment payments, credit cards, and other debt.

What is more alarming is that African Americans have easy access to securing consumer loans, but are routinely denied debt capital that would help increase their net worth. Many African American families may have several credit cards, but they are denied mortgages. In addition, while many African Americans can easily get a car loan, many find it very difficult to get a business loan.

This situation becomes the African American's fiscal nightmare. Too often, after being bombarded with so much easy credit and credit cards, African American households experience employment disruption, economic hardship, or uncontrollable family situations that affect their ability to repay their obligations in a timely manner. Before long, the African American households are overextended on their credit and undercapitalized. They start robbing Peter to pay Paul, as they try to figure a way out of their financial quandary, or they eventually file bankruptcy.

Bankruptcy offers a moment—and only a moment—of emotional and economic ease, but debtors soon return to the same credit mismanagement merry-go-round. Their credit history is then marred by late payments, mispayments, uncollectible debts, and a bankruptcy claim, all of which remain on their credit reports for five to seven years. Poor credit reports limit their ability to use debt financing as a way to secure equity-building assets like a home, a security, or a business.

The following adage evokes an understanding of how credit management and human perception operate in our society: "There was a time when a person used cash and people referred to them as being thrifty. Today if a person uses cash, people refer to them as not having any credit." In spite of what the adage implies, it is time for African Americans to become thrifty, especially in their use of credit.

African Americans must begin to follow a simple plan of credit management that will help us reduce consumer credit, increase our cash flow, and improve our ability to invest. Even more important, good credit management will help us reserve available credit for major purchases that will increase our net worth.

After implementing such a program, you need to make a commitment to preserve your credit for major wealth-building assets in the form of a home, a security, a business, and (to a lesser extent) a car. Other investments backed by collateral may also be included. The ones I recommend are antiques, major works of art, and rental property. However, the major investments that have historically helped African American families increase their net worth include securities, homes, and businesses. Therefore, we must preserve our debt capital (borrowed funds) until we have secured these assets for our families. I recommend that you

- Go from credit card to debit card.
- Go from being a day late and a dollar short with credit obligation to paying your debts a day early and, after doing so, have a dollar to invest.
- Go from fear of not having enough to pay your bills to understanding where you are spending every dollar.
- Go from being a bewildered credit consumer to becoming an informed person committed to controlling your debts and securing your financial future.

To help achieve these smart credit management moves, you will have to remember that your financial security comes first and your creditor comes second. Remember this, because as you try to lower your credit payments, your creditors will try to make you feel bad. However, you must reduce your credit payments and invest the difference in order to protect your family's future. Understandably, creditors will not jump at the chance of taking less per month or going without a payment or two, but you must get your credit situation in line with your ultimate goal of financial security.

To do so, you must address your smaller credit problems before they become larger problems and keep your new commitment to increase your savings, all at the same time. Eventually future creditors will see you as a low risk, and they will advance you the loans you need to buy your home or business because you now have something you didn't have before—equity. You have money in the bank and that always makes lenders feel secure. The lesson is one you hear often in this book: You can use a little financial discipline now and avoid a lot of financial discomfort later. With credit, the financial discomfort is a bad credit rating and limited access to debt financing. I believe it is better to choose to bite the credit management bullet than be forced to swallow it. You may find comfort in knowing that you are not the only one having to make this hard choice.

In his great book, *How to Get Out of Debt, Stay Out of Debt & Live Prosperously,* author Jerrold Mundis says that "Consumer debt soared to a staggering 72 percent of personal income in 1985. Personal bankruptcy rose by 35 percent in 1986. . . . [The] trouble with debt is [that it] cuts across all social strata. Some of us are earning more than $100,000 a year, others are on unemployment. . . . But debt is debt, no matter how much we earn or who we owe . . . sooner or later it . . . poisons our lives."

I had the opportunity to hear Mr. Mundis speak. In the presentation he shared the principles that help members of Debtors Anonymous—a self-help organization that views debt as an addiction much like Alcoholics Anonymous looks at alcoholism. You can contact them at:

> Debtors Anonymous
> P.O. Box 20322
> New York, NY 10025-9992
> (212) 642-8222

These two groups share many of the same notions about how to treat their addictions, the most noticeable being to take it "one day a time." As Mr. Mundis puts it, "Every day is a day I must choose to be debt free."

To help people fight the habit of abusing their credit cards, Mr. Mundis outlines some of the common reasons people believe that they must have a credit card:

- To rent a car.
- To avoid carrying cash.
- For identification.
- To make purchases over the telephone.
- For business reasons.
- In case of emergencies.
- To make life easier.

Mr. Mundis lists a number of reasons and ways a person can make it in life without a credit card. One way is to get a debit card. Debit cards strongly resemble the regular bank credit cards. The main difference is that you are not borrowing money from a banking institution. Instead, you make deposits into an account and use a debit card to pay for purchases. Debit cards allow you to do everything you can do with a credit cards except they won't put you in the credit doghouse. The only money you spend comes directly from your checking or savings account.

Although Mr. Mundis opposes the use of credit cards, he does offer some good advice if you have them.

- Keep credit cards in a drawer at home.
- Know what you are going to use them for before you take them out of the drawer.
- Use them only for the intended purposes.
- Return cards to the drawer after usage.
- Immediately write a check to pay for charges you made with the card.

Another national organization that is committed to helping Americans win their war against debt is the National Association of Credit Counselors. This nonprofit group helps families cope with indebtedness by helping them create a monthly budget and arranging a repayment plan with creditors. Both the National Association of Credit Counselors and Debtors Anonymous like to have people understand where they are spending their money and then help them adjust their monthly expenses in order to meet their long-term goals. This is the same concept that financial planners use to help families create budgets and what I call the no budget budget concept.

Knowing where your money is going will help you decide how much you can afford to pay creditors and how much you can afford to invest for your long-term objectives.

Knowing your financial situation will also help you maintain your commitment to become debt free and wealthy. As documented by the Joint Center for Political and Economic Studies in its report entitled "Banking on Black Enterprise," few African American households have ready available capital to invest. The report indicated that in 1984, "For every dollar of wealth in the median white family, the median black family had nine cents." Unfortunately, not much has changed since the center published its report. If your family is brave enough to manage its credit and reposition dollars that are now going to pay for consumer purchases to your investment account, mortgage, and business enterprise, your family will be one of the few African American households that will one day be debt free and financially secure.

TYPES OF CREDIT

Credit is a means of buying a service or merchandise NOW and paying LATER. It allows us to enjoy our purchases immediately and pay for them while we enjoy them. It enables millions of Americans to buy a new home or a car, get married, put a child through college, or make home improvements.

Is credit good or bad? Well, it depends on how it's used. Credit-card debt has tripled in the last ten years, and the Gross National Product (GNP) has only doubled. Personal bankruptcy filings have increased tremendously and are expected to continue to increase over the next few years.

Although credit abuse has been escalating significantly, credit continues to be an important financial tool in today's society.

Credit comes in a variety of forms. Some of the credit tools available include the following:

- Personal loans.
- Lines of credit.
- Mortgages.
- Store charge accounts.
- Credit cards.

All forms of credit fall into one of two categories: open-end credit plans or closed-end credit plans.

OPEN-END CREDIT PLANS
Open-end credit plans are also known as charge, or revolving-credit, accounts. They allow repeated debits on an account up to the credit limit. Payments may be minimum installments, generally based on a percentage of the credit balance, or paid in full. There is usually a finance (interest) charge on the balance. Credit cards, retail store charge cards, and lines of credit are all examples of open-end credit plans.

There are three different types of credit cards available today—bank cards, retail cards, and travel and entertainment cards.

BANK CARDS
Bank cards are credit cards offered by financial institutions such as a bank or a savings and loan association. Bank cards include VISA, Master-Card, and Discover. Bank cards grant credit to individuals that allows them to purchase services or goods from third parties. They generally allow us to pay a minimum balance, larger installments, or the balance in full. There is usually a charge such as an annual fee for this service.

RETAIL CARDS
Retail cards are credit cards issued by department stores and gasoline companies. Credit is extended to the customer directly from the merchant authorizing the credit. There are usually no annual fees associated with this type of card.

TRAVEL AND ENTERTAINMENT CARDS
Travel and entertainment cards include American Express, Carte Blanche, and Diners Club. They are credit granted by third parties and require balances to be paid in full. There is also an annual fee associated with the use of travel and entertainment cards.

CLOSED-END CREDIT PLANS
Closed-end credit plans, also known as installment plans, are characterized by personal loans, mortgages, home equity loans, and car loans. Principal and interest payments are usually amortized over the life of the loan, there's a predetermined number of equal payments, and loans are based on a fixed interest rate of the outstanding balance. Usually the item being purchased serves as collateral for the loan.

A mortgage is an example of a closed-end credit plan where the real property is used as collateral for the loan. Loan interest payments are tax deductible on loans secured by a residence—up to $1 million of such debt.

Home equity loans are especially popular since the interest on loans up to $100,000 is entirely tax deductible while other types of interest payments are no longer deductible. Home equity loans allow you to borrow money based on the equity you have in your home. In most cases, financial institutions allow you to borrow up to 70 to 80 percent of the current value of your home minus any current indebtedness not to exceed $100,000 and use the money for any purpose.

SECURED LOANS

Secured loans require property to be used as collateral to support the loans. The asset pledged will be forfeited in the event of a default by the borrower.

UNSECURED LOANS

Unsecured loans do not require collateral. Loans are based on the applicant's income and ability to repay the loan. These are frequently referred to as "signature loans."

DEBIT CARDS

With debit cards you are actually debiting money you have deposited with a financial institution in a money market or savings account. You are using your own money, and there are no interest charges with these types of accounts. However, the institution may impose transaction fees.

SECURED CREDIT CARDS

As the name implies, secured credit cards are secured by a deposit you make with the financial institution issuing the card. For example, the creditor will allow you to charge up to $1,000, but you must also maintain an account balance of $1,000 with the creditor that issued the card. In the event you default, the creditor uses your $1,000 deposit as collateral. These cards are generally used by individuals with adverse credit ratings and frequently have expensive transaction fees and application fees.

SMART CREDIT MANAGEMENT MOVES

It's easy to get credit! As long as there are no adverse entries on your credit report, credit companies make getting credit extremely easy. It is equally easy to stay in debt. Creditors like to grant credit since that's how they make money.

Most institutions will grant car loans because they can repossess the car if you fail to meet the payments. It is customary with most institutions to finance 80 percent of the purchase price, with a 20 percent down payment. If this is your first loan, you may have to put down more than 20 percent.

SHOPPING FOR CREDIT CARDS

Most people spend more time shopping for their peanut butter than they do for credit. Making the correct credit purchase decision is essential to our financial well-being. The cost of using a credit card can significantly increase the cost of a purchase if all factors involved in purchasing credit are not evaluated. For example, some credit cards charge higher interest rates—in some cases, as high as a 21 percent annual percentage rate (APR)—while others have annual percentage rates as low as 12.5 percent.

Since lending institutions are highly competitive and new products are constantly being offered, it is well worth your time and effort to periodically compare credit products. Interest rates vary from company to company, and fees and grace periods also vary; these factors could have a significant effect on your actual cost to borrow. Ask yourself the following important questions when shopping for credit:

- What is the grace period, if any?
- What is the annual percentage rate?
- What annual or monthly fees/charges, if any, are associated with this card?
- What balance computation method is the company using?
- What is the line-of-credit amount?
- Are there personal check-cashing privileges?
- How widely accepted is the card?
- Is there insurance protection?
- Does the card have access to money-machine networks?

FEES AND CHARGES

Be conscious of the fees and charges credit companies impose on credit cards. Some of these charges include monthly fees whether you use the card or not, late-payment fees, over-the-limit penalties, and transaction fees.

INTEREST RATE CALCULATIONS

Revolving lines of credit offer us very convenient repayment schedules. They are also very expensive. To understand the high cost of revolving lines of credit, it's important to know how the minimum payment plus interest is calculated. With a revolving line of credit, interest is computed on the monthly balance. As the balance falls, so does the amount of your minimum payment; therefore, it takes longer to pay off the balance. It could take you many months or even years before your balance is paid, which would cause you to pay a substantially larger amount of interest than you would pay on an installment loan. In the early years of an installment loan, your payments go mostly toward interest; in the later years, more of the total payment goes toward the balance and less to interest.

Let's look at how monthly interest is calculated in order to understand how the interest expense in revolving lines of credit defeats your goal of getting out of debt. Your credit card company charges you an annual percentage rate. This annual percentage rate is divided by twelve (months) and applied to your balance; any payments are subtracted.

For example, you have a $5,000 credit card balance and your credit card company charges an annual percentage rate of 19 percent. You have wisely decided to stop using your card and want to know how long it's going to take you to pay off your balance. Your credit card company requires you to pay a monthly payment of at least 3 percent of the outstanding balance.

You must first determine the monthly rate. Your minimum, as we stated earlier, is no less than 3 percent of your outstanding balance. Therefore, your minimum payment is

$$\$5,000 \times 3\% = \$150$$

How long will it take you to pay off your balance if you continue to pay only your minimum payment and never use your card again? Well over fifteen years!

HOW CREDITORS GRANT CREDIT

RATING SYSTEMS

Many people think of banks as service organizations. If you remember that banks are in business to make a profit and that they determine their loan policies and decisions on the risks they face, you will be better prepared for the process of submitting a credit application.

A creditor scores your credit application to determine whether you will be a good credit risk before it grants you credit.

In the past, creditors have relied on the "three C's": character, credit capacity, and collateral. Character indicates your willingness to pay, your credit history, stability, and reliability. For example, your application score is based on how long you have lived at your current residence, whether you rent or own a home, current and prior employment history, current liability amounts, and whether you pay your bills on time. Credit capacity indicates whether or not you can afford these additional loan payments. Your monthly expenditures, income, and employment history are measured. For example, what is your job description, your current monthly income and expenses, and total number of dependents.

Collateral means property that may be used to support the debt should you fail to repay. It could include items such as savings accounts, a home, or investments.

Many creditors have recently instituted an elaborate computer rating system whereby an applicant receives different values or grades for various personal criteria. Creditors will rate you based on as few as six or as many as twenty different components. You receive a grade for the various components. and then your score is totaled. If your total exceeds the passing score, then you will more than likely be extended the credit. On the other hand, if your score falls short, you will be denied the credit.

All creditors use different credit-scoring systems. It is possible to be granted credit from one creditor and denied credit from another based on identical information. Creditors are not required to reveal your scores, and they may use whatever scoring system they choose so long as they do not discriminate.

Some lenders will assume more risk than others, meaning you might find one creditor that will extend you credit while another won't. The one that granted the easy credit is taking more risk and, therefore, you will pay a higher rate of interest in most cases.

Remember, lenders make money by granting loans. They like loans on their books. Why? Because lenders make money by paying you 5 percent interest on a savings account and loaning the money out at 10, 11, or 12 percent. This difference is called the "spread." The spread must be large enough to pay the lender's operating expenses, occasional credit defaults, and still yield a net profit. A creditor does not want to lend money to someone who won't repay the loan.

IMPROVING YOUR CREDIT RATING

Under the Equal Credit Opportunity Act (ECOA), when you apply for credit, your prospective creditor must process your application within thirty days. If the credit amount requested is reduced or your application is declined, the creditor must give you specific reasons for the rejection. If the original rejection letter does not give specific reasons for the credit refusal, you should ask for an explanation within sixty days of the rejection. The creditor then has thirty days to respond to your request.

If you believe your application was evaluated unjustly, you should appeal the decision with the credit grantor. Be sure to direct your time and efforts to the decision maker(s).

The first step is to write a letter explaining in detail the reasons you believe the application should be reevaluated. By personalizing your appeal, you are demonstrating your confidence in yourself and your repayment capabilities.

You should include with your letter any supplemental information that might increase your chances for approval. For example, you can prove that you own assets by attaching recent bank statements or deeds to property. Provide evidence of other income sources, too. If your credit history is sparse, use receipts of paid bills, former accounts, or accounts under former names. Later in this chapter we will highlight steps you can take to remove negative comments from credit reports.

Finally, don't have what is called "the wrong attitude" when appealing an adverse credit decision. Be sure to show confidence and responsibility without having a "chip on your shoulder."

CREDIT DISCRIMINATION

The ECOA states that creditors are not permitted to discriminate against you because of age, sex, race, religion, national origin, color, or marital status. However, they are still permitted to grade your financial and personal data, such as income, expenses, and work history.

You also cannot be denied credit because you receive public assistance or because you are a woman who might become pregnant and have to leave her job.

Any group, individual, or organization who extends credit or arranges financing is bound by this act. Thus, financial institutions such as banks, credit unions, and savings and loans; department stores; credit card companies; mortgage companies; airline and gasoline companies; real estate and loan brokers are bound by this act.

COSIGNING

Cosigning a loan means becoming responsible for payment on the loan. Your name may not appear on the title of the account or property, but if the primary applicant fails to meet payment, you will be held liable. Before you cosign on a loan, consider the following:

- Is the person you are cosigning for a responsible individual in terms of managing his or her finances?
- If you did have to repay a loan, could you get the money back from the person?
- Make sure that you have the ability to pay in the event of a default. You can be sued if you also fail to pay.
- Cosigning becomes part of your credit record. You may have difficulty in obtaining a future loan because the lending institution may view you as having reached your credit potential.

IF YOU DO DECIDE TO COSIGN
- Get a commitment from the creditor that you will be notified as soon as possible if any payments are missed.
- Get any documents that pertain to the loan.
- Find out from the creditor if you will be responsible for the principal portion only or principal and interest.

STAYING CURRENT

To assure favorable reporting of your account, you should always make your payments on time. Mail your payment a couple of days before the due date or, if possible, personally deliver the payment to the creditor by the due date to assure your payment is received on time. Some credit companies will charge a late-payment fee for payments not received by the due date. If you notice you're being charged late-payment fees, call your creditor to determine when these fees are assessed. Most creditors allow a five- to ten-day grace period beyond the payment due date before charging the fee, but some charge the fee on the payment due date.

Always follow the creditor's instructions when paying the bill. Make sure you mail your payment to the correct address. Always write your account number on your check and return any detachable portions of the statement with your payment.

If your creditor does not supply you with return payment stubs, include a note to the creditor stating your name, address, account number, and amount of your remittance with your payment.

If you are going to be late on a payment, try to make at least a partial payment by the due date. Always make a phone call to explain your tardiness.

Finally, when you receive a statement, always make sure your payment has been credited to your account.

REPAYMENT PRIORITIES
All debts should be paid according to the terms of your agreements. Note that the less you pay and the longer you delay your payments, the more it costs you to borrow.

If you are having difficulty reducing your indebtedness, contact your creditor and request an increase to your credit limit. This should avoid any additional over-the-limit fees. Be careful in taking this step though as a higher credit limit can be just the ticket for getting deeper into debt.

HIGH INTEREST RATES
Interest rates have fallen dramatically since the early 1980s, but borrowers still continue to pay as much as 21 percent on credit cards. If you loan money to an entity such as the government or a corporation in the form of a bond, your objective is to loan the money for the longest period of time at the highest rate possible. When a creditor loans you money, the objective is the same. If you begin to get in the habit of thinking that paying off a debt is the same as earning money, you are on the right track. If you pay off an 18 percent credit card, in essence you have earned 18 percent.

The first step to earning a "guaranteed" interest rate is to list all your obligations from the highest interest rate to the lowest. Then, repay the highest rate of interest debts first. You might even want to consider taking out a lower rate personal loan or shopping for a lower interest rate credit card. Remember, high interest rates are costing you money.

Another important consideration when setting debt repayment priorities is to remember that interest payments on consumer debt are not tax deductible. Therefore, one of your primary goals in repaying debt should be to pay off all consumer debt as soon as possible.

SOLVING BILLING DISPUTES
Review your billing statements from creditors every month. People do make mistakes and so do computers. Some of the items you should be looking for include the following:

- Duplicate billing on the same item.
- Incorrect billing amount for an item.
- Returned items that are not credited.
- Payments that are not credited.

CHARGES FOR ITEMS NEVER PURCHASED

If any of the above have ever happened to you, you should immediately exercise your rights and protections under the federal Fair Credit Billing Act. This act entitles you to certain rights in the event of billing disputes on open-end credit accounts, which include store charge cards, bank cards, and lines of credit. It does not apply to billing disputes on closed-ended credit accounts such as mortgages, car loans, and other fixed payment obligations.

If you find a billing error, you must write to the creditor within sixty days of receiving the statement containing an error. Also send copies of any documentation to prove the error. Consider using certified mail, return receipt requested, to verify proof of mailing.

REVIEW YOUR CREDIT REPORT

A good credit report is essential when you apply for a loan. On the other hand, a bad credit report can lead to denial of requested credit. It is up to you to maintain a good credit history as well as to monitor your credit report for errors.

HOW THE CREDIT REPORTING SYSTEM WORKS

The first time you applied for credit, your credit history started ticking. Each time you take out a loan, make a payment, or apply for new loans or credit, your report is updated.

Credit agencies are the bureaus that retrieve, handle, and disperse personal credit information. It seems as if credit bureaus know everything about us! Personal finances are not the only pieces of information contained in credit reports. Past work history, employment history, and a reflection of personal lifestyle are included as well.

The function of credit agencies is to supply information to various businesses such as stores, lending institutions, and employers. The credit agency itself does not rate your credit; it only supplies the information, including past and current obligations, paid-in-full obligations, and negative or positive information. There are many credit bureaus and they do not necessarily contain the same information.

CHART 31: FOUR MAJOR CREDIT AGENCIES

TRW Credit
Chilton Corporation
(now merged with TRW)
505 City Parkway West, Suite 110
Orange, CA 92613-5450
(714) 991-6000

Credit Bureau, Inc./Equifax
5501 Peachtree Dunwoody Road
Suite 600
Atlanta, GA 30356
(404) 250-4000

Trans Union Credit
444 North Michigan Avenue
Chicago, IL 60611
(312) 645-0012

Associated Credit Bureaus, Inc.
Member Services Department
P. O. Box 218300
Houston, TX 77218
(713) 492-8155

There are also many regional and local credit agencies.

YOUR REPORT

Periodically, you should review your credit report. Many times there may be errors, deletions, or additions to your credit report that may cast an unfavorable view on your credit history. It is estimated that the credit reports of approximately 100 million Americans have incorrect information. Remember, your report can determine an acceptance or denial of credit you request.

You should review your credit report approximately every three years; many times there will be errors. For instance, your credit card balance may be $200, but your credit report might show $2,000. Also, if you have been divorced, you will want to check your credit record to make sure your personal credit history reflects only your past and current obligations. In some cases, your report may contain negative records that don't even belong to you!

Credit agencies handle a tremendous volume of data, and errors can occur. Negative information can stay on your file for seven to ten years. Even if you haven't had any problems with late or missed payments, you should still review your own personal file. Everyone has the right to review his or her own personal credit report. Credit agencies charge a fee (usually between $8 and $15) if you request a copy of the credit report.

However, if you have been denied credit within the last thirty days, you can request a copy of your credit record at no charge.

Make sure to include the following in your request:

- Current date.
- Full name (and any other previously used names).
- Current address.
- Former address (if you have lived at your current address for less than two years).
- Date of birth.
- Social Security number.
- Signature.

You should receive a report back within two to three weeks.

If you prefer to meet with someone in person, you need to make an appointment and take along proper identification.

Most credit agencies will require a written request, rather than a telephone request. Telephone may be handy in asking specific questions. However, there is usually a long holding period.

TRANSLATING YOUR CREDIT REPORT

When you receive a copy of your credit report, you will probably be confused by the numbers and special coding on computer-printed paper. In addition, each credit bureau's report may look a little different. So how do you begin to sort through all of the facts and figures?

First of all, credit reporting agencies must staff fully trained individuals to assist with the interpretation of credit reports. Also, an explanation of how to interpret your credit report should accompany the report itself. The information may look overwhelming at first, but it is well worth your while to understand the credit information that is being supplied to any potential lender.

The purpose of your review is to make sure the information you see is accurate and up-to-date.

- **Employment:** Look to see that past, as well as present employer information is correct.
- **Salary:** Your past and current salary figures have an impact on future credit requests.

- **Address:** If there is a conflict between what you claim as an address and what a credit bureau has on its records for your address, you may run into problems with future creditors.
- **Accounts:** Are they yours? Sometimes, because of account numbers or name similarities, there may be accounts listed on your report that don't belong to you.
- **Balances:** Do accounts that have been paid off reflect the payoff, or do they show an old balance?
- **Past-due amounts:** If you have past-due amounts, are the figures correct?
- **Date of Last Activity (DLA):** This may be the final payment date, referral to a collection agency date, or date you closed an account. This shows your activity with past creditors.
- **Duplications:** Each piece of information should be reflected on your credit statement one time only.
- **Public/court records:** If you question any legal entries, you must petition the court of the appropriate jurisdiction before anything can be removed.
- **Status reports:** Make sure the status column indicates your current status.

If you find any errors or misstatements in any of the above, it is up to you to initiate action to make a correction on your statement. Most credit bureaus have correction spaces on the credit report itself.

You may wonder why an inquiry led to a denial of credit that you requested. Each creditor has a different set of requirements for granting or extending of credit. Some creditors use a "point" system, while others may take a general look at your ability to pay on a timely basis. A credit agency does not make credit-granting decisions, and creditors do not report to the agencies that you were declined or why you were declined.

REMOVAL OF NEGATIVE COMMENTS

If you have an account that was handed over to a collection agency, you may have developed a repayment plan with the agency or creditor. Your repayment will not necessarily remove the negative comment on your credit report. The following steps may assist in the removal of a negative entry:

- When you propose a payment plan to a creditor, ask for a letter promising the removal of the derogatory information on your credit file. Keep a copy of that letter.
- Make timely payments.
- Ask the creditor how long it will be before it contacts the credit agency to request the removal.
- Make sure to follow up with the credit bureau by requesting a copy of your credit report.
- If you find there is still a negative comment after a reasonable time period, contact the original creditor in writing and include a copy of the promissory note.
- If the creditor doesn't act, write to your state's Department of Consumer Affairs. Send any and all documentation to the department and send a copy of the letter back to your creditor.

If you see negative or unfavorable remarks that you want to delete from your credit report, you must dispute the notation rather than give a reason. For instance, if you missed three months of payments and listed the reason as an illness, the remark will not be lifted from your credit record. On the other hand, if you don't think that an entry belongs on your statement, you must file a written notice with the credit-reporting agency. Make sure to keep copies for your records as proof that you filed a dispute.

If the above actions don't clear up your dispute, you may still file a statement that will be included as part of your current credit file. This statement should be one hundred words or less and as clear and concise as possible. Again, the statement cannot be a reason that explains the circumstances leading to the nonpayment or late payment.

If your dispute results in action by the credit agency (e.g., deletion, revision), the credit bureau must notify creditors, at your request, who received a copy of your credit report during the last six months. It may take up to six months to investigate and correct an error.

FAIR CREDIT REPORTING ACT

The Fair Credit Reporting Act (FCRA) was passed by Congress to protect consumers against the circulation of inaccurate or obsolete information and to ensure that consumer reporting agencies adopt fair and equitable procedures for obtaining, maintaining, and giving out information about consumers. Under the FCRA you have the following rights:

- To be told the name and address of a consumer reporting agency that was used to deny you credit.
- To find out the nature, substance, and sources of the information that has been collected about you.
- To obtain, free of charge, a copy of your credit file if you have been denied credit within the last thirty days.
- To be told who has received a report within the last six months (or two years if used for employment purposes).
- To dispute inaccurate or incorrect information.

INFORMATION TIME SPAN

Unfortunately, negative information tends to stay on a credit report longer than some favorable pieces of information. There are some rules that protect the individual from permanent, adverse credit information. The following pieces of information can only be reported for their respective time periods:

Delinquent accounts have a maximum reporting time of seven years. This time period begins from the date of the last regularly scheduled payment.

Collection accounts, or those accounts that have been referred to a collection agency, will remain on your credit record for seven years. This period begins when the creditor refers the account to an outside collector.

Accounts charged to profit and loss have a seven-year time limit beginning from the time the creditor takes action to write off the account.

Lawsuits cannot be reported for more than seven years from the date the suit was initiated, unless the governing statute of limitations has not expired.

Judgments remain for seven years from the date the judgment was rendered.

Bankruptcies remain on your credit report for ten years.

Bankruptcies, garnishments, tax liens and court judgments may be reported to a credit agency. Banking activities, such as checking and savings accounts, are not reflected on a credit summary.

CREDIT PROBLEMS

Buying on credit is a necessary and convenient way of life. If an emergency arises and we don't have enough cash to purchase a new furnace, for instance, we might purchase the furnace on credit. Or possibly we'd like to take a family vacation but don't have the full amount of cash to pay for the trip. Financing enables us to use something today and pay for it in installments over a period of time.

If you occasionally miss a payment, but pay the amount as soon as you realize your error, you probably are not in serious credit trouble. The situation may be remedied with a quick phone call to the creditor explaining the reason for the missed payment and an assurance that it has been mailed. However, if you find yourself routinely missing payments, then you may be headed for credit trouble.

The following young woman I spoke to knows firsthand what having bad credit is like, but she also knows how to get out of credit trouble.

After I had gone through my divorce, I had to reestablish my credit. The first thing (in reestablishing credit) is to have a lot of common sense. Don't spend what you don't have. A lot of people think that money from a credit card is theirs, but it isn't.

I had credit problems in my marriage and I learned my lesson. The credit cards were in my name, but my husband used the cards for his own business. Eventually, we had to consolidate the debts and get a loan.

After my divorce, I had to set goals for myself. To buy a home, I had to have good credit. It's amazing what they put you through when you make an offer on a home.

The creditors knew nothing about me when I made an offer on the suburban home I'm in now. I had reestablished an excellent credit line, but since I was a divorcée from the city, wanting to purchase a home in the suburbs, they thought: How could she afford this by herself?

I've talked to other single minorities, and they've gone through this same kind of trouble. They've had to suffer through stereotypes put on them by creditors, mortgage companies, and real estate companies because they are single and trying to purchase property. I've come to believe that it's easier when you're purchasing a home as a couple and you've got a solid credit background.

I eventually convinced the mortgage company that my credit was good and that I could take on the responsibility of paying for a new home. As assurance, I took my credit report with me whenever I would make an offer on a house.

DANGER SIGNALS

It is very important to be in control of your financial health. Being aware of credit danger signals and looking out for signals is imperative to your financial well-being. The following are some warning signs that you may be losing control.

- Are you allowing yourself to neglect your savings?
- Do you spend more and more of your take-home pay to pay monthly bills?
- Do you borrow money from family and/or friends?
- Are you near the edge of your credit limits?
- Do you hold off sending out checks because of cash flow problems—paying bills in sixty or ninety days that you once paid in thirty?
- Are you able to make only minimum payments on your debt obligations?
- Do you worry that your credit card transactions might be declined?
- Do you have adequate savings for an emergency?
- Are you charging miscellaneous, small purchases or entertainment expenses because you don't have the cash to pay for them?
- Are you consistently withdrawing from savings to pay current obligations?
- Are you finding that you are unable to pay your bills in their entirety and deferring part of the payment to the following month?
- Do you put off dental or doctor visits because you can't afford them?
- Are you routinely receiving late-payment notices or phone calls from creditors?
- Do you have negative marks on your credit rating?
- Have you recently been denied credit?
- Are you unable to estimate how much you owe on your installment debts?
- Do you constantly worry about money?
- Do your monthly installment payments exceed 20 percent of your monthly take-home pay?

If you are, or suspect someone else is, a chronic spender, you should consider looking into a program structured for chronic debtors. You can find these groups listed in the white pages of your telephone directory. Attendance is free or call Debtors Anonymous and the National Association of Credit Counselors.

TURNING CONSUMER DEBT INTO DREAM CAPITAL

Credit can be a valuable net worth–building tool. It allows families to finance the purchase of their wealth-building assets.

We have already seen how families can use their credit for entertainment and consumer purchases. However, African American families may be better served if they save their available credit to purchase assets such as education, antiques, works of art, homes, automobiles, rental property, securities, and businesses that will ultimately have a positive impact on the family's net worth. Notice that all of these items are appreciating assets and will increase your net worth. Credit for dining out, vacations, or consumer items should be used sparingly and judiciously, because you run the risk of reducing your credit limit and endangering your credit rating.

Of course it also pays to have access to cash or credit for emergencies when you might be short on cash. However, you should not neglect to build an emergency fund. If you abuse your credit, you may find yourself with an emergency or an opportunity and not have access to credit or the financial resources to respond to these situations.

The other advantage of having a favorable credit rating and access to credit is that it provides a positive state of mind. Knowing that you have access to credit gives you confidence when you are discussing the purchase of a major net worth–building asset. It also helps to have a good relationship with your banker and to know just how much money your family can afford to borrow for a home, car, or business. One of the greatest benefits of reducing your monthly allocations to repay your consumer debt is that it will free up more capital you can use to secure your dreams.

In the chapters concerning home and business ownership, you learned how other African American families leveraged their credit to increase their net worth. Your family can do the same thing! Just remember to always know your credit limit, avoid credit problems, and save your credit for appreciating assets. You should also remember that by controlling your short-term pleasures, you can secure your long-term financial security.

EIGHT

SMART TAX MOVES

Discretion shall preserve thee, understanding
shall keep thee.
                    —Proverbs 2:11

"There are some things in life that will never change," my grandmother Ethel Boston used to say. "As long as you live you can always look forward to being black, paying taxes, and meeting death." This chapter will focus on two inevitable events in life—being black and paying taxes. We discussed being black and dying in Chapter 5, "Insure Your Financial Future."

Recent tax proposals seem to suggest that many African Americans will not have to worry about tax relief for their families. In the current tax reform debate, the Republicans and Democrats have defined middle-income households as households that earn more than $200,000 a year. Politicians feel it is these middle-income households that need tax relief.

Only 5 percent of the African American population earns in excess of $200,000. However, it is my belief that more than 5 percent of African Americans need help *controlling* their federal income tax obligation.

Every American taxpayer must work forty-five days just to pay his or her annual Federal tax bill. Imagine how much money we could save if we had to work only two weeks a year, as opposed to almost four weeks a year, to pay that annual bill. For example, the average American paid approximately $1,300 in taxes last year. Over a ten-year period that amount is $13,000. If we could reduce that amount by half, to $650 a year, we would have an additional $650 a year to invest. On the surface $650 doesn't look like much, but when we consider this amount over a ten-year period, it becomes $6,500. In addition, if we were able to have those funds compound at a rate of 10 percent annually, the $6,500 would grow in value to $16,000. Now we're talking money!

This example illustrates the importance of trying to control your taxes. Our primary aim is to find additional money to invest for your family's economic well-being. Keep this goal in mind as you review the following smart tax moves, because reducing your income tax obligation will enable you to invest additional money in a smart manner. You want to move money from the federal government's bank account into your own investment account.

Our example also illustrates how a small sum of money can grow into a significant sum if invested wisely. For now, we will review ways to control your tax bill. Perhaps these hints will result in your having more money to invest. Throughout this book, we will look at some smart ways to invest the money your family saves in taxes.

In this chapter you will learn three things:

1. How to reduce your tax bill by $50 to $200 a month.
2. How to correct common tax problems.
3. How to benefit from year-round tax planning.

There will always be tax changes, but every day should be viewed as a day for you to reduce your tax bill. Remember the old adage, "A penny saved is a penny earned!"

TAX RULES ALWAYS CHANGE

In 1995 Congress debated a new tax reform bill, and there will be another tax reform bill in a few years. Congress likes to pass tax reform legislation during presidential elections. Everyone needs to keep abreast of the tax legislation debate. Make sure your congressional representatives know how you feel.

During these tax debates, you may say to yourself, "I don't have to worry about it because the laws are all going to change anyway." That thinking may sound rational, but unfortunately it may also increase your tax obligation. First, rarely will Congress make tax law changes retroactive—Congress will give the public a year or two to adjust to the new tax legislation. Second, in order to take advantage of most new laws, you have to understand how the new laws are related to the laws they replace, modify, or eliminate. Third, tax laws are like seasons, they always change.

The ever-changing nature of Congress, and tax legislation, presents a unique opportunity for smart investors. The informed taxpayer pays less income tax than the less informed taxpayer. One way to stay informed about new tax laws is to follow the tax debate as it unfolds in Congress by watching CNN, CNBC, and C-SPAN and reading the *Wall Street Journal, Money* magazine, and your local newspaper.

CHART 32: TAX CALENDAR

The following dates have tax significance for calendar-year taxpayers:

January 16 — Last day for paying final installment of your past year estimated tax. If you miss this deadline, you may avoid a penalty by filing your final return for past year and paying the balance of your past year tax by January 31, current year. Farmers and fishermen pay their full estimated tax for past year.

January 31 — Forms W-2 and 1099 should have been received by this date. Final past year return may be filed, rather than filing January 16 estimate.

March 1 — Last day for farmers and fishermen to file past year returns instead of filing past year estimate on January 16.

March 15 — Due date of calendar-year corporation returns.

April 17 — Due date of past year income and self-employment tax returns and calendar-year partnership returns. Payment of first installment of current year estimated tax. Last day to establish and contribute to an IRA for past year.

June 15 — Payment of second installment of current year estimated tax. Due date of income tax returns of citizens abroad and nonresident alien individuals not subject to withholding.

August 15 — Last day to file income tax returns on automatic extension.

September 15 — Payment of third installment of current year estimated tax.

October 16 — Last day to file income tax returns on second extension.

December 31 — Last day to establish a Keogh (H.R. 10) plan for current year.

January 15 — Final installment of current year estimated tax. Farmers and fishermen pay current year estimated tax in full.

April 15 — Due date of current year income tax return.

Tax planning is a year-long process that ends with the filing of your April 15 return. The annual tax calendar in Chart 32 will help you remember the significant tax-paying dates. Remember to transfer them from the tax calendar to your personal calendar.

Planning helps reduce your tax liabilities and your tax expenses. However, if you are uncertain about the tax law or treatment of certain deductions, consult a qualified tax professional. The following suggestions may help you in reducing your yearly income tax liabilities or expenses.

HOW TO REDUCE YOUR TAX BILL

There are three major ways to reduce your taxes.

1. Earned Income Deferral: Use salary reduction plans to defer income.

2. Interest Income Deferral (interest and dividends):
   a. Exclusion: Use municipal bonds or municipal bond mutual funds to exclude taxes.
   b. Deferral: Use deferred-income techniques, such as EE Bonds, T bills maturing in the next tax period, deferred annuities, or public utility stocks, to defer income to a future period.

3. Income Shifting: Use the Uniform Gift to Minor Act (UGMA) or joint property titling to shift income to another, lower-bracket individual, such as a parent or child.

Let's take a closer look at each of these tax saving strategies.

DEFERRING EARNED INCOME

One of the best ways to reduce your current income tax bill is to defer a portion of your annual income. People do this by investing in an Individual Retirement Account (IRA), a 401(k) plan, a tax-sheltered annuity, or any other pension plan. With every dollar you invest in such plans, you are deferring a portion of your earnings to another time period on the assumption that when you need these funds you will be in a lower tax bracket or have an opportunity that will more than pay for your tax obligation.

Today, most taxpayers have the opportunity to put money into deferred savings or retirement plans, yet very few take advantage of these programs. Many people believe that they should not tie up their money for that long a period of time because they will not be able to touch the money without penalty until retirement. However, let me point out that in programs like your 401(k), a family can use the funds for certain emergencies, education, or a mortgage down payment. Even if you can't touch the money for some time, that does not mean that you should not place a portion of your earning into a tax-deferred program, especially, when many of these programs will allow you to dollar-cost average into an equity mutual fund.

Investments that offer tax-deferred compounding usually grow faster than non-tax-deferred investments. The reason is that you have more money compounding, and you are not taking a portion out every year to pay for income tax. Chart 33, "The Power of Tax-Deferred Compounding," gives a good example of the impact of tax-deferred interest compounding.

CHART 33: THE POWER OF TAX-DEFERRED COMPOUNDING

· TYPE OF INVESTMENT

	Tax/Taxable Earnings (Example: Passbook Savings Account)	After-Tax/Tax Deferral on Earnings (Example: Nondeductible IRA)	Pretax/Tax Deferral on Earnings (Example: 401(k) Plan)
Value at end of:			
5 years	$903	$1,014	$1,469
10 years	$1,181	$1,490	$2,159
15 years	$1,545	$2,189	$3,172
20 years	$2,021	$3,216	$4,661
25 years	$2,644	$4,725	$6,848
30 years	$3,459	$6,943	$10,063
35 years	$4,524	$10,202	$14,785
40 years	$5,919	$14,990	$21,725
Amount invested	**$690**	**$690**	**$1,000**

Assumptions: The individual earned $1,000 before taxes, is in the 31 percent tax bracket, and is earning 8 percent interest.
Reprinted by permission of Educational Technologies, Inc.

When I was a financial planner I helped a family friend who felt that he was paying too much in income tax. Andy was single and at the time making a decent income at a hospital. Every year he would end up owing Uncle Sam more money. To remedy the problem, I suggested that Andy increase his monthly contribution to his tax-sheltered annuity plan at work. The result was that his savings increased substantially, and Uncle Sam began to send him a small refund every year.

It might sound almost incredible that a small adjustment in where a person places his savings could make such a big impact on a household's tax picture, but it happens all the time. Let me use another example. Suppose you earn $25,000 a year. With no exemptions or dependents, your taxable income will remain $25,000. This figure puts you into the 28 percent tax bracket, and your tax obligation will be $4,050.

Now, if you placed $2,000 into a tax-deferred saving program, your taxable income falls to $23,000, and your tax obligation will be $3,490. Your tax rate falls to the 15 percent level. The difference is you are able to save $560 a year in federal income taxes. That's the advantage of income deferral and why it is so important for every African American taxpayer to take advantage of it.

There is a limit on how much you can put into various tax-deferred accounts, but whatever the amount you should make the most of your tax-deferred savings, 401(k), savings plan, tax-sheltered annuity (TSA) or IRA, or 457. Most African American families still qualify for the popular IRA deduction. You can find the IRA rules in the *Resource Guide*.

DEFERRING INTEREST INCOME

You can also defer your interest income by placing your investments in vehicles that offer income-deferred accumulations. Here are some investments your family might chose to defer income:

• **Treasury Bills.** If your situation warrants short-term deferral of income, treasury bills may provide some help. Since Treasury-bill interest is not taxed until the rated security matures, you would be able to defer the recognition of this interest by one tax year. If you anticipate a lower marginal tax rate next year, this strategy would allow you to incur the tax on the interest at a lower rate.

• **Savings Bonds.** A longer-term benefit can be derived from the purchase of Series EE savings bonds. The investor can choose to recognize the income of these bonds, which are bought at a discount, when the bonds are cashed in. As the holding period required to receive the minimum guaranteed interest is longer term, the income is deferred for a longer period if the bond is held to maturity. All savings bonds must be held five years before they can be cashed in. Most bonds mature in thirty to forty years.

• **Life Insurance Policies.** Whole-life, variable-life, and universal-life policies generally provide a tax-free accumulation of investment funds over long time periods. Life insurance policies are not appropriate for short-term investing because of the substantial up-front sales costs and surrender charges.

• **Annuities.** Annuities are a cousin of life insurance policies. In a typical annuity contract, the insurer agrees to make payments to you as long as you or your designated beneficiary lives, sometimes for a fixed minimum number of years.

Both life insurance and annuities are complicated arrangements involving many provisions and factors. Before you make a withdrawal or take out a loan in relation to either, you should discuss the effects of these actions with your insurance and tax advisers.

INCOME SHIFTING

Beginning in 1993, family members may pay substantially different tax rates—from a low of 0 percent to a high of 39.6 percent. Differences in tax brackets may encourage shifting income and assets from high-bracket individuals to low-bracket individuals, who may include your children and grandchildren, as well as your parents. Individuals over age thirteen are taxed at 15 percent of their income up to $22,750. A good strategy to implement is paying children and parents for work they perform at your place of business. Here are several popular ways to shift income:

• Use a Uniform Gifts (or Transfers) to Minors account to shift income to children or grandchildren.
• If possible and applicable, pay children a wage for services actually rendered to gain business.
• Give outright lifetime gifts to charity of appreciated property to create an income tax deduction (within limits) and get income (from the property) out of your return.
• Give gifts to children or other family members. There is a $10,000 per donee exclusion ($20,000 if a joint gift is made) from the Uniform Gift/Estate taxes.
• Just a reminder. If you have a favorite church, black college or university, or nonprofit organization, you can also make it the beneficiary of one of your life insurance policies. Your payments will be tax deductible, and the organization will benefit from the face value of the policy.

OTHER TAX-SAVING MEASURES

- Purchase municipal securities (notes, bonds, money markets or funds) to avoid income taxes on interest.
- Time sales of investment property to utilize capital losses up to the annual $3,000 limit.
- "Lump" property tax payment by paying two winter payments in one taxable year. Pay estimated state income or intangible taxes before year end. Also, always keep in mind that the tax deductibility of mortgage payments makes home ownership a great tax move as well as a smart money move.
- Reallocate interest to change its nature from nondeductible consumer interest to deductible home-equity or mortgage interest. Whenever possible, use a home equity loan to make car payments, vacations, and the like.
- Make a year-end property contribution of clothes, used furniture, etc. Remember IRS documentation rules. If the value is over $175, get a receipt and attach it to your return. If the value is over $500, an additional form is required. If the value of the property is over $3,000, an appraisal is required. Because many African Americans make their greatest contribution to African American churches, remember to claim these contributions on your tax form. Tax deductibility will not make your tithe any less devout.
- Contribute appreciated property to maximize the deduction and avoid capital gains. Certain income limits apply. This tax-saving measure also works for personal property that you no longer want. For example, donate your old car to a nonprofit organization and deduct the contribution on your income tax.
- "Lump" contributions into a given year by making advance contributions before year end.
- "Lump" deductions subject to Adjusted Gross Income (AGI) floors. For example, miscellaneous deductions are subject to a floor of 2 percent of AGI. If the payment of these deductions can be managed and "lumped" into a particular period, you might be able to utilize deductions that would not be available otherwise.

When you evaluate investment options you should consider the effect of your investments on income taxes, in addition to investment issues such as risk. You want to make investments that will generally decrease your investment return, although in varying amounts at various times. Be sure you are comparing "apples with apples," and evaluate investment performance on an *after-tax basis* so that you can make valid comparisons among investment options.

AVOIDING TAX PROBLEMS

African American families need to be aware of common tax problems in order to avoid or correct them. According to Cheryl Frank, author of *How to Survive an IRS Attack,* families who are having problems should consult a tax accountant or lawyer. She told me once on *The Color of Money* that the IRS has many payment plans to help families pay their back taxes. She also said that "Taxpayers should never ignore a notice from the IRS and always respond to the IRS in writing." In some cases, the IRS will even forgive some of the taxes owed. However, in order to take advantage of these programs you must stop ignoring the problem—it will not go away by itself. Here is a list of some of the common mistakes taxpayers make by trying to ignore the IRS:

1. They fail to file taxes for several years.
2. They fail to pay taxes for several years.
3. They fail to discuss the tax implication of a marriage or a divorce.

It may take several meetings with your tax advisor to correct your tax problems. However, they are correctable. When dealing with the IRS, it helps to remember that even delinquent taxpayers have rights. All taxpayers have the right to

- Prompt, courteous, and impartial treatment.
- An explanation of the collection process.
- Certain information as provided under the Privacy Act of 1974.
- Confidentiality.
- Representation.
- Request that your case be transferred to another IRS office.
- Request and receive receipts for any payment and copies of any agreements.
- Have tax penalties and interest abated if they are not owed.
- File a claim for a refund or a credit.

- File a suit for a refund if the claim is rejected.
- Submit an offer in compromise.
- Appeal a decision or an action of an IRS employee to his or her immediate supervisor.
- Designate the application of a payment made voluntarily.

INCREASE YOUR NET WORTH
USING TAX SAVINGS

The sooner you correct your IRS problems, the more money you will save on interest penalties to the IRS, which ultimately means more money for your family to invest and thereby increases your net worth. You can increase your net worth in an effective manner when you:

1. Defer a portion of your earned income by participating in a company pension plan.
2. Defer a portion of your interest income by using tax-deferred investments, which include transferring funds that earn interest to investments that may generate capital gains. (The capital gain is not taxed as ordinary income and offers tax-loss deductions if they are needed.)
3. Maximize allowable deductions, especially mortgage payments.
4. Shift income and gifts to other individuals and nonprofit organizations.

Many people are skeptical about tax planning. They wonder if it really is beneficial and if they will incur the wrath of the IRS if they plan. It is beneficial to try to save money on your annual tax bill, especially if you plan to invest the tax savings in the American free enterprise system. As eager as our government is to have you pay your tax bill, it is also eager for you to invest in long-term investments that ultimately help create more employment opportunities, viable businesses, and a stronger economy. To this end, every dollar invested in an American company helps protect the American dream.

Let's see how these smart tax moves can help your family. Imagine that your family earns $50,000 a year and includes two children. Your effective tax rate will be 28 percent or $11,760 in federal tax. (Keep in mind that good tax planning may help reduce your state and local tax bills as well.) Nevertheless, your family will be able to save on your tax bill in the future because you bought a new home, started investing $100 per month in a tax-deferred plan (IRA or 401[k]), moved money from a savings account into a mutual fund, and made a $1,000 contribution to your church. Let's see the tax benefits of these actions.

CHART 34: YOUR FAMILY'S CURRENT TAX OBLIGATION $11,760

Strategy	Savings
1. $600 Mortgage ($100,000 adjustable rate mortgage at 6%)	($2,016)
2. Tax-deferred savings	($336)
3. Reposition $5,000 from 6 percent savings account to a mutual fund	($300)
4. $1,000 church contribution	($280)

New tax obligation: $8,828
Tax Savings: $2,932 or $244.33 a month
Tax savings if invested every year at 10 percent for ten years: $29,320

Most African American families can effectively reduce the federal tax bill by purchasing a home, and investing in an individual retirement account (IRA) and/or (401[k]) plan at work.

If your family is committed to investing, you could make an adjustment on your W-4 (withholding) tax form and have most of this monthly savings come directly to you. In doing so, the family can begin a monthly investment program. I advise this strategy only for clients who are committed to investing their savings. Otherwise, the family might have additional taxes to pay at the end of the year and not accumulate any investment capital.

Nevertheless, you can clearly see how smart tax moves can help increase your family's net worth by transferring dollars you now send to the U.S. government to your family's long-term investment account. Diligent tax planning can provide thousands in tax money for your investment.

Many African American households are reluctant to try to reduce their tax bills because they are afraid of the IRS. Keep in mind that the difference between tax exclusion and tax evasion is about ten years. I know it's an old joke but it clearly illustrates the point.

As Justice Oliver Wendell Holmes once wrote, "Every American only has to be responsible to pay their fair share of taxes." There is nothing wrong or illegal in trying to reduce your tax liability as long as you do it legally and effectively. It's important to keep good records (for at least three years) and utilize some tax management plan.

Taxes will always be with us, but that does not mean that we can't diminish the amount of money we must pay in taxes every year. In order to control our taxes we must watch for every legal tax-saving opportunity.

This reminds me of a story about the late civil rights leader Dr. Martin Luther King, Jr. He was leading a march in Cicero, Illinois, to protest that community's long-standing practice of housing discrimination. During the demonstration local white residents threw rocks and bottles at him and the other marchers. Dr. King kneeled down, closed his eyes, and started praying beside a parked car. After the police disbanded the attackers, a reporter asked Dr. King, "Weren't you worried about getting hit with a rock?" "No," replied Dr. King, "but I kept my eyes open just in case."

When it comes to reducing income taxes, we want to do the same thing: *Always keep our eyes open*—just in case there is a new tax law that will reduce our tax obligation or another taxable dollar we can defer or deduct from our overall tax bill. Doing so can help you turn dollars intended for tax coffers into additional dream capital for your family.

NINE

WEALTH-BUILDING STEPS FOR AFRICAN AMERICAN WOMEN

Woman . . . be it unto thee even as you wish!
—Matthew 15:28

Before reviewing the wealth-building steps for African American women, we should remember the first rule of economic survival, "God bless the child who has his own." This chapter underscores the importance of African American women having their own financial resources. Many readers may wonder why a book on money management includes a chapter devoted to African American women. Yes, African American women and men share the same financial concerns but there are some money issues that African American women face that are germane to them alone.

In her book *Money Harmony,* author and psychotherapist Olivia Mellan highlights the different cultural orientation men and women have about money. She writes: "In spite of the societal changes over the last twenty years, I think it is still fair to say that many women were raised with the belief, whether overt or unconscious, that dealing with finances was a man's job. Many of us were told, either directly or in subtler ways, that if we were lucky, we would find some rich man to take care of us and to deal with the unpleasant tasks of money management. We (women) were raised to be nurturers of these men first, and competent achievers second or not at all."

Much like their white counterparts, the financial decisions made by African American men and women are influenced by their cultural orientation. That African American women see themselves as nurturers is evidenced by their perspective on money: They tend to recognize African American men as breadwinners and masters of the family treasury.

In this scenario the African American female's role is mainly that of a "caregiver" while her significant other is viewed as the primary "provider" of the African American household. According to a survey conducted by Louis Harris and Associates, African American women overwhelmingly define success in terms of "family." Shelby White writes in *What Every Woman Should Know About Her Husband's Money* that "Men equate money with power and self-esteem. . . . In contrast, women think the definition of femininity is being able to balance work and home and to care for people."

The dissimilar monetary views of African American men and women affect African American households in many ways. While African American men will take greater financial risk with their financial resources than will African American women, acknowledging their financial naiveté may be the most disadvantageous behavior that separates African American women from men. African American women are quick to acknowledge their lack of financial acumen; African American men, on the other hand, are quick to let others believe that they know more about investments, real estate, and managing the family's finances than they really do. In some households the financial interest of the families may be better served if a woman controlled the family purse strings.

Defining the financial provider in a household is not always easy, especially in African American households where the woman's income can either equal or surpass that of her spouse. Nevertheless, old gender-based stereotypes take a long time to change. Until these stereotypes are changed, families may find guidance in a *Newsweek* article entitled "The New Providers." The authors wrote that "In the land of the two-earner family, mutual respect is more important than mutual funds."

African American women have other reasons, besides gender-based biases, to control their own financial futures. Many of these reasons are directly tied to social factors that have a negative impact of their economic lives:

• More than half of the African American work force is female (50.6 percent) while white women are 44.7 percent of the white work force. Fifty-six percent of African American women have steady jobs, and their median annual earnings are $18,720.

• The typical African American single-female-headed household has changed from mostly married-but-separated or widowed in 1970 to mostly single or divorced in 1987.

• Forty-two percent of African American wives do not work full time.

• The average life expectancy of African American women is seventy-four years. This is eight years longer than African American men, whose average life expectancy is sixty-six years.

• There are 1.2 million African American women among the working poor.

• Thirty-nine percent of families receiving welfare are African American. In 1973, 1.6 million female-headed families received Aid to Families with Dependent Children (AFDC).

• Many black women find it difficult to find a mate.
  – There are only eighty-five African American men for every one-hundred African American women in the twenty-five to forty-four age group.
  – African American men face high unemployment rates and are less likely to get college degrees than African American women.
  – In 1988, one in three of African American men age fifteen to twenty-four were living in poverty compared to one in one-hundred white men.
  – Owing to the current job market, marriage does not guarantee economic security for African American women.
  – Eleven percent of African American women are divorced.
  – In 1960, nearly 80 percent of African American families were headed by married couples. Many sociologists believe that the decline in two-parent African American families is a result of several factors including the increased unemployment of African American men and growing female independence.

• A 1992 population survey indicated that forty-seven percent of African American families are headed by married couples, 46 percent are female-headed households, and 7 percent are male-headed households. For whites, 82 percent are married, 14 percent are female-headed households, and 4 percent are male-headed households.

• Two thirds of all African American children are born to single women.

The above statistics give us a better understanding of the economic issues facing African American women. Many women are single for a significant portion of their lives, they live longer than their male companions, and they often have the responsibility of heading single-family households.

In some respects the white female must also deal with the same economic issues; however, the African American female's situation is more precarious than her white counterpart because the African American female usually earns less. Furthermore, unlike her white counterpart, the African American female cannot rely on a marriage or an inheritance to improve her financial situation.

SEVEN WEALTH-BUILDING STEPS FOR AFRICAN AMERICAN WOMEN

It is clear that African American women have financial concerns that are far different from those of the African American males, and they must take certain steps to safeguard their financial futures. African American women can take seven wealth-building steps to help them cope with their unique money management concerns:

1. Don't wait for Mr. Right to get your financial house in order.
2. Use your time to earn more money.
3. Never surrender your economic power.
4. Learn more to earn more.
5. Participate in an investment club.
6. Take control of your retirement now.
7. Always use your dollars *and* sense.

Let's see how each step can help African American women build their personal net worth.

STEP 1: DON'T WAIT FOR MR. RIGHT
TO GET YOUR FINANCIAL HOUSE IN ORDER

Remember, we want to dispel the myth that taking care of investments is a man's job. African American women must be self-reliant when it comes to making basic money management decisions.

Women cannot continue to believe that men know more about money matters than they do. The reality is that most African American females spend many years as singles or as single parents, and need to become financially astute. To do otherwise is to rely on someone else to safeguard your financial future—someone who might not be as interested in your future security.

Darice's mother helped her cultivate a passion for paintings and sculptures, and Darice started collecting art when she was in college. She could have waited until she was married before starting to build her art collection, but she didn't. She bought her first painting a few days before her twentieth birthday. Unbeknownst to her, Darice was starting to make smart money moves. From there, her acquisitions were sporadic. She wasn't necessarily buying for investment purposes or buying art that would appreciate. She was just drawn toward art.

Her buying pattern went on until she was spending "serious dollars." Darice then started reading about and studying art in her spare time. Art collecting became an obsession and a hobby, albeit an expensive one. She discovered that the works of African American artists were undervalued compared with European and white artists. That's because the art business is like any other: It's about who you know, the right connections, and being exposed to the right people—collectors who will buy your work. Consequently, Darice decided to support African American artists with her dollars. "At this point, I got really serious," she says.

Collecting became her life. As she puts it, Darice "transformed into someone who worked to buy art." Her job required her to travel a lot, so she was able to visit galleries around the country and meet many artists. Whenever she had a free moment she would read about art or go out to look at it. That was really where the fire in her life came from. She started thinking that maybe she should collect art for a living because it was what she really enjoyed. She nursed that idea for about five years before she actually gave it a try.

In the fall of 1993, she opened a gallery in downtown Chicago. The gallery has 5,000 square feet of space, 3,000 of it is for exhibition space. The rest is for memorabilia and historical items.

At age thirty-five, Darice has finally consummated and expanded what she's done all of her adult life: buy and sell art. Her personal collection is worth about $225,000, and most of it hangs in her home.

Remember, if the African American woman learns to depend on herself, she never has to wait for Mr. Right to make the right money move.

STEP 2: USE YOUR TIME TO EARN MORE MONEY

It is a reality that African American women live longer than African American men. In Chapter 4, you learned the time value of money—the more time a dollar has to compound, the more the dollar will grow. For example, a $1,000 investment earning 10 percent will double in value in seven years—to $2,000. Nevertheless, if that same $1,000 is allowed to compound for fourteen years at 10 percent, it will increase to $4,000. The only factor that caused the money to grow more was the element of time, and that is called the time value of money.

In the investment chapter I also pointed out that time is the greatest asset small investors have. Author of *Money Dynamics,* Venita Van Caspel's formula for financial success is

Time + Money + Compound Interest = Financial Success.

It, therefore, behooves the African American female to look for ways to use her longer life span to increase her wealth. African American women can benefit from their longer life expectancy when pursuing the following smart money moves:

- African American women may want to take a long-term attitude when investing in the stock market. For example, you may not want to move all of your stock investments (or mutual funds) to a conservative investment just because you are reaching retirement age. Instead, to offset inflation and maintain your purchasing power, you may want to have a portion of your portfolio remain more aggressive after your retirement.

- African American women may also decide to take more risks with their investments. There is really no need to invest every dollar in fixed assets, especially when these funds may not be needed for twenty or thirty years. By assuming more risk in their long-term investment portfolios, African American women can also increase their returns and, it is hoped, maintain their future purchasing power.

- Because it is likely that you will outlive your mate, you will need more retirement money than he will. As a rule, when discussing your insurance and retirement goals, always use age seventy-seven as a minimum age requirement.

- Purchase a decreasing term policy to age eighty-five or ninety to have more time to become self-insured and increase your financial assets.

• Take a part-time job after you retire (some type of work that you really enjoy) to help you continue to save money after you "retire."

• Always consider a longer life expectancy when reviewing your retirement needs. You don't want to retire with just enough money to last a certain number of years. Retirement would be a terrible time to learn that you don't have enough money to enjoy the necessities of life.

• Take care of yourself now to make sure you live a long and healthy life. The best way to ensure a longer life expectancy is to take care of your body by eating right, exercising, and avoiding habits that reduce your life span.

STEP 3: NEVER SURRENDER YOUR ECONOMIC POWER

African American women make important financial contributions to their families. Whether in two-income families where both husband and wife work, one-income families where the female stays home, or the single-parent female-headed household where the African American female is the sole provider, it is not uncommon for African American women to give up most, if not all, of their economic power. For example, the African American woman may give up or sacrifice her financial security for a college education for her children or let the man assume the role of provider and master of the family treasury.

A better way to manage the family's financial resources may be to understand that married couples are also financial partners. Both should share economic power, and one partner should not surrender power to another. Such sharing would encourage more team work among black married couples. More importantly, sharing economic power would help either partner manage the family's financial resources should one of them become disabled or pass away.

Many families today have two incomes, making it easier for the working wife to assume the position of "co-provider." On the other hand, we must not overlook the economic benefits a nonworking wife contributes to the family. Whether a married woman is working or not, she should consider herself a co-provider and not surrender her economic power.

Besides having a say in the major financial matters of the household, a female co-provider should also exercise her own economic powers by doing the following:

- Maintain a separate savings and checking account.
- Become the owner of your spouse's life insurance policy.
- Maintain your own credit card and open lines of credit.
- Have your own will.
- Have your own lawyer and financial advisor.
- Arrange a prenuptial agreement, if you are single.
- Maintain your own investment portfolio.
- Learn your rights as an ex-spouse (if you are divorced) in the state in which you reside.
- Retain a portion of all of your earnings before contributing to joint accounts.

Two approaches that co-providers may want to avoid are the "let's-share-everything" scenario and sacrificing their financial future for the children. In the let's-share-everything scenario where one spouse earns more than the other, there is nothing fair about equally sharing expenses. What normally happens in such cases is that the lower-income spouse exhausts his or her savings trying to keep up with the higher-income spouse and the savings of the higher-income spouse continue to grow because the lower-income spouse is subsidizing household expenses. The solution is to decide on an arrangement that is fair to both of you based on current income levels. What would a fair sharing arrangement be? Look at what percentage of the total household income each partner provides and divide the expenses accordingly. For example, if the female spouse brings home 40 percent of the family income and the male brings in 60 percent, the couple would share expenses 40/60. Remember to be flexible because incomes can fluctuate due to circumstances beyond your control.

Many couples believe that the equal-sharing arrangement is fair, because if a divorce occurs, each can claim half of the estate. However, my advice in case of divorce is to ask only for what represents your financial contribution to the relationship and move on. If the wife cannot afford to maintain the house on her income, then the former spouse should buy her share of the house. History has shown that a divorced woman cannot depend on a former spouse to pay the mortgage. Women should not depend solely on child support or alimony payments for financial stability.

Another issue female providers must contend with is sacrificing your financial future for the children. This may mean not pursuing an education, employment opportunity, or investment program in order to be a caregiver to your offspring, and occasionally to your aging parents. In the long run, such actions will only hurt, not help, your children. African American female providers must make every effort to increase their incomes in order to move their children as far from the poverty line as possible.

Not only is this idea sound financially but it also helps children appreciate the value of a dollar when they have to earn their own money. Make it clear that you will assist your children in getting a college education, but not pay the total bill. The children will value their education more, and you will continue to invest in your future. I know that holding back from your children may sound selfish, but the moral lessons are as important as financial lessons. Never overlook the opportunity to teach your children the value of financial planning and the power of earning.

Here are several other factors about being a co-provider or sharing economic power for you to consider:

- Many men view marriage as a business merger. African American women's financial interests may be best served if they view marriage the same way.
- Men respect women who are financially savvy.
- The best thing you can do for poor folks is not to be one. This includes the poor folks who may live under your roof.

Surveys have cited money as being one of the leading reasons many marriages end in divorce. By not surrendering your economic rights, you will keep money from ending your marital bliss.

STEP 4: LEARN MORE TO EARN MORE

In Chapter 10, "Expanding Your Human Capital," we discuss the economic value of a formal education and intellectual capital. The fact that an African American college graduate's income is almost on par with her white counterpart illustrates the importance of getting a formal education. Recent figures indicate that African American college-educated women earn an average of $18,000 and that their white counterparts earn $20,000. There can be little doubt that education has helped African American females increase their earning power, and we hope the salary gap will decrease even more.

Conversely, the African American female who does not have a formal college education has one of the lowest earning potentials in America. Many are forced to depend on government assistance programs to provide a steady income. Households headed by these women, with an annual income of approximately $5,000 a year, represent a large portion of the poorest African American households.

Whether you already have a college degree or are still trying to earn a GED, you must always take the time to pursue additional education and training. Study after study indicates that the more formal education and training a person has, the more money that person can earn. More importantly, recent surveys have pointed to the fact that our nation is divided by two sectors—the well educated and well paid and the poorly educated and poorly paid. The choice for African American women is clear; you can learn more and earn more, or you can learn less and earn less.

One source for earning and learning is your personnel department. Many corporations have tuition reimbursement programs and will pay for an advanced degree and additional training that will benefit your career.

Also check your local library and the *Resource Guide* to find information on colleges, government agencies, and African American women's professional and business organizations that are partial to helping women obtain a higher education.

Many investment companies also offer seminars to help you educate yourself about finances. Two leaders in this field are the Oppenheimer Fund and the Calvert Group. The Calvert Group has developed an informative investment guide for women, *A Personal Economy and Financial Program for Women.* Call the Calvert Group at (800) 743-4683 for a free copy.

Remember to be cautious about taking advice from any money manager, because as Lynda Williams, Director of the Calvert Women's Investment Program, said, "Women are oversold and underserved by the financial services community." Another good reason to find a financial planner you can trust.

STEP 5: PARTICIPATE IN AN INVESTMENT CLUB

Investment clubs are almost becoming a rage in America. The National Association of Investment Clubs has over 200,000 members. The association does not categorize its members by race, but by gender, and has noted that all-female investment clubs outperform all-male investment clubs. The Breardstown Ladies Club has even written a best-selling book about itself and its investment strategy.

Investment clubs are first and foremost a place to meet friends and learn how to invest in the stock market. According to Kenneth Janke, president of the National Association of Investors, the official governing body of investment clubs, "These clubs average about 10 to 12 people each investing $50 a month." The association guides investment clubs with rules and regulations, provides a monthly newsletter, and offers regional investor meetings.

Although investment club members do well in selecting and owning stocks, you can't expect to become wealthy by being an investment club member. However, if you apply the information you learn in the club to your personal investment selections, you can become more savvy about the stock market.

Like most investors, the Washington, D.C., based Washington Women's Investment Club (WWIC) started out small. Composed of twenty-one African American women, the club saw strength in its numbers rather than in its financial savvy. Most investment clubs appeal to those who are interested in investing, but don't want to assume the responsibility of a financial risk by themselves. The WWIC gave a sense of security to professional African American women in the Washington area. Chapter 1 of the group's instructional book, *How to Start an Investment Club*, explains that African Americans can achieve their financial goals by systematically increasing their net worth. Maurita Coley, vice president of the legal department at Black Entertainment Television in Washington, D.C. and WWIC member agrees.

"If you look at how much money you want to invest in a year, you can determine on what scale you see yourself. For us, we wanted it to be money we wouldn't miss," said Coley.

She continues, "The majority of the group's initial membership was composed of attorneys and media professionals. We put our heads together and decided to pool our resources. Thus the WWIC was born."

Coley says that starting an investment club should be fun and easy and that "a club is the most efficient way to find good investments and get involved. It's an excellent way to share the risks, and it tends to be less scary."

Additional information on WWIC can be found in our *Resource Guide*.

STEP 6: TAKE CONTROL OF YOUR RETIREMENT NOW
I mentioned earlier that African American women live on average eight years longer than African American men. This longer life span offers women additional opportunities, but it also gives them additional re-

sponsibilities. One of the additional responsibilities is to oversee their pension assets.

Most Americans retire at age sixty-five. Enjoying a comfortable retirement will be determined by the amount of money you have in your retirement accounts, including your pension plan, 401(k) plan, IRA, Tax Shelter and Annuity (TSA), Social Security, plus any other accounts you have earmarked for your retirement.

African American women must take control of their assets by first taking an inventory of every pension account they have. You will want to write to every fund administrator to find out what type of investment you have, what the return is, when these funds will be available, and what options are available to you.

Also contact the Social Security Administration to get a report of your Social Security payments. By reviewing the list, you will know if all of your past employers made their payments to your Social Security account. This information is important because you may reach retirement age and find out that your Social Security payments are less than you expected or even that you don't quality for Social Security because you do not have enough Social Security credits.

Many women leave retirement plans up to their husbands, assuming they will share in their husband's pension and social security, but in today's environment this is not wise. Not only is divorce common but downsizing, mismanagement of company pension plans, and the uncertainty of our Social Security system also make it very important for every African American female to control her own pension. If you are married, implement the following procedures:

- Have and annually fund your own spousal IRA.
- Have your husband's employer include you in his pension plan. Legally you are entitled to a portion of his pension.
- In a divorce decree, don't give up any pension rights.
- Work part-time in order to save for your retirement.
- Know everything about your husband's retirement plan and what rights you have under it.

"The High Cost of Motherhood," Chart 35, illustrates the impact of not working and not putting money into your pension account. Use this chart as a reminder not to miss making an annual investment into your pension account, even if you take time off to have children.

CHART 35: THE HIGH COST OF MOTHERHOOD:
At a 10 Percent Yield, Who Has More at 65?

	HUSBAND		WIFE	
Age	Contribu-tions	Value at Year-End	Contribu-tions	Value at Year-End
21	$2,000	$2,200		$0
22	$2,000	$4,620		$0
23	$2,000	$7,282		$0
24	$2,000	$10,210		$0
25	$2,000	$13,431		$0
26	$2,000	$16,974		$0
27	$2,000	$20,872		$0
28	$2,000	$25,159		$0
29	$2,000	$29,875		$0
30	$2,000	$35,062		$0
31		$38,569	$2,000	$2,200
32		$42,425	$2,000	$4,620
33		$46,668	$2,000	$7,282
34		$51,335	$2,000	$10,210
35		$56,468	$2,000	$13,431
36		$62,115	$2,000	$16,974
37		$68,327	$2,000	$20,872
38		$75,159	$2,000	$25,159
39		$82,675	$2,000	$29,875
40		$90,943	$2,000	$35,062
41		$100,037	$2,000	$40,769
42		$110,041	$2,000	$47,045
43		$121,045	$2,000	$53,950
44		$133,149	$2,000	$61,545
45		$146,464	$2,000	$69,899
46		$161,110	$2,000	$79,089
47		$177,222	$2,000	$89,198
48		$194,944	$2,000	$100,318
49		$214,438	$2,000	$112,550
50		$235,882	$2,000	$126,005
51		$259,470	$2,000	$140,805
52		$285,417	$2,000	$157,086
53		$313,959	$2,000	$174,995
54		$345,355	$2,000	$194,694
55		$379,890	$2,000	$216,364
56		$417,879	$2,000	$240,200
57		$459,667	$2,000	$266,420
58		$505,634	$2,000	$295,262
59		$556,197	$2,000	$326,988
60		$611,817	$2,000	$361,887

	HUSBAND		WIFE	
Age	Contributions	Value at Year-End	Contributions	Value at Year-End
61		$672,998	$2,000	$400,276
62		$740,298	$2,000	$442,503
63		$814,328	$2,000	$488,953
64		$895,761	$2,000	$540,049
65		$985,337	$2,000	$596,254
Total	$20,000	$985,337	$70,000	$596,254

Given all of the nuances of pension management, several investment companies offer retirement-only financial plans. These plans will help you collect and review all of your pension data and calculate how it will grow over your life span. Companies like American Express Financial Services and Merrill Lynch offer these retirement-only financial plans at a cost. Independent financial planners offer the same service but at a higher cost. Nevertheless, if you want your pension funds to grow and be assured that these funds are available when you need them, then you must take control of your pension.

STEP 7: ALWAYS USE YOUR DOLLARS *AND* SENSE

Financial advisors often shake their heads in disbelief after hearing how one of their clients made a foolish or costly consumer purchase. We call these people "penny foolish." In other words, had they taken their time, researched the situation, and shopped for the best deal, the decision would have been less costly and it would have left more money in their pockets. Instead, they moved ahead quickly, did not research the situation, and paid too much for an item that will probably pay only a minimum return on their investment.

Few African American females can afford to be penny foolish when making consumer purchases; to the contrary, they need to be "dollar wise." Making smart consumer purchase decisions will leave you with investment capital even after you make the purchase. In truth, many women are naturally dollar wise because they shop for bargains, wait for sales, use coupons, and shop at warehouses and outlets.

However, after saving money on one purchase, don't turn around and use the savings to make another purchase! For example, if you purchase a pair of shoes on sale and save $100, would you use the $100 savings toward the purchase of another pair of shoes, or would you invest the $100 in your investment account? The dollar-wise consumer would invest in her mutual fund and not in another pair of shoes.

Like their white counterparts, many African American women did not expect to be stretching dollars once their income rose to the middle-class level. While income levels have not changed over the course of twenty years, the purchasing power of those income dollars has changed. Thus, someone with a $25,000 to $50,000 income in 1995 cannot afford to purchase the same home, car, or consumer items she or he could purchase in 1975. According to the U.S. Department of Labor, inflation is causing the cost of living to rise faster than the salaries of American workers.

So whether we want to or not, we must all try to be dollar-wise consumers. We must look for cost-effective ways to purchase the items we want, and we must plan to use much of the money that we save on our major purchases to invest for the long term. This means that as we make decisions about credit cards, clothing, personal care, housing, food, and so on, we are going to take our time, research the situation, shop, and then make a dollar-wise move.

MAKING ENDS MEET

As a way of honoring and learning about how the African American female made dollar-wise decisions in the past, I asked historical researcher Deborah A. Atkinson to share some of the money-saving ideas African American women traditionally utilized. Of course, many of our female ancestors were trying to survive and provide for their families, and they were not able to build a financial nest egg. But I list their sacrifices as tribute to their frugality in the face of all odds.

Some of these activities have been passed down from generation to generation. Many factors have precipitated the demise of thrift activities but some of our historical thrift measures have survived.

- Using an herbalist or midwife instead of physicians.
- Planting home gardens for vegetables and fruits: beans, corns, tomatoes, sweet potatoes, potatoes, peas, collard greens, blackberries, cherries, raspberries, apples, peaches, and tobacco.
- Buying items such as sugar, salt, rice, and flour in bulk twenty-five- and fifty-pound sacks.

- Canning fruits, vegetables, and relishes in the summer for winter consumption.
- Combining with several other families to purchase large quantities of beef, produce, staples, and dry goods at a reduced rate.
- Walking or using public transportation.
- Purchasing clothing and shoes in bargain department stores, consignment shops, yard and garage sales, or discount outlets.
- Renting room(s) or basement apartments in their primary residences.
- Buying home furnishings at sales, vintage or used furniture stores, or outlets and discount stores.
- Making minor home repairs (e.g., electric, plastering, painting, wallpapering, and plumbing) themselves.
- Maintaining their own lawn and gardens.
- Keeping blinds or drapes closed in summer to shelter rooms from the hot sun and open in winter to warm rooms with the sun.
- Washing some clothing items by hand.
- Bartering, for example, sewing in exchange for market items, painting a house in return for automobile repairs, baby sitting in exchange for canned goods.
- Going to a beauty salon school for hair care because the cost is lower.

TO BE A WOMAN

Perhaps the best way to honor the African American female providers and co-providers of the past and present is with a poem I wrote about African American women.

TO BE A WOMAN
It takes more than just being a lady,
to be a woman.
Takes more than high fashions and soft hands,
to dignify a race,
taken from their homeland.
And to be polite is nice.
And to like good wine is fine.
But these qualities alone won't do,
When your baby's hungry,
your man is laid off,
and the monthly bills are due.
A lady must put on airs,
Too cute to do this
and too refined to do that.
But a woman ain't got time to spare.
She has too much to do,
and too much to share.
Which females do people really admire?
Which ladies achieve real fame and success.
Is it the debutante?
Is it the beautiful Madame?
Or, is it just
A woman more or less.

The first rule of economic survival is "God bless the child that's got his own." Now, let the blessings of God shine upon you while you use these seven steps to increase your financial reserves and increase your net worth. Because God also blesses the child that's got *her* own.

EXPANDING THE FACETS OF OUR HUMAN CAPITAL

But there is a spirit in man . . .
　　　　　　　—Job 32:8

Up to this point, everything we have discussed concerning wealth creation involved your earning ability and your financial resources. An important wealth-building resource often taken for granted or totally overlooked is *human wealth*—your ability to learn, work, and produce income for your family.

Human wealth can be divided into three distinct forms of human capital: *Intellectual, Physical, and Spiritual.* Few African Americans understand how to use human wealth to enrich their lives. When you consider human capital in relation to financial resources, you realize that a person's human capital represents 50 percent of his or her ability to accumulate wealth. This means that 50 percent of what people need to be financially successful has nothing to do with money.

Here is my formula:

	Investment capital	25%
+	Human capital	50%
+	Investment know-how	25%
=	Financial well-being	100%

So far we have spent our time learning about the 25% financial knowledge needed to invest the 25% investment capital. Now, we need to learn more about the 50% wealth-building resources associated with your human capital.

There are three ways to enhance your human capital and transform your human capital into wealth. This chapter will show you how to increase your intellectual capital, protect your physical capital, and better understand your spiritual capital.

INTELLECTUAL CAPITAL

Intellectual capital is using your mind and consciousness to increase your net worth. This includes placing a value on your education and specialized training. In his book *Success Runs in Our Race*, author George Fraser estimated that "Based on educational and professional achievement alone, an African American's intellectual capital is valued at ten dollars an hour. It also means our intellectual capital is approximately valued at five trillion dollars. Intellectual capital would also include your ability to use your consciousness to attract good fortune, and mental toughness to focus on your long-term goals."

Recent books on the power of positive thinking have added to the general public's understanding and appreciation for the life-enriching powers of the mind. In the following discussion, I will explore three areas concerning the wealth-building attributes of the mind that have not been widely discussed, especially in the African American community:

- The right of consciousness.
- Conditioning the mind for financial success.
- Myths and misconceptions that impede African American progress.

Naturally when one considers intellectual capital, the first thing that comes to mind is education. We have already touched on the learn-more-to-earn-more theory. According to 1991 census data, an African American with a high school diploma earned $18,000. An African American male college graduate earned $24,000, an African American with a master's degree earned $35,000, and an African American with a Ph.D. earned $45,000 annually. Clearly, an advanced college degree is the best investment you can make.

The *Resource Guide* contains a listing of black colleges and universities along with information regarding scholarship and tuition. In addition, Kraft Foods has published a free book titled *Choosing to Succeed* that provides information about the ninety-seven historically black schools. To receive a copy write to:

Kraft Foods
P.O. Box 23430
Kankakee, IL 60902

It won't take you long to realize that a college education from one of these institutions represents a good investment.

Reading is also important to success. It is the way most people learn. Many successful African American entrepreneurs who never went to college are avid readers.

In 1994, several news sources reported that a successful entrepreneur sold his share of a cable operation, for a cool $100 million. For over fifty years, this entrepreneur has been a successful real estate developer, politician, cable operator, and the first African American to own a major interest in a river-boat casino—and he achieved all of this without a college education. His secret: he loves to read financial reports and industry information. A friend of his once said, "It is remarkable that despite not having a degree, no one can interpret a financial statement as accurately as him." Of course, he is the exception and not the rule. Therefore, we must insist that our children receive a college education.

However, the lesson is clear. If you cannot attend college, you can still increase your intellectual capital by reading. To use a phrase from Dr. Dennis Kimbro, "Readers are leaders." According to Dr. Kimbro, "Normally the leaders in any given fields are there because they have read more and applied their reading more than anyone else in their field."

While increasing our financial wealth, it stands to reason that we would want to read more about personal finances, economic issues, and successful African Americans. I do believe that such reading is important because if, as the saying goes, "Knowledge is power," then financial knowledge must represent "financial power."

A college education, reading, and an openness to learning are obvious ways to increase your intellectual capital. What is not so obvious is the importance of conditioning your consciousness.

Consciousness, as defined by Webster is the "state of being aware of something within oneself." Much has been written about the powers of the subconscious mind and the effects of sleep on our daily lives. Nevertheless, we need to explore the notion of conditioning our conscious and its impact on increasing our intellectual capital.

Give special consideration to the phrase "being aware of something within oneself." The phrase suggests the importance of preparing to experience prosperity, affluence, and wealth. Could this be true? Does a person have to be aware mentally of something internally before he or she can live it externally? I believe the answer is yes.

To me, the saying "First there is the inner and then there is the outer" is a valid statement. First we think it and then we do it. We experience in our mental world before we experience in our physical world. For this reason, many writers suggest that what we experience in our outer world is nothing but a reflection of an earlier thought or mind-set.

My own observations about consciousness and wealth have helped me understand that everything I own, I own by right of consciousness. This means that until I am prepared mentally to enjoy my car, my condo, or my business, I will not have it, or if I do have a car, condo, or business, I will not keep it for long. If this concept is applied to the general population, then everything we own, we own by right of consciousness—not by constitutional right, not by right of citizenship, not by affirmative action, not even by civil rights or congressional decree—*only* by the right of consciousness.

Now you can understand why conditioning your consciousness for financial success is important. Your financial well-being begins and ends with your mind. Your ultimate financial success does not depend on your personnel officer, your banker, or the government's economic advisors; it depends *on your mind.*

Hence, it is necessary to control the types of information you allow to enter your consciousness. Unity minister and author Eric Butterworth wrote in *Spiritual Economics,* "Your negative thoughts of fear and worry are depleting your goods faster than inflation erodes the value of the dollar. And your positive, optimistic thoughts add to your good more dramatically than compound interest increases your bank savings."

Conditioning your mind with prosperous thoughts is wise; however, in a world where five minutes of the nightly news can offer enough depression to last a lifetime, it is unlikely that anyone can fill his or her mind only with thoughts of success and prosperity. Nevertheless, try to bring some prosperous thinking into your life on a regular basis. Read books, listen to motivational tapes, and associate with people who have a prosperous view of life.

You have read how computers were created to duplicate the human mind with the ability to calculate and retrieve information. There is another similarity between the computer and human consciousness. You cannot expect an outdated computer running outdated software to provide the same information and power as a newer model. Furthermore, computers are only as good as their software and data—if you put junk in, you are going to get junk out. The same holds true with our consciousness.

We must constantly be aware of the junk, that is, the wealth-restricting thoughts, that other people try to program into our consciousness. This may be especially true for African Americans. During the course of our history, we have created, permeated, and incorporated into our daily lives many myths and misconceptions about wealth and have programmed our personal mental computers with limited "wealth-building software."

TWENTY-ONE MISCONCEPTIONS ABOUT MAKING MONEY

During my career as a financial planner, entrepreneur, and host of the *Color of Money* television program, I have often wondered why there are so few financially successful African Americans. I now understand that part of the problem stems from African Americans' beliefs about money. Unfortunately, many of these beliefs are contrary to what a person needs to become financially successful. I make it a point to discuss these misconceptions from time to time on my show. Twenty-one of the most often cited misconceptions are discussed below.

1. "MONEY IS THE ROOT OF ALL EVIL."

Here is a Bible verse that is often misread and often taken out of context. In fact, it is just one of many misconceptions about money that are in some way related to the Bible. The correct reading, from the book of Timothy, is "For the *love* of money is the root of all evil." This of course refers to the notion that loving anything more than loving God may present a moral dilemma. It does not mean that there is anything intrinsically wrong with money, just in how you relate to it and how you use it. The point: money is not evil. It is just a means of exchange, a tool for you to achieve your own well-being.

2. "A RICH MAN CAN'T GET INTO HEAVEN."

Here is another Bible verse, this time from Mark, that suggests that being financially successful means that you are unworthy. You can also take this to mean that wealthy people are dishonest. Nonsense! Despite the number of biblical references to good stewardship and prosperity, somehow many of us have fixated on the poverty-focused verses. Do you need biblical justification to achieve prosperity? Fine. Consider a reading from Proverbs 14:23: "All hard work brings a profit, but mere talk leads only to poverty." God did not mean for you to be poor.

3. "YOU CAN'T TAKE IT WITH YOU."

To put it another way, it's okay to spend every dime you have on the here and now, because you're going to die anyway. That's true, but the heart of amassing wealth is planning, and you can't do that if you have little thought for what happens down the road. I remember an African American Seventh Day Adventist telling me, "I don't need to invest for the long term because the savior is going to come any day now and it will all be over." I said, "Yes, but suppose the savior doesn't get here until you're seventy years old?" While it is true that we can't take our worldly possessions with us when we die, it is also true that our financial responsibilities don't expire at our death. There are still bills to be paid, children to be raised, and spouses to be supported. You may leave the world with nothing, but do you want to leave your loved ones without financial resources?

4. "YOU MEET THE SAME PEOPLE ON THE WAY UP THAT YOU MEET ON THE WAY DOWN."

People who believe this have a defeatist attitude because they assume that no matter how high they rise, they will always fall in the end. This is far from the truth. Success is not fleeting. It can bring lasting rewards. There may be setbacks along the way (and it would be surprising if there weren't any), but setbacks are not synonymous with failure—unless, of course, you choose not to try to succeed again.

5. "YOU CAN'T ESCAPE BEING BLACK."

This is, to my way of thinking, a terribly insidious and self-defeating way of thinking. It is a way of internalizing forever the idea that African Americans do not deserve success. Why? Because the assumption underlying the statement is that after a person of color becomes successful, he or she will abandon the African American community. There is overwhelming evidence that the assumption just isn't true. While a few will turn their backs on other African Americans, most successful people never forget their community and many fight battles every day to help others. African

American developers build low-income housing, business owners hire workers, and executives try to correct the negative stereotypes many whites have about African Americans in the workplace. Being African American is no excuse for not striving to become financially successful.

6. "THE WHITE MAN'S ICE IS ALWAYS COLDER."

This popular saying means, of course, that African American goods and services are inferior to those available to white people. Utter nonsense, of course, but some of us still believe it. What bothers me most about this lie is what it says about the African American who believes it, for he or she is someone whose self-defeating attitude will hold back not only one individual but also a race. African Americans can never achieve greatness believing that what they do isn't as good as what white folks do.

7. "MY GOD WILL TAKE CARE OF ME."

When I consider this statement I remember the story about the minister who died in a flood while waiting for God to save him. The man was already surrounded by flood waters when two men in a jeep drove by and offered to drive him to safety. The minister refused their offer, saying, "My God will save me." Later, as the water was still rising, a man in a rowboat floated by the minister's house and tried to convince him to row to dry land. Again, the minister refused saying, "My God will save me." When the rising tide forced the minister to get on his rooftop, a helicopter flew by and dropped a ladder for him to climb aboard. He waved the helicopter off, shouting once again, "My God will save me." Shortly after that, the minister was drowned by rushing flood water. Angrily, he stood before St. Peter at the Pearly Gates and shouted, "Why didn't you save me?" To which St. Peter replied, "We tried. We sent a jeep, a rowboat, and a helicopter, and you wouldn't board any of them."

When you are getting your financial house in order do not expect a thunderclap, a burning bush, or a deep voice from the heavens. God will take care of you by sending you the tools to do the job. Learn how to recognize them and learn how to use them.

8. "YOU MUST KNOW SOMEBODY
TO MAKE IT IN THIS WORLD."

Many African Americans feel that their careers or income will be limited because they lack "connections." I would be the last to suggest that strategic relationships are not important, but it is important for people to understand that these relationships develop over time. I didn't know anyone in the television business when I started out six years ago. Now my Rolodex holds hundreds of business cards. We can all connect to the right people eventually. Besides, the most important person you need to know to be successful is yourself. Once you are confident in your own abilities, no one else need define you and you won't need false praise to validate your accomplishments.

9. "I'LL GET MY REWARD IN HEAVEN."

This may make sense to some people, but if you really believed it, you wouldn't be reading this book now, would you?

10. "THERE IS MORE TO LIFE THAN MAKING MONEY."

This rationalization is often used by people who are afraid that having money will somehow change them. It will—they will become richer. Unfortunately, being single minded about amassing wealth can be frightening to some people. This is their way of covering up their fear that something will happen to them that they cannot control. Everyone should have a balanced life, but don't use that as an excuse for staying broke.

11. "YOU CAN'T BEAT THE SYSTEM."

For many African Americans the American economic and political system is an enemy that cannot be beaten. To these folks, America's capitalist system is corrupt and designed to keep them poor and powerless. It isn't hard to understand why even many sophisticated and affluent African Americans believe this. There is certainly some truth to it. America's historically wretched treatment of its darker tenth of a nation is obvious. But for every brother or sister who says that capitalism is evil, I suggest you talk to citizens of the former Soviet Union, inhabitants of the countries recently liberated from the Iron Curtain, or even those in China where capitalism is now flourishing and bringing new wealth. And if you can't find them, talk to the African American men and women in this country who have become successful, and they will tell you that the system is not so bad. It is far from perfect, but don't let the ill will of its critics dissuade you from trying to accumulate wealth. As hard as it may be, if you lived in any other type of system, accumulating wealth would probably be impossible.

12. "THE BEST THINGS IN LIFE ARE FREE."

Nothing is free. For everything we receive, there is a price that must be paid. To receive love, you must give love. To enjoy the beauty of nature, you must work to preserve it. To enjoy the experience of spiritual enlightenment, you must offer time to meditate. You don't pay for everything with money, but the bottom line is that you must pay. When we believe that good things come without a price, we have already dealt ourselves a blow in the march to accumulate wealth.

13. "LIVING WELL IS THE BEST REVENGE."

Many of us use this dangerous idea as justification for overindulging in anything—from constant mall-trawling to nonstop partying. We might say that we grew up poor and missed the so-called good life, so now we're making up for it by living extravagantly. Or we might believe that a lavish lifestyle is a principled act of rebellion in a system that has oppressed us. One word best defines this sort of thinking: Foolish. Cavalier spending habits not only leave us poorer than before; they also frequently go hand-in-hand with physical overindulgence that can be life threatening. It's not a big leap from spending too much on material goods to going overboard when it comes to gratifying the senses. African Americans consume too many fatty foods, smoke too many cigarettes, and drink too much alcohol. The result is that thousands of us die every year before we are old enough to amass the wealth we want.

The irony is that living well isn't the best revenge. Living long is. The most important thing you need to make money is time. Time allows the interest on your savings to compound and grow. Time lets you collect the benefits of retirement and build an estate. Start thinking about how long you will live, and begin planning for your life. You will inevitably end up living better.

14. "ALL I NEED IS A GOOD JOB."

Maybe there was a time when all an African American needed to become financially secure was a good job, but that certainly isn't the situation today. The economy is bubbling along nicely, but even many successful corporations are considerably leaner than they were fifteen years ago. That means that good jobs are not easy to come by and the jobs that are available often do not offer the same level of security, employment or retirement benefits they once did.

Now if the treatment you get in the private sector doesn't make you realize that financial planning is a necessity, there is always the treatment you can look forward to from the public sector's largest pension plan, Social Security. That should be enough to frighten anyone into learning how to amass wealth.

15. "MY SOCIAL SECURITY WILL TAKE CARE OF ME."

Who started this rumor? Someone's well-meaning great-aunt who lived through the Depression? President Roosevelt? I don't know. But the fact is that the Social Security system is going broke and doesn't even take care of the needs of the people it is supposed to protect right now. Sixty percent of the African American elderly are poor. For many, Social Security is their only income. These are the people who counted on Social Security to make their retirement years a little easier. Sadly, the one thing we know about the ailing Social Security system is that it is not expected to get much better in the future.

In short, Social Security will not take care of you. By the time you are ready to retire it may not be able to take care of anybody except the people who administer it. Your grandmother may not have had this problem, but you will. So, start planning now.

16. "IT IS OKAY IF I AM POOR."

Many African Americans are fixated on living a pious life. For some reason, such an existence is considered a holy experience. George Subria, the author of numerous books on African American business, referred to this as the Porgy and Bess syndrome: *"I got plenty of nothing and nothing's plenty for me."* Well, I don't think so. Having plenty of nothing means just that—no savings, no home, and no retirement accounts, except for social insecurity.

17. "THE POOR WILL ALWAYS BE WITH YOU."

For the life of me, I can't understand why any African American would utter the words, "The poor will always be with you." It is in the Bible, but when Jesus Christ spoke these words, maybe he was reminding the people of his time to always remember the poor and less fortunate in the world.

In any case, I don't believe Jesus was proclaiming that all African Americans are destined to be poor and stay poor.

18. "I AM ALWAYS A DAY LATE AND A DOLLAR SHORT."

I don't know where this one came from. I have heard African American businesspeople use it, as a way of saying, "I am poor, I can't get a break, and I want you to help me." There is supposed to be a hint of humor in it, but I don't get it.

Why, as a consumer, would I want to do business with someone who is always a day late and a dollar short? Maybe that is the problem—I do get it.

19. "I DISTRUST CAPITALISM."

There are many reasons why many African Americans distrust capitalism. One of the major reasons stems from slavery in America. Capitalism is also cited as the reason African Americans endured racial and economic injustices—so it is with good reason that African Americans distrust the capitalist system. Nevertheless, we must raise the question, "Is it the system that is bad or is it the men who control the system?" I do not believe capitalism is bad any more than I believe money is evil. Furthermore, I don't believe that African Americans should be ashamed to call themselves capitalists.

20. "NEITHER A LENDER NOR BORROWER BE."

It will be very difficult to increase your net worth if you refuse to lend or borrow money from time to time. This is especially true if you need to buy a car, home, or business—all of which may require you to borrow a substantial amount of money. There are times when lending to others (bond investments) may be profitable. You should not pass up these opportunities solely because you were instructed never to be a lender or a borrower.

21. "THE COSTS ASSOCIATED WITH SUCCESS ARE TOO HIGH."

I should point out here that the biggest price a person must pay for success is time. It takes time to complete your college education, build a business, or become the best in your chosen field. But I should also point out that there is a high cost associated with not being successful. The largest price is the economic reality that poorer African Americans on average pass away sooner than their middle-income counterparts.

But all of this talk about the cost of success is trivial, because as novelist James Baldwin observed, "Anyone who has ever struggled with poverty knows how extremely expensive it is to be poor."

These are the fallacies about money that my television guests have heard in the African American community. You may hear them quoted with slight variations in different parts of the country, or you may hear some of them more often than others. Even if you do not hear them at all, the evidence that people believe them will be all around you when you see how your friends and family have internalized these roadblocks to increasing their wealth. They say that they want to become millionaires, but they behave in ways that will keep them financially insecure.

Keeping your head on straight about money matters is not easy, even after you begin to realize the unconscious pitfalls that clutter your path. Read as much as you can about building wealth: the more you immerse yourself in this subject the easier it will be to achieve your goals. There are many good books and magazines on the subject, and I have listed some of them in the *Resource Guide*.

If your consciousness is programmed with misconceptions don't panic. Begin to reprogram your consciousness with prosperous thoughts. Read inspirational books and biographies of successful African Americans, and always keep in mind the value of human capital, be it intellectual, physical, or spiritual.

Quotes from Famous African Americans About Success

1. "We can't live in a capitalist society without capital."
   Rev. Jesse Jackson
2. "The best thing you can do for poor folks is not be one."
   Rev. Ike
3. "Black men and women need to create their own economic base. Without economic power there is no political power."
   Luther Campbell
4. "Social and political power can not be protected without economic power."
   Joshua Smith
5. "Without money, you have no control. Without control, you have no power."
   Spike Lee
6. "Words are nothing but words; power lies in deeds."
   Mali Griot

7. "Money talks, nonsense walks."   *traditional saying*
8. "Men must not only know, they must act."   *W.E.B. Du Bois*
9. "Romance without finance has no chance."   *traditional saying*
10. "At the bottom of education, at the bottom of politics, even at the bottom of religion, there must be economic independence."
    Booker T. Washington
11. "In the fifties Negroes in America wanted to integrate socially; in the sixties and seventies black Americans wanted to integrate politically. Now, in the nineties African Americans want to integrate economically. We have finally realized how important it is to integrate the money."
    Andrew Young, Former U.S. Ambassador to the United Nations
12. "The color of freedom is green."   *Tony Brown*
13. "In a material world we easily forget that life is lived from within, not from without."   *Susan Taylor*
14. "The world we live in is first and foremost shaped by the mind."
    Charles Johnson
15. "Men may not get all they pay for in this world, but they must certainly pay for all they get."   *Frederick Douglass*
16. "A race which cannot save its earnings can never rise in the scale of civilization."   *Frederick Douglass*
17. "Dollars not only count, but they rule."   *Charles T. Walker*
18. "Money is life. Once upon a time freedom used to be life. Now it's money."   *Lorraine Hansberry*
19. "Money is the manifestation of power."   *S. E. Anderson*
20. "Not poor, just broke."   *Dick Gregory*
21. "Politics doesn't control the world, money does. . . . We ought to begin to understand how money works and why money works."
    Andrew Young
22. "When you can count your money, you ain't got none."
    Don King
23. "The issue is no longer, can you check into the hotel, it's whether you got the money to check out. The issue is no longer whether you can go to the University of Mississippi, but whether you can pay the tuition. The issue in no longer whether you sit on the bus or whether you can drive it: it's whether you can develop the capital to own the bus company."   *William Gray*
24. "Our crown has been bought and paid for, all we have to do is wear it."   *James Baldwin*

25. "I've been rich and I've been poor and I have to admit that rich is better." *John H. Johnson*

26. "Anytime you see someone more successful than you are, they are doing something that you aren't." *Malcolm X*

27. "When we are noted for enterprise, industry, and success, we shall no longer have any trouble in the matter of civil and political rights." *Frederick Douglass*

28. "There is no force like success, and that is why the individual makes all effort to surround himself throughout life with the evidence of it; as of the individual, so should it be of the nation." *Marcus Garvey*

29. "Success in life revolves around recognizing and using our abilities, our raw material." *Benjamin Carson*

30. "Success has a power of its own." *Cordiss Collins*

31. "Clarity is not a thought process but a way of life." *Keorapetse Kgostitsile*

32. "In God we trust, all others pay cash." *traditional saying*

33. "Get wisdom, but with all you're getting, get wealth." *Rosa Bowser*

34. "The pretense of wealth prevents the accumulation of real wealth." *Nathan Hare*

35. "Wealth is really what you own and control, not how much you have in your pockets." *John H. Johnson*

36. "The fundamental difference is the attitude white people have about acquiring wealth and the attitude Black people have. White people know that wealth brings power, so they do everything possible to gain more wealth and thus more power. Black people, too often, seek wealth to have enjoyment, to buy pleasure. There's a big difference between power and pleasure, and since power lasts longer than pleasure, whites have gained control of practically everything." *Raymond St. Jacques*

37. "Wealth isn't what a man has, but what he is." *Charles Johnson*

38. "Wealth will never come to those who fail to appreciate it." *Father Divine*

39. "You get out what you put in." *traditional saying*

40. "There's nothing mysterious about success. It's the ability to stay mentally locked in." *Montel Williams*

41. "Nothing succeeds like success." *Alexandre Dumas père*

42. "Actually we are slaves to the cost of living." *Carolina Maria DeJesus*

43. "Man cannot live by profit alone."   *James Baldwin*
44. "The haves and have nots can often be traced to the did's and didn't dos."   *William Raspberry*
45. "Chance has never yet satisfied the hope of a suffering people. Action, self-reliance, the vision of self and the future have been the only means by which the oppressed have seen and realized the light of their own freedom."   *Marcus Garvey*
46. "We realize that our future lies chilly in our own hands. We know that neither institutions nor friends can make a race stand unless it has strength in its own foundation; that races like individuals must stand or fall by their own merit; that to fully succeed they must practice the virtues of self reliance, self respect, industry, perseverance, and economy."   *Paul Robeson*
47. "Education is our passport to the future, for tomorrow belongs to people who prepare for it today."   *Malcolm X*
48. "When I discover who I am, I'll be free."   *Ralph Ellison*
49. "Great triumphs are achieved by those who believe in their dreams and persevere."   *African proverb*
50. "Anyone who has ever struggled with poverty knows how extremely expensive it is to be poor."   *James Baldwin*
51. "God bless the child that's got his own."   *traditional saying*

PHYSICAL CAPITAL

Apart from our minds, we must also look to our bodies for physical capital. Most African Americans avoid any discussion concerning death; nevertheless, there are some things we must discuss for our financial well-being, and maintaining our physical capital is one of those areas. We will review the physical aspect of our human wealth and the three factors that have historically eroded the creation of wealth for African Americans:

- Failure to decrease preventable deaths in the African American community.
- Failure to view good health as a wealth-building opportunity.
- Failure to understand the value of time.

Physical capital revolves around a person's ability to earn a living and to invest. It also revolves around disability, sickness, and death because these three occurrences could have an impact on your family's financial well-being.

Of the three, untimely death appears to be the major factor limiting the ability of African American families to substantially increase their net worth. What is most alarming is that many of these deaths result from preventable illnesses such as lung cancer, hypertension, heart attack, or diabetes, and that for a majority of our youngest African American men, ultimately death comes in the form of gunshot wounds.

The economic impact of physical capital can be understood when you realize that time, not money, is the most important factor in becoming financially successful. Every family needs time to recover from financial mistakes, establish a career, build an investment portfolio, have the children grow up and leave home, accumulate money in a retirement plan, and let financial assets compound and appreciate. Time is especially important if you are investing only a small amount of money every month. Unfortunately, the African American community jeopardizes its physical capital by refusing to join the good health craze and failing to have regular medical examinations.

The best way to address this issue is to recognize good health as a wealth-building tool because illness robs the African American community of billions of dollars of physical capital every year. Therefore, we must protect our health to increase our physical capital because

- Longevity nurtures prosperity.
- Good health is the best investment you can make.
- Good health drives your earning capacity.
- Good health gives you a longer time frame for building an estate.
- Good health gives your funds time to compound and appreciate.

SPIRITUAL CAPITAL

Spiritual capital is the energy—or lack of it—that results from your relationship with the almighty and the way this relationship helps you live a prosperous life. Job 32:8 reads "There is a spirit in man." The value of spirit or spiritual capital cannot be underestimated. Many successful African Americans credit their success to their strong belief in God.

When author George Wallace completed *Black Wealth Through Black Entrepreneurship* and delivered it to his publisher, the publisher asked Mr. Wallace why he made so many references to God in the book.

Mr. Wallace responded, "Because every black entrepreneur I interviewed credited his success to God." The religious faith of African Americans and their success is everywhere. We pray for everything. If there is something we want badly enough, we will pray for it. We pray for houses, new clothes, and even good fortune at the casino. In almost every African American community, business, and organization on almost any day you can hear, "God's will be done." "It is in God's hands now," or "In God we trust."

THE SPIRIT OF SUCCESS

What I find interesting is that with all of this praying many African Americans haven't realized how to maximize the spirit of success. Several reasons appear to account for this situation:

- Many see God as some super being living in the sky ready to punish or reward them depending on their actions.
- Many still believe that a poor life is a Christlike life.
- Many view their relationship with God as interpersonal and not intrapersonal, in other words, a relationship that is inside of them and limited, rather than a part of all that they are and all that they do.
- Many see God as a being to depend on instead of a God that empowers.
- Many believe that in this world we must suffer and be rewarded for our suffering in the next world. These notions about God undermine the ability of some African Americans to enhance and understand their spiritual capital.

Many successful African Americans, such as Oprah Winfrey, Arsenio Hall, Dr. Benjamin Carson, Terry Williams, and Susan Taylor, understand and readily use their spiritual capital. Most have a calming presence about them. At first, this calmness may appear as confidence, but there is something unique about the way they talk, walk, and act—a demeanor that announces to the world, "I am one with God."

Deepak Chopra wrote in *The Seven Spiritual Laws of Success* that "Our internal reference point is our own spirit, and not the objects of our experience. When you are in touch with your spiritual self you will not let outside situations, circumstances, people, or things keep you from enjoying your highest good or economic potential."

You can measure spiritual capital by:

- The manner in which you face the challenges of daily living.
- The way you demonstrate the Christian principle of love for yourself and others.
- That your God wants you to succeed.
- The faithful manner in which you live and manage your personal and business affairs.
- The nature of your relationships with your family, friends, and co-workers.

I have separated people who use spiritual capital from those who don't into two groups. The difference between the two groups is that some people are constantly testing God, while others understand that because their God is, they are what they are and who they are.

An example of this occurred during the late sixties. The Reverend Jesse Jackson reminded America's African American youth, they were somebody. Regardless of where they lived or their economic condition, they were somebody. It was a great message and it inspired and still inspires many young people. Nevertheless, Jackson's message raises one question: Where did they get my "somebodiness" from?

The first group of petitioners to God are still asking this question, while the second group of nonpetitioners already know the answer. Their somebodiness came from the divine spirit that is their constant companion wherever they go. They understand that, "The kingdom of God is within you" (Luke 17:21). This gives the second group the awareness that their God wants them to be successful and is constantly active to make sure that they achieve success.

Hence, the second group believes that If I do my best then my God will do the rest. "For with God nothing shall be impossible" (Luke 1:37), while the first group believes, If I try then my God will help me by and by. The second group knows that it will definitely happen, the first group thinks that it might be a possibility. This assurance, by the way, is carried over into every aspect of our well-being, including our financial well-being.

According to the Reverend Eric Butterworth, the connection between spirit and prosperity is natural. Butterworth writes in his book *Spiritual Economics,* that in Latin the word *prosperity* means "according to hope or to go forward hopefully." He concludes that "considered in the broadest sense, prosperity is 'spiritual well-being.' "

Charles Filmore, the father of the Unity Church movement, created a storm of controversy when he proclaimed that "It is a sin to be poor." Many people took his words literally, but Mr. Filmore was speaking figuratively. He was trying to say that it would be incorrect for a Christian to have a *"poor self-image*—a contradiction to believe in the purpose of Jesus Christ and yet believe that this belief compels you to live in poverty." This mandate invites every person to experience the spirit of success.

According to Deepak Chopra, "The first spiritual law of success is the Law of Pure Potentiality. This law is based on the fact that we are, in our essential state, pure consciousness. Pure consciousness is pure potential; it is the field of all possibilities and infinite creativity."

Understanding the spirit of success is important since the majority of African Americans are Christians. Some use the Christian principle to obtain prosperity, while others use it to justify their poverty.

USING HUMAN CAPITAL
TO INCREASE YOUR NET WORTH

To see how African Americans are using their spiritual powers to increase their net worth, we could look at the millions of African Americans who attend church every Sunday and compare that number to the lack of millions of dollars in their individual bank accounts. However, a more dismal factor may be reflected in the financial state of African Americans' spiritual foundation—the African American church. In the introduction to *Economic Empowerment Through the Church,* Eric Lincoln writes that "The black church takes in well over two billion dollars a year in dues, donations, and charitable giving . . . and yet, the black church as an institution is always on the edge of insolvency."

According to George C. Fraser, author of *Success Runs in Our Race,* African Americans receive "less than a one percent return on their collective intellectual capital." Mr. Fraser came to this figure by dividing the number of hours African Americans had in formal education and professional training (500 billion hours) by the $21 billion African American businesses produce in sales and services. In the June 1995 issue of *Black Enterprise,* economist Andrew F. Brimmer stated that African Americans share of money income was projected to be $353 billion or 8 percent of the total U.S. money income. I think that Mr. Fraser should also include the collective income and wealth of African Americans to make his calcu-

lations reflect the true return we are getting from our collective education. Nevertheless, to his credit Mr. Fraser also states, "You can argue
with my mathematics, but you cannot argue against my contention that
African Americans can do better with their (intellectual) resources."

We also vicariously witness the lethal destruction of African American's
human capital on nightly newscasts. These reports of drug-related slayings
in the African American community have almost become a regular feature.
There is a saying in the industry: "If it bleeds, it leads the nightly news." Too
often the stories that bleed come from the African American communities.

We can point to times throughout history when African Americans relied on their self-determination to create and enlarge their political and
economic opportunities in America. They used their intellectual, physical, and spiritual power to end slavery, Jim Crowism, and segregation.

We now call on these same personal powers to help African Americans increase their individual and collective net worth. Whenever people
increase their human capital, they also increase their capacity for economic self-determination. Let's see how:

CHART 36

	Before	After
INTELLECTUAL CAPITAL		
By increasing our educational achievement, we increase our earning capacity.	No degree: Earn less than $9,000 a year	Master's degree: Earn $35,000 + a year.
By filling our consciousness with prosperous software, we increase our capacity to enjoy prosperity.	Constantly trying to correct unfavorable financial situations.	Constantly enjoying financial situations.
PHYSICAL CAPITAL		
Choosing a healthier lifestyle increases life expectancy, which increases earning potential. We have more time to earn a living, invest and have our earnings grow.	Live to age 55. Work for 30 years and average $20,000: total earnings = $600,000	Lives to age 65 +. Work for 40 years and average $20,000: total earnings = $800,000°

°As you can see, time is money. The longer you live, the more time you have to earn money and see the
money grow.

	Before	**After**
SPIRITUAL CAPITAL		
When our spiritual understanding allows us to enjoy financial success, we increase our capacity to experience success. It is okay to use the spiritual aspect of our nature to improve our economic situation.	Piousness and poverty are linked to spiritual fulfillment.	Affluence and prosperity are linked to spiritual fulfillment.

Let's see how your family can use its human capital to increase its net worth. Again I will refer to you and your spouse as Mr. and Mrs. Money. Let's assume that Mrs. Astor Money decided to return to night school and complete her college education. Armed with a college degree, she feels that her company will increase her salary from $18,000 to $30,000.

After reading an article that explained how African American men can live longer, Mr. Money thinks that it may be time for him to begin a regular exercise program and change his diet. He also wants to lose about thirty pounds. Mr. Money plans to work until age sixty-two and then retire. At that point, he'll watch his money grow, and these actions will help him add at least $250,000 to his earning power.

Both Mr. and Mrs. Money are also thinking about attending a new church in their community where the minister is quite progressive and the members are pleasant and successful. The Moneys want to surround themselves with successful people.

We are all spiritual beings with a spiritual relationship with God. It is our choice to use it. Being aware of your spiritual capital is beneficial. Intellectual and physical capital, along with spiritual capital, represent a significant wealth-building resource that African Americans often underutilize. I hope that your family will not be one of the millions of African American families that fails to use the most important net worth–building resources—intellectual, physical, and spiritual capital—to increase its net worth.

ELEVEN

A PILGRIM DISCOVERS
THE PROMISED LAND

Save when there shall be no poor among you.
—Deuteronomy 15:14

While I was writing *Smart Money Moves for African Americans,* most of my attention had to be focused on financial concepts that would help you increase your net worth. In so doing, I did not mean to suggest that African Americans should spend all of their time trying to accumulate money. Neither was I trying to negate some of the joys that money can't buy.

I agree with author Marshall Sinetar, who wrote that to be whole, every human being must find not only "financial stability" but also "inner fulfillment." I also believe that this sense of inner fulfillment is fostered when one enjoys financial stability. Having both creates a sense of security. One of the major purposes for writing this book was to help more African Americans achieve emotional and economic security.

While pursuing this long-term objective, you can take solace in knowing that over a ten-year period the stock market has historically produced a ten percent annual rate of return that doubles the value of your stock portfolio. In addition, the equity in your home should increase substantially, and your business should be stable and grossing over $1 million in annual sales. Of course, you could reach all of these goals sooner, but if you don't, you have the benefit of knowing that other investors, homeowners, and entrepreneurs usually reap the rewards of their investments in about ten years. No doubt, ten years is a long time to work toward a goal, but knowing that in ten years you and your family will be financially secure should help you stick to your wealth-building plan.

Now let's see how your net worth might grow if you follow the smart money moves outlined in this book. Should your assets appreciate at the same rate as they have in the past, you could wake up ten years from now with a net worth over $200,000.

At that time, you could have $70,000 in cash reserves and mutual funds; $30,000 in home equity; and a business that is valued at $100,000—for a total of $200,000.

Imagine owning a net of this magnitude all from following the steps in this book. I know it sounds as though it cannot be achieved. But believe me, it can be achieved . . . and you can achieve it. Because as Theodore J. Miller, author of *Invest Your Way to Wealth,* noted: "The fundamental key to creating wealth is buying a broad mix of quality assets and giving them time to grow."

Should you not follow the net worth–building concepts outlined in this book, you are likely to find yourself in the same financial situation in ten years as you are in now. You will be ten years older, without a wealth-building plan, with limited financial resources, and your net worth will show little increase from where it is today. Shakespeare once said that "life is a dream." If this is so, then we all have an opportunity to live our dreams.

African Americans often speak about the promised land. During slavery, African Americans looked to the northern cities of the United States as the promised land where slavery was illegal and they could live as free people. Today, many African Americans see the promised land as having a good job, medical insurance, and a comfortable retirement plan. Still other African Americans will always see the promised land to be their final resting place.

When African Americans say that they are going to the promised land, they are trying to find a place; however, they should be looking at the promised land as a passion they must experience. Many African Americans have separated their human experiences from the metaphor and have forgotten that they *are* the promised land.

Joseph Campbell explains, "The mystery that you are looking for and you think is somewhere external to yourself is not out there at all. It's what you are. You don't have to go anywhere to find God, and you don't have to go anywhere to find the Promised Land. It's here, inside every human being. It's where you are. It is what you are."

This brings me to the second but perhaps the primary reason this book was written: to help guide African Americans to the only place where they can find their economic *promised land*—their self-sustaining nature.

For this reason the train ride to abundance has been more soulful than corporal. The itinerary was designed to have an impact on your thoughts and feelings. I hope this holistic and largely spiritual concept to wealth building will better prepare you to take the smart money moves suggested in this book.

Many African Americans are beginning to understand why a holistic approach is needed to help African Americans become empowered economically. Noted African American theologian Eric Lincoln writes, "Unless we try to help African Americans from a holistic way, we are only solving part of their problems."

When viewed in its totality, the investment program outlined in this book is a holistic way to achieve prosperity. It recognizes the African American investor as more than a person with an income. It acknowledges that the African American investor also has intellectual, physical and spiritual capital to invest. African American investors can combine their human capital with their financial capital to enhance their financial well-being. *Smart Money Moves for African Americans* is a valuable resource that should not be allowed to collect dust in a bookcase. You should refer to it often and share it with your friends and family members.

I recently learned the value of using the phrase, "I envision" from my friend Justin Becket when talking about the future. Justin is a vice president at Sloan Financial Group, the country's largest African American–owned money management company with more than $1 billion under management.

Whenever Justin, who is only thirty-three, speaks about a future project he always uses the words, "I envision." Three years ago Justin shared information about a mutual fund he wanted to start. It would be the first open-ended Pan African Mutual Fund managed by African Americans. The fund Justin envisioned would be called the New Africa Fund. The name suggests the new and greatest emerging market in the world—Africa. On April 12, 1995, Justin and his partner The Calvert Mutual Fund Group launched the world's first open-ended Pan African Mutual Fund. Justin was named president of the New Africa Fund.

Justin's use of the term "I envision" initialed my use of this phrase to affirm a future hope or desire. Let's consider it for a moment. Wouldn't it be great if when asked about your future plans, you could respond, "I envision myself being financially successful" or "I envision owning a multimillion-dollar company." Now, whenever I discuss the future I use the words, "I envision."

Let me share what I envision for your future, before your train pulls into the Abundance train station. I envision you owning a home, investing in the stock market, leading a healthy lifestyle, building a business, and insuring your financial future.

I can also envision African American women forming investment clubs and African American families setting up their own college and small-loan funds. It's a wealth-filled life for you and your family, where you can afford to send your children to college, support your favorite charities, and retire with financial dignity. Lastly, I envision your actions and the actions of other African American investors helping to bridge the great economic gap that now separates African Americans and whites. This is what I envision for your financial future if you follow the smart money moves outlined in this book. Nevertheless, what I envision for you is secondary to what you envision for yourself.

Our train ride to Abundance has come to an end; the train is pulling into the station. We have reached our final destination. As the doors open, we can hear the conductor shout, "Last stop—Abundance."

In spite of our expectations we are still hesitant about leaving the train and uncertain about what to expect as we step into the promised land. Nevertheless, we move forward knowing that regardless of the political climate, the economic forecast, or the financial storm we may encounter, if we invest our resources wisely, we will be able to enjoy our financial dreams.

We move toward the front of the train, and I whisper so that only you can hear my words, "Pursue your dreams." Taking your hand to say good-bye, I remind you that, "Every payday is your day to save a dollar and a dream."

POWER INVESTING
RESOURCE GUIDE

The Smart Money Moves Library
Bibliography
Smart Money Glossary
1. African American Financial Institutions
2. African American–Managed Mutual Funds
3. African American Publicly Traded Companies
4. 1995 Black Enterprise Top 100 African American–Owned Businesses
5. African American–Owned Insurance Companies
6. Small Business Association Loans
7. Small Business Association Regional and District Offices
8. Minority Business Development Centers
9. Historically Black Colleges and Universities
10. Investment Associations
11. Women's Special Employment Assistance
12. The IRA
13. African American CPA Firms
14. A++ Rated Insurance Companies
15. African American Women Professional Groups
16. Important Phone Numbers
17. Life Expectancy at Birth by Race and Gender
18. N.A.I.C. Dividend Reinvestment Program Companies

THE SMART MONEY MOVES LIBRARY

I am often asked to recommend financial reading material that will help people increase their net worth. The following is a list of books and periodicals that can serve as the foundation of your power-investing library. Whenever you can, add to this collection and share it with your family and friends. Building your investment library is a smart tax move.

1. *Think and Grow Rich: A Black Choice*
   by Dennis Kimbro and Napoleon Hill
2. *Succeeding Against the Odds*
   by John H. Johnson
3. *Black Wealth Through Black Entrepreneurship*
   by Robert L. Wallace
4. *Why Should White Guys Have All the Fun*
   by Reginald Lewis and Blair Walker
5. *Gifted Hands* and *Think Big*
   by Ben Carson M.D.
6. *Acts of Faith: Daily Meditations for People of Color*
   by Iyanla Vanzant
7. *One Up on Wall Street* and *Beating the Street*
   by Peter Lynch
8. *Money Dynamics for the 1990s*
   by Venita Van Caspel, CFP
9. *Black Enterprise* Magazine
10. The *Wall Street Journal*
11. *Money* magazine
12. *High Finance on a Low Budget*
    by Mark Skousen and Jo Ann Skousen
13. *USA Today* newspaper
14. *Black Women's Guide to Financial Independence*
    by Cherly Bousard
15. *The Personal Touch*
    by Terry Williams
16. *Success Runs in Our Race*
    by George Fraser
17. *Live Your Dreams*
    by Les Brown
18. *Success* magazine
19. *The African American Address Book*
    by Tabatha Crayton
20. *Don't Believe the Hype*
    by Farai Chideya
21. *In the Spirit*
    by Susan Taylor

22. *The Power of Your Sub-Conscious Mind*
    by Joseph Murphy
23. *Spiritual Economics*
    by Eric Butterworth
24. *The Entrepreneurial Mind*
    by Jeffry A. Timmons
25. *A Letter to My Children*
    by Marian Wright Edelman
26. *The Color of Money* magazine
27. *Economic Empowerment Through the Church*
    by Gregory J. Reed
28. *An Introduction to Business for African-American Youth*
    by Abner McWhorter
29. *Black Labor*
    by Claud Anderson, Ed.D.
30. *The Black Man's Guide to Good Health*
    by James W. Reed, M.D., Neil B. Shulman, M.D., and Charlene Shucker
31. *How to Start An Investment Club*
    by Washington Women's Investment Club
32. *Transform Your Life*
    by Barbara King

BIBLIOGRAPHY

Adams, Russell L. *Great Negroes Past and Present.* Chicago: Afro-American Publishing, 1963.

Anderson, Claude. *Black Labor–White Wealth: The Search for Power and Economic Justice.* Baltimore: Duncan & Duncan, 1994.

Barr, Alwyn, and Robert A. Calvert. *Black Leaders: Texans for Their Times.*

Bates, Timothy Mason. *Banking on Black Enterprise: The Potential of Emerging Firms for Revitalizing Urban Economies.* Washington, D.C.: Joint Center for Political and Economic Studies; Lanham, Md.: Distributed by University Press of America, 1992.

Bell, Janet Cheatham. *Famous Black Quotations and Some Not So Famous.* Chicago: Famous Black Quotations, 1986.

Bennett, Claudette E. *The Black Population in the United States: March 1992.* Washington, D.C.: U.S. Department of Commerce, Sept. 1993

Berg, Adriane G. *Your Wealth-Building Years.* 2nd ed. New York: Newmarket Press, 1992.

Black Biographical Dictionaries. Library of Congress. Washington, D.C., n.d.

Blum, Laurie. *Free Money.* New York: John Wiley, 1993.

Boa, Fraser. *The Way of Myth-Talking with Joseph Campbell.* Boston: Shambala Publications, Inc., 1992, 1994.

Butterworth, Eric. *Spiritual Economics*. Unity Village: Unity, 1983.

Case, Samuel. *The First Book of Investing*. Rocklin, Calif.: Prima Publishing, 1994.

Chideya, Farai. *Don't Believe the Hype: Fighting Cultural Misinformation about African-Americans*. New York: Plume, 1995.

Chopra, Deepak. *The Seven Spiritual Laws of Success: A Practical Guide to the Fulfillment of Your Dreams*. San Rafael, Calif.: Amber-Allen Publishing/New World Library, 1994.

Crayton, Tabatha. *The African-American Address Book*. New York: Berkley Publishing, 1995.

Dacey, Norman F. *What's Wrong with Your Life Insurance*. New York: Macmillan Publishing Co., 1963, 1989.

Deloitte & Touche, LLP. *Personal Tax Planning 1994–95*. Waterford, N.J.: Prentice Hall, 1994.

Diggs, Anita Doreen. *Talking Drums: An African-American Quote Collection*. New York: St. Martin's Press, 1995.

Dunnan, Nancy. *How to Invest $50–$5,000*. 4th ed. New York: HarperCollins, 1993.

Estell, Kenneth. *The African-American Almanac*. 6th ed.

Frank, Cheryl R. *How to Survive an IRS Attack*. Dubuque: Kendall/Hunt, 1995.

Franklin, John Hope, and Alfred A. Moss, Jr. *From Slavery to Freedom: A History of African Americans*. 7th ed.

Fraser, George. *Success Runs in Our Race*. New York: William Morrow, 1994.

Frazier, E. Franklin. *Black Bourgeoisie*. New York: Collier, 1975.

Hagstrom, Robert G., Jr. *The Warren Buffett Way: Investment Strategies of the World's Greatest Investor*. New York: John Wiley, 1994.

Hill, Napoleon. *Think and Grow Rich*. New York: Fawcett Crest, 1960.

Humphrey, Phyllis. *Wall Street on $20 a Month: How to Profit from an Investment Club*. New York: John Wiley, 1986.

IDS Financial Services, Inc. *Money Matters: Your IDS Guide to Financial Planning*. New York: Avon Books, 1990.

Ingrassia, Michele, and Pat Wingert. "The New Providers." *Newsweek*, May 22, 1995.

Investment Company Institute. *1995 Mutual Fund Fact Book*. Washington, D.C.: Investment Company Institute, 1995.

Katz, William Loren. *Eye Witness: The Negro In American History*. New York: Pitman Publishing, 1967.

Keene, Julie. *Women Alone*. Carson, Calif.: Hay House, 1995.

Kimbro, Dennis. *Daily Motivations for African-American Success*. New York: Ballantine, 1993.

King, Dean. *Penny Pincher's Almanac: Handbook for Modern Frugality*. New York: Simon & Schuster, 1992.

Lavine, Alan. *Your Insurance Options*. New York: John Wiley, 1993.

Lebreque, Leon. *Building Your Financial Future*. Troy, Mich.: Educational Technologies, Inc., 1991.

Leonard, Frances. *Women and Money*. Menlo Park, Calif.: Addison-Wesley, 1991.

Little, Jeffrey, and Lucien Rhodes. *Understanding Wall Street.* New York: Liberty Hall Press, 1991.

Lynch, Peter, and John Rothchild. *One Up on Wall Street: How to Use What You Already Know to Make Money in the Market.* New York: Penguin, 1989.

Lynch, Peter, and John Rothchild. *Beating the Street.* New York: Simon & Schuster, 1993.

Mather, Frank Lincoln. *Who's Who of the Colored Race.* Vol. 1. 1915 republished by Detroit: Gale Research, 1976.

Mellan, Olivia. *Money Harmony.* New York: Walker Publishing Co. 1995.

Miller, Theodore J. *Invest Your Way to Wealth.* Washington, D.C.: Kiplinger Books, 1994.

Mundis, Jerrold. *How to Get Out of Debt, Stay Out of Debt, and Live Prosperously.* New York: Bantam Books, 1988.

National Urban League. *1994 State of Black America Report.* New York: National Urban League, 1994.

New English Bible (New Testament). New York: Oxford University Press, n.d.

O'Hara, Thomas E., and Helen J. McLane. *Taking Control of Your Financial Future: Making Smart Investment Decisions with Stocks and Mutual Funds.* Homewood, Ill. Irwin, 1995.

Price, John Randolph. *Practical Spirituality.* Austin: Quartus, 1985.

Reed, Gregory J. *Economic Empowerment Through the Church.* Grand Rapids: Zondervan Publishing House, 1993, 1994.

Reed, James W., Neil B. Shulman, and Charlene Shucker. *The Black Man's Guide to Good Health: Essential Advice for the Special Concerns of African-American Men.* New York: Perigee, 1994.

Riley, Dorothy Hinbush. *My Soul Looks Back, Lest I Forget.* New York: HarperCollins, 1991.

Roger, John, and Peter McWilliams. *Wealth 101.* Los Angeles: Prelude Press. 1992.

Rugg, Donald D., and Norman B. Hale. *The Dow Jones-Irwin Guide to Mutual Funds: How to Diversify Your Investments for Maximum Return and Safety in Any Kind of Market.* Homewood, Ill.: Dow Jones–Irwin, 1983.

Ryrie, Charles Caldwell. *The Ryrie Study Bible. King James Version.* Chicago: Moody Press, 1978.

Savage, Terry. *New Money Strategies for the '90s: Simple Steps to Creating Wealth and Building Financial Security.* New York: HarperBusiness, 1993.

Schlayer, Mary Elizabeth, and Marilyn H. Cooley. *How to be a Financially Secure Woman.* New York: Ballantine, 1978.

Sewell, George Alexander. *Missisippi Black History Makers.* Jackson, Miss.: University Press of Mississippi, 1977.

Shinn, Florence Scovel. *The Game of Life and How to Play It.* Marina del Rey: DeVorss, 1925.

Sinetar, Marsha. *To Build the Life You Want, Create the Work You Love.* New York: St. Martin's Press, 1995.

Skousen, Mark, and Jo Ann Skousen. *High Finance on a Low Budget.* Dearborn Financial Publishing, 1993.

Stowers, James E. *Yes You Can . . . Achieve Financial Independence.* Kansas City: Andrews and McMeel, 1994.

Timmons, Jeffrey A. *The Entrepreneurial Mind.* Andover, Md.: Brick House, 1989.

Tyson, Eric. *Mutual Funds for Dummies.* Foster City, Calif.: IDG Books, 1995.

U.S. Department of Commerce. *1987 Economic Censuses: Survey of Minority-Owned Business Enterprises.* Washington, D.C.: U.S. Department of Commerce, August 1991.

U.S. Small Business Administration. *Checklist for Going into Business.* Washington, D.C.: U.S. Small Business Administration, 1993.

VanCaspel, Venita. *Money Dynamics for the 1990s.* New York: Simon and Schuster, 1988.

Wade, Jack Warren. *When You Owe the IRS.* New York: Penguin, 1983.

Wallace, Robert L. *Black Wealth through Black Entrepreneurship.* Edgewood: Duncan & Duncan, 1993.

Washington Women's Investment Club. *How to Start an Investment Club.* Washington, D.C.: WWicked, 1993.

White, Shelby. *What Every Woman Should Know About Her Husband's Money.* New York: Random House, 1995.

SMART MONEY GLOSSARY

Accidental Death Benefit—A benefit in addition to the face amount of a life insurance policy, payable if the insured dies as the result of an accident (sometimes referred to as "double indemnity").

Accounts Payable—Money owed by the business for goods and services the business has received.

Accounts Receivable—Money owed to the business for good and services the business has sold.

Actuary—Someone professionally trained in the technical aspects of insurance and related fields, particularly in the mathematics of insurance (the calculation of premiums, reserves, and other values).

Adjusted Gross Income (AGI)—All taxable income as defined by the Internal Revenue Service.

Adjustable Life Insurance—A type of insurance that allows the policyholder to change the plan of insurance, raise or lower the face amount of the policy, increase or decrease the premium, and lengthen or shorten the protection period.

Advance–Decline Line—A line that charts the difference between the number of stocks whose prices rise (advance) and the number of stocks whose prices fall (decline) in each day's trading. May indicate the relative strength of the market.

Agent—A sales and service representative of an insurance company. Life insurance agents many also be called life underwriters or field underwriters.

Aging Schedule—A listing of accounts receivable or accounts payable by amount and time outstanding.

Annual Report—A booklet produced once a year by a public corporation, which contains financial reports and statistics, including findings of the auditors, and information about the corporation's business activities during the preceding year.

Annuitant—The person during whose life an annuity is payable, usually the person to receive an annuity.

Annuity—A contract that provides a periodic income at regular intervals for a specified period of time, such as for a number of years or for life.

Annuity Certain—A contract that provides an income for a specified number of years, regardless of life or death.

Annuity Consideration—The payment, or one of the regular periodic payments, an annuitant makes for an annuity.

Application—A statement of information made by someone applying for life insurance. The information gathered helps the life insurance company assess the acceptability of risk.

Asked Price—The lowest price someone will take for securities at a specific time.

Assets—Cash on hand; in checking and savings accounts, trusts, stocks, bonds, and other securities; real estate, home (if owned) and income-producing property; and business equipment and inventory. Anything owned that has monetary value, such as cash, marketable securities, ownership interests, machinery, equipment, building, etc.

Assignment—The legal transfer of one person's interest in an insurance policy to another person.

Associate Degree—The degree given for many two year programs, particularly common at junior and community colleges. Many can be later applied to a four-year baccalaureate degree.

At the Market—Current price at which a stock is selling.

Audit—Participation in a course for content purposes only. No credit is given although a fee is generally charged.

Automatic Premium Loan—A provision in a life insurance policy that any premium not paid by the end of the grace period (usually thirty-one days) is automatically paid by a policy loan if there is sufficient cash value.

Averages—Statistics (such as the Dow Jones Industrial Average, the Standard & Poor's Composite Index, the New York Stock Exchange Composite Index, etc.)

comprising the daily average of the closing prices of representative groups of stocks; used to indicate the relative strength or weakness of the market.

Averaging—Buying the stock of a company at intervals. Averaging down means buying a company's stock at successively lower prices; averaging up means buying as the price is rising.

Baccalaureate or Bachelor's Degree—The degree awarded for successful completion of a four- or five-year program of study. Examples include bachelor of arts, bachelor of science, and bachelor of business administration.

Balance Sheet—A financial statement showing the financial position of a business or individual at a given point in time, including assets, liabilities, and owner's equity.

Bear—A "bear market" is one in which most stocks are falling in price. A "bear" is a person who believes that stock prices will go lower in the future.

Beneficiary—The person named in the policy to receive the insurance proceeds at the death of the insured.

Blue Chip—A description of companies that are usually large and considered quite safe investments.

Bond—Similar to a promissory note, a bond issued by a corporation is a certificate that indicates how much money you have loaned to the company, the interest it will pay on this loan, and the date of maturity (when the loan must be paid).

Book Value—The assets of a company divided by the number of shares of stock that company has outstanding.

Broker—The person at a stock brokerage firm who handles your account. Also, a sales or service representative who handles insurance for clients, generally selling insurance of various kinds and/or several companies.

Bull—A "bull market" is one in which most stocks are rising in price. A "bull" is someone who believes that stock prices will rise in the future.

Business Life Insurance—Life insurance purchased by a business enterprise on the life of a member of the firm. It is often bought by partnerships to protect the surviving partners against loss caused by the death of a partner, or by a corporation to reimburse it for loss caused by the death of a key employee (also known as "key person insurance").

Business Plan—A structured, written approach to the operation of a business, covering both day-to-day operations and plans for the future.

Capital Gain—Profits earned by selling certain assets, such as real estate, stocks, or bonds, are considered gain in capital when those assets have been held a certain length of time (currently six months or longer). Taxes on capital gains are less than taxes on dividends or other earned income.

Cash Surrender Value—The amount available in cash upon voluntary termination of a life insurance policy by its owner before it becomes payable by death or maturity.

Certificate—The piece of paper that is issued by a corporation indicating how many shares of its stock you have purchased. Also, a statement issued to individuals insured under a group policy, setting forth the essential provisions relating to their coverage.

Certified Financial Planner (CFP)—A designation awarded to those specializing in all aspects of financial planning.

Certified Public Accountant (CPA)—Accountants who pass a national exam, but are licensed by the state. A CPA with a designation of Accredited Personal Financial Planning Specialist (APFPS) has passed a national exam on all aspects of financial planning.

Chartered Financial Analyst (CFA)—A designation for those specializing in securities analysis.

Chartered Financial Consultant (ChFC)—A designation awarded to those specializing in financial planning.

Chartered Life Underwriter (CLU)—A designation awarded to those specializing in all aspects of life insurance.

Chartered Property Casualty Underwriter (CPCU)—A designation awarded to those specializing in property and casualty insurance.

Chartist—Someone who uses charts and graphs to plot the movement of stock prices and uses this movement as an indicator of when to buy or sell stock.

Churning—If a broker does an excessive amount of buying and selling for an account, the broker is said to be "churning" the account to increase his or her commission income.

Claim—Notification to an insurance company that payment of an amount is due under the terms of a policy.

Close—The price at which a stock sells at the last trade of the day.

Commission—The fee charged by a broker to transact your buy and sell orders.

Commodity—A tangible product, such as coffee, sugar, gold, etc., which can be traded in a commodity exchange.

Common Stock—The shares of stock of a publicly owned corporation. *(See Preferred Stock.)*

Convertible-Term Insurance—Term insurance that can be exchanged, at the option of the policyholder, and without evidence of insurability, for another plan of insurance.

Cost Index—A way to compare the costs of similar plans of life insurance. A policy with a smaller index number is generally a better buy than a comparable policy with a larger index number.

Cost-of-Living Rider—An option that permits the policyholder to purchase increasing term insurance coverage. The death proceeds increase by a stated amount each year, to coincide with an estimated increase in the cost of living.

Credit Life Insurance—Term life insurance issued through a lender or lending agency to cover payment of a loan, installment purchase, or other obligation in case of death.

Current Assets—The assets of a company that can be turned into cash relatively quickly.

Current Liabilities—The debts and other expenses of a company that must be paid within the year.

Debt—Money owed to others that requires repayment at specific times of the original amount borrowed and interest.

Debt Service—The total payments on debts over a given period, including the original amount borrowed and interest.

Declination—The rejection by a life insurance company of an application for life insurance, usually for reasons of health or occupation.

Default—Failure to repay a loan according to the terms agreed to when signing the promissory note.

Deferment (of loan)—A condition during which interest and payments do not accrue on the loan and repayment is extended by the length of the deferment period.

Deferred Annuity—An annuity providing for the income payments to begin at some future date.

Disability Benefit—A feature added to some life insurance policies providing for waiver of premium, and sometimes payment of monthly income, if the policyholder becomes totally and permanently disabled.

Disbursement—The process of paying financial aid funds to students.

Discriminatory—In a loan application review, basing a decision upon race, sex, age, color, national origin, religion, marital status, receipt of public assistance, or the exercise of rights under consumer protection law. (It is not illegally discriminatory to base a loan decision upon the applicant's financial circumstances, financial history, or ability to repay.)

Diversification—The practice of investing in the stocks of different types of companies and industries in order to spread risk.

Dividend—A share of the profits of a company, distributed to the stockholders in proportion to the shares of stock owned; usually paid quarterly. (*See Stock Divi-*

dend.) Also, a return of part of the premium on participating insurance to reflect the difference between the premium charged and the combination of actual mortality, expense, and investment experience. Such premiums are calculated to provide some margin over the anticipated cost of the insurance protection.

Documentation—Written information and statements submitted with the financial aid application to clarify and substantiate information reported on the need analysis form.

Dow Jones Averages—The most widely known of the indicators of the direction of the stock market as a whole.

Earnings Per Share—A figure that represents the profitability of a company, found by dividing the company's net profit by the number of shares of outstanding stock in the company.

Endowment—Funds invested by a college or university to produce revenue for institutional constituents. Also, life insurance payable to the policyholder if living, on the maturity date stated in the policy, or to a beneficiary if the insured dies prior to that date.

Face Amount—The amount stated on the face of the insurance policy that will be paid in case of death or at the maturity of the policy. It does not include additional amounts payable under accidental death, other special provisions, or acquired through the application of policy dividends.

Factoring—Selling accounts receivable to an unrelated party at a price less than the full value of the invoice (a common way of obtaining working capital).

Family Policy—A life insurance policy providing insurance on all or several family members in one contract, generally whole-life insurance on the principal breadwinner and small amounts of term insurance on the spouse and children, including those born after the policy is issued.

Grace Period—The time period immediately following graduation or withdrawal from school during which no loan payments are required. The grace period differs for different loans; borrowers should review their promissory note for specific details. Also, a period (usually 30 or 31 days) following the premium due date, during which an overdue premium may be paid without penalty. The policy remains in force throughout this period.

Guarantee—Legal agreement obligating the signer ("guarantor") to repay a debt of a borrower upon default of the borrower.

Guaranteed Insurability—An option that permits the policyholder to buy additional stated amounts of life insurance at stated times in the future without evidence of insurability.

Income—The amount remaining after all expenses have been deducted from sales (commonly referred to as "earnings" or "profits").

Individual Policy Pension Trust—A type of pension plan, frequently used for small groups, administered by trustees who are authorized to purchase individual level-premium policies to annuity contracts for each member of the plan. The policies usually provide both life insurance and retirement benefits.

Insiders—People within a company, such as directors or employees with influence, who own stock in the company.

Institutional Investors—Banks, pension funds, and other groups that have large sums of money to invest.

Insurability—Acceptability to the company of an applicant for insurance.

Insurance Examiner—The representative of a state insurance department assigned to participate in the official audit and examination of the affairs of an insurance company.

Insured or Insurer Life—The person on whose life the policy is issued.

Interest—The sum of money earned on investment.

Investment Banker—A person or firm that buys newly issued stock of a company either for itself or to resell to the public.

Investment Club—A group of persons who join together to invest in the stock market.

Lapsed Policy—A policy terminated for nonpayment of premiums. The term is sometimes limited to a termination occurring before the policy has a cash or other surrender value.

Liabilities—Amounts owed to other people or businesses. The debts and other obligations of a company or individual.

Lien—Legal claim on property as security (collateral) for a debt.

Life Annuity—A contract that provides an income for life.

Life Expectancy—The average number of years of life remaining for a group of persons at a given age according to a particular mortality table.

Life Insurance in Force—The sum of the face amounts, plus dividend additions, of life insurance policies outstanding at a given time. Additional amounts payable under accidental death or other special provisions are not included.

Limit Order—An order placed with a stock broker that specifies the price the buyer is willing to pay for a stock.

Liquidity—The ability to turn an investment into ready cash.

Listed—Stocks are listed when they are offered for sale through the stock exchanges.

Load—The advance fee charged by some mutual funds when you buy shares in the fund.

Long—A person who owns shares of stock is said to be "long" on those shares, as opposed to being "short" when the shares are sold.

Lot—The number of shares purchased. A "round lot" is one hundred shares; less than this is called an "odd lot."

Master Policy—A policy that is issued to an employer or trustee, establishing a group insurance plan for designated members of an eligible group.

Mortality Table—A statistical table showing the death rate at each age, usually expressed as so many per thousand.

Moving Average—Adding a certain number of daily closing prices of a stock (or a stock index, such as Dow Jones) and dividing by the number of days in the sample produces an "average" for that stock or index. On subsequent days, the new closing price is added, the oldest dropped, and a new average is produced. A line connecting averages gives the "moving average."

Mutual Fund—A company that buys shares in many companies and then sells shares in this "pool" of stocks to the public. A diversified and professionally managed portfolio of securities that may include stocks or bonds. Policyholders have a choice of investing their cash values in stock or bond mutual funds when they own a variable- or universal-variable life insurance product.

Net Worth—The remainder after all liabilities are subtracted from all assets.

New Issue—Stocks that are offered by a company to the public for the first time.

Nonforfeiture Option—One of the choices available if the policyholder discontinues premium payments on a policy with a cash value. This, if any, may be taken in cash, as extended-term insurance or as reduced paid-up insurance.

Opening—The first price of the day for a particular stock.

Option—The right to buy shares in a company at a specific price on or before a specific date.

Ordinary Life Insurance—Life insurance usually issued in amounts of $1,000 or more with premiums payable on an annual, semiannual, quarterly, or monthly basis.

Over-The-Counter (OTC)—Stocks that are usually not listed on an exchange but can be purchased from certain dealers.

Owner's Equity—In a business, the same as "net worth."

Paid-Up Insurance—Insurance on which all required premiums have been paid. The term is frequently used to mean the reduced paid-up insurance available as a nonforfeiture option.

Permanent Life Insurance—A phrase used to cover any form of life insurance except term; generally insurance that accrues cash value, such as whole life or endowment.

Personal Financial Statements—A listing of personal assets, liabilities, and net worth.

Point—In relation to the price movement of stocks, a point is one dollar.

Policy—The printed legal document stating the terms of the insurance contract that is issued to the policyholder by the company.

Policyholder—The person who owns a life insurance policy. This is usually the insured person, but it may also be a relative of the insured, a partnership, or a corporation.

Portfolio—A collection of stocks held by an individual, an institutional investor, or an investment club.

Preferred Stock—Certain stock of a company that is treated preferentially to common stock; for example, it may have a fixed rate of dividends and provide owners with more safety of investment.

Premium—The payment, or one of the periodic payments, a policyholder agrees to make for an insurance policy.

Prerequisite—Usually means a course that must be taken before subsequent courses can be taken.

Price-Earnings Ratio—A figure gained by dividing the price of a share of stock by its earnings for the year.

Prime Rate—The interest rate a lender uses as a basis for establishing interest rates on loans; the interest rate on most business loans is set as the current prime rate plus a set margin.

Promissory Note—Legal document that binds a borrower to the repayment obligations and other terms and conditions governing a loan.

Proxy—A form that allows a shareholder to vote on matters affecting the company in which he or she owns a stock without attending the shareholders' annual meeting or to allow the corporation's officers to vote on his or her behalf.

Rate—A percentage indicating the amount of interest paid or received on an investment.

Registered Representative—A person who works at a brokerage house and handles buy and sell orders for its clients. Sometimes called a broker.

Reinstatment—The restoration of a lapsed policy to full force or effect. The company requires evidence of insurability and payment of past due premiums plus interest.

Reserve—The amount required to be carried as a liability in the financial statement of an insurer, to provide for future commitments under policies outstanding.

Retained Earnings—The accumulated income (which has not been paid out as dividends) of the company from the time it was organized through the current reporting date.

Rider—A special policy provision or group of provisions that may be added to a policy to expand or limit the benefits otherwise payable.

Rights—Additional payment from a company in which you hold stock, which gives you the "right" to purchase more shares at a certain price for a certain length of time.

Risk Classification—The process by which a company decides how its premium rates for life insurance should differ according to risk characteristics of individuals insured (e.g., age, occupation, sex, state of health) and then applies the resulting rules to individual applications. *(See Underwriting.)*

Securities and Exchange Commission (S.E.C.)—The federal agency that regulates the activities of the stock market.

Seed Capital—Funds invested to start a business.

Separate Account—An asset account established by a life insurance company separate from other funds, used primarily for pension plans and variable-life products. This arrangement permits wider latitude in the choice of investments, particularly in equities.

Settlement Options—The several ways, other than immediate payment in cash, which a policyholder or beneficiary may choose to have policy benefits paid.

Short—Having sold a stock, you are said to be "short," as opposed to "long," when you own or have purchased it.

Specialist—A person on the floor of the stock exchange whose responsibility is to conduct an orderly market in the buying and selling of a certain group of securities.

Stock Dividend—Sometimes, in lieu of cash, a company will issue additional shares of stock to shareholders in proportion to those they already own.

Stock Split—In order to reduce the price of shares of its stock, a company may "split" them (usually two for one, but other ratios are possible) and issue additional shares to stockholders in accordance with the number they already own. Unlike a stock dividend, however, the value of your holding has not increased. The earnings of the company are simply divided among a larger number of shares.

Stop Order—A request to your broker to sell a stock for you when it reaches a specified price.

Straight-Life Insurance—Whole-life insurance on which premiums are payable for life.

Street Name—If you leave your stock certificates with your broker, rather than have them delivered to you, they will be listed in "street name," that is, in the name of the brokerage house.

Suspend Trading—In rare instance, because of problems of some kind, trading will be suspended by the S.E.C. for a period of time in a certain stock.

Symbol—The capital letter (or letters) used to identify a company's stock for trading purposes.

Tender's Offer—An offer, by another company, to buy stocks from current shareholders, usually at an increased price, in order to take over or merge with the object company.

Term Insurance—Life insurance payable to a beneficiary only when an insured dies within a specified period.

Term Rider—Term insurance that is added to a whole-life policy at the time of purchase or that may be added in the future.

Underwriting—The process by which a life insurance company determines whether it can accept an application for life insurance, and if so, on what basis.

Universal-Life Insurance—A flexible life insurance policy under which the policyholder may change the death benefit from time to time (with satisfctory evidence of insurability for increases) and vary the amount or timing of premium payments. Premiums (less expense charges) are creditied to a policy account from which mortality charges are deducted and to which interest is credited at rates that may change from time to time.

Variable Annuity—An annuity contract in which the amount of each periodic income payment may fluctuate. The fluctuation may be related to securities market values, a cost-of-living index, or other variable factor.

Variable-Life Insurance—Life insurance under which the benefits relate to the value of assets behind the contract at the time the benefit is paid. The amount of death benefit payable would, under variable-life policies that have been proposed, never be less than the initial death benefit payable under the policy.

Volume—The number of shares of a certain stock sold or the number of total stocks sold in the market for a particular period of time.

Waiver of Premium—A provision that under certain conditions an insurance policy will be kept in full force by the company without further payment or premiums. It is used most often in the event of total and permanent disability.

Warrants—A company will occasionally offer rights to buy shares for a specific price. Similar to "Rights," but valid for a longer period of time and can be traded.

Whole-Life Insurance—Life insurance payable to beneficiary at the death of the insured, whenever that occurs. Premiums may be payable for a specific number of years (limited-payment life), or for life (straight life).

Working Capital—Money used for ongoing business expenses such as payroll, utilities, and rent.

Yield—The rate of return on your investment in a stock, expressed as a percentage.

1. AFRICAN AMERICAN FINANCIAL INSTITUTIONS

Advance Federal Savings & Loan Association
1405 E. Cold Spring La.
Baltimore, MD 21239
(301) 323-9570

American Federal Savings & Loan Association
701 E. Market St.
Greensboro, NC 20071
(919) 273-9753

American State Bank
PO Box 6389
Tulsa, OK 74148
(918) 428-2211

American State Bank
PO Box 12348
Portland, OR 97212
(503) 282-2216

Berean Federal Savings Bank
5228 Chestnut St.
Philadelphia, PA 19139
(215) 472-4545

Boston Bank of Commerce
133 Federal St.
Boston, MA 02110
(617) 457-4400

Broadway Federal Savings & Loan Association
4501 S. Broadway

Los Angeles, CA 90037
(213) 232-4271

Carver Federal Savings & Loan Association
75 W. 125th St.
New York, NY 10027
(212) 876-4747

Carver State Bank
701 Martin Luther King Jr. Blvd.
Savannah, GA 31401
(912) 233-9971

Citizens Bank
401 Charlotte St.
Nashville, TN 37219
(615) 256-6193

Citizens Federal Savings Bank
300 N. 18th St.
Birmingham, AL 35201

Citizens Federal Savings Bank
1728 3rd Ave. N
Birmingham, AL 35203
(205) 328-2041

Citizens Trust Bank
PO Box 4485
Atlanta, GA 30302
(404) 659-5959

City National Bank of New Jersey
900 Broad St.

Newark, NJ 07102
(201) 624-0865

Columbia Savings & Loan Association
2000 W. Fond du Lac Ave.
Milwaukee, WI 53202
(414) 374-0486

Commonwealth National Bank
2214 St. Stephens Rd.
Mobile, AL 36601
(205) 476-5938

Community Bank of Lawndale
1111 S. Homan Ave.
Chicago, IL 60624
(312) 533-6900

Community Federal Savings & Loan Association
4490 Main St.
Bridgeport, CT 06606

Development Bank of Washington
2000 L St. NW, #702
Washington, DC 20036
(202) 332-9333

The Douglass Bank
1314 N. 5th St.
Kansas City, KS 66101
(913) 321-7200

Drexel National Bank
3401 S. King Dr.
Chicago, IL 60616
(312) 225-9200

Dwelling House Savings & Loan Association
501 Herron Ave.
Pittsburgh, PA 15219
(412) 683-5116

Emerald City Bank
2320 E. Union St.
Seattle, WA 98122
(206) 329-3434

Enterprise Savings & Loan Association
1219 E. Rosecrans Ave.
Compton, CA 90282
(213) 591-5641

Family Savings & Loan Association
3683 Crenshaw Blvd.
Los Angeles, CA 90016
(213) 295-3381

First Commerce Savings Bank
PO Box 3199
Jackson, MS 39205

First Federal Savings & Loan
7990 Scenic Highway
Baton Rouge, LA 70874
(504) 775-6133

First Independence National Bank
44 Michigan Ave.
Detroit, MI 48226
(313) 256-8250

First Southern Bank
PO Box 1019
Lithonia, GA 30058
(404) 987-3511

First State Bank
PO Box 640
Danville, VA 24543
(804) 793-4611

First Texas Bank
PO Box 29775
Dallas, TX 75229
(214) 243-2400

Founders National Bank of Los Angeles
3910 W. Martin Luther King, Jr., Blvd.
Los Angeles, CA 90008
(213) 295-3161

Gateway National Bank
3412 Union Blvd. N
St. Louis, MO 63115
(314) 389-3000

Golden Coin Savings & Loan Association
170 Columbus Ave., #210
San Francisco, CA 94133
(415) 397-8988

Greensboro National Bank
PO Box 22046
Greensboro, NC 27420
(919) 373-8500

Harbor Bank of Maryland
21 W. Fayette St.
Baltimore, MD 21201
(410) 528-1800

Heritage National Bank
6393 Penn Ave.
Pittsburgh, PA 15206

Highland Community Bank
1701 W. 87th St.
Chicago, IL 60620
(312) 881-6800

Home Federal Savings Bank
9108 Woodward Ave.
Detroit, MI 48202
(313) 873-3310

Ideal Federal Savings Bank
1629 Druid Hill Ave.
Baltimore, MD 21217
(301) 669-1629

Imperial Savings & Loan Association
211 Fayette St.
Martinsville, VA 24114
(703) 638-7545

Independence Bank of Chicago
7936 S. Cottage Grove
Chicago, IL 60619
(312) 487-4700

Independence Federal Savings & Loan Association
1229 Connecticut Ave. NW
Washington, DC 20036
(202) 622-5500

Industrial Bank of Washington
4812 Georgia Ave. NW
Washington, DC 20011
(202) 722-2014

Liberty Bank & Trust Company
3939 Tulane Ave.
New Orleans, LA 70160
(504) 483-6601

Life Savings Bank
7990 Scenic Highway
PO Box 74108
Baton Rouge, LA 70874

Mechanics & Farmers Bank
PO Box 1932
Durham, NC 27702
(919) 683-1521

Metro Savings Bank
715 Goldwin Ave.
Orlando, FL 32805

Mutual Federal Savings & Loan Association
205 Auburn Ave. NE
Atlanta, GA 30303
(404) 659-0701

Mutual Savings & Loan Association
112 W. Parrish St.
Durham, NC 27701
(919) 688-1308

New Age Federal Savings & Loan Association
1401 N. Kings Highway Blvd.
St. Louis, MO 63113
(314) 361-4100

New Atlantic Bank
415 St. Paul's Blvd.
Norfolk, VA 23510
(804) 623-6155

North Milwaukee State Bank
5630 W. Fond du Lac Ave.
Milwaukee, WI 53216
(414) 466-2344

Omnibank
10474 W. Jefferson Ave.
River Rouge, MI 48218
(313) 843-8856

Peoples National Bank of Commerce
3275 N.W. 79th St.
Miami, FL 33147
(305) 686-0700

People's Savings & Loan Association
101 N. Armistead Ave.
Hampton, VA 23669
(804) 722-2575

Seaway National Bank of Chicago
645 E. 87th St.
Chicago, IL 60619
(312) 487-4800

Sound Savings and Loan Association
1006 2nd Ave.
Seattle, WA 98114

Standard Savings & Loan Association
PO Box 8806
Houston, TX 77288
(713) 529-9133

Tuskegee Federal Savings & Loan Association
301 N. Elm St.
Tuskegee, AL 36088
(205) 727-2560

United Bank and Trust Company
2714 Canal St.
New Orleans, LA 70119
(504) 827-0060

United National Bank
PO Box 1450
137 Gillespie St.
Fayetteville, NC 28302
(919) 483-1131

United National Bank of Washington
3940 Minnesota Ave. NE
Washington, DC 20006
(202) 828-4300

Unity National Bank
2602 Blodgett St.
Houston, TX 77004
(713) 526-3971

Victory Savings Bank
1545 Sumter St.
Columbia, SC 29201
(803) 733-8100

Washington Shores Federal Savings & Loan Association
715 Goldwin Ave.
Orlando, FL 32805
(305) 293-7320

2. AFRICAN AMERICAN–MANAGED MUTUAL FUNDS

1. ARIEL CAPITAL MANAGEMENT, INC.

Ariel Growth Fund
Goal: Long-term, superior growth of capital. Focusing on investments in areas of unrecognized value.
Suitable Investor: Person looking on the long-term horizon. Willing and able to place money in long-term investment.
Minimum Investment: $1,000.
Automatic Investment Plan: $50 per month.
Fund Manager: John W. Rogers, Jr.
Years in Operation: Since November 1986.
Telephone Number: 1-800-292-7435.
City: Chicago, Illinois.

Ariel Appreciation Fund
Goal: Long-term capital appreciation.
Suitable Investor: Long-term investor.
Minimum Investment: $1,000.
Automatic Investment Plan: $50 per month.
Fund Manager: Eric McKissack.
Years in Operation: Since November 1986.
Telephone Number: 1-800-292-7435.
City: Chicago, Illinois.

2. BROWN CAPITAL MANAGEMENT

Brown Capital Management Mutual Funds
Corporate and public pension funds
Equity: Medium investor.
Balanced: Conservative investor.
Small Company: More aggressive investor in small to growing companies.
Minimum Investment: $10,000.
IRA: $2,000.
Keogh: $2,000.
Fund Manager: Brown Capital Management.
Years in Operation: Company began operation in 1983. Fund started in 1992.
Telephone Number: 1-800-809-FUND.
City: Baltimore, Maryland.

3. AFRICAN AMERICAN PUBLICLY TRADED COMPANIES

1. **United American Health Care**
   City: Detroit
   Exchange: NYSE
   List Symbol: UAH
   Products/Services: Health Care Services

2. **Caraco**
   City: Detroit
   Exchange: NASDAQ
   List Symbol: CARQ
   Products/Services: Generic drug manufacturer and distributor

3. **Granite Television**
   City: New York
   Exchange: NASDAQ
   List Symbol: GBTVK
   Products/Services: Television Broadcasting

4. **Black Entertainment Television**
   City: Washington, D.C.
   Exchange: NYSE
   List Symbol: BTV
   Products/Services: Cable television network

5. **Envirotest Systems Corp.**
   City: Phoenix
   Exchange: NASDAQ
   List Symbol: ENVI
   Products/Services: Automobile emissions tester

6. **Carver Federal Savings**
   City: New York
   Exchange: NASDAQ
   List Symbol: CARV
   Products/Services: Savings and loans

7. **Pyrocap International Corp.**
   City: Woodbridge, Va.
   Exchange: AMEX
   List Symbol: PYREC
   Products/Services: Manufacturers and markets fire-suppressant compounds

4. 1995 BLACK ENTERPRISE TOP 100 AFRICAN AMERICAN–OWNED BUSINESSES

Advanced Systems Technology, Inc.
3490 Piedmont Rd., NE
Atlanta, GA 30305-4810
(404) 240-2930
Computer systems services

Advantage Enterprises Inc.
5030 Advantage Blvd.
Toledo, OH 43612
(419) 727-0027
*Project integrator for health care and
construction*

**African Development Public
Investment Corp.**
1635 N. Cahuenga Blvd.
Hollywood, CA 90028
(213) 461-0330
African commodities and charter service

Am-Pro Protective Agency, Inc.
PO Box 23829
Columbia, SC 29224
(803) 741-0287
Security guard services

Amsco Wholesalers, Inc.
6525 Best Friend Rd., #A
Norcross, GA 30071
*Wholesale distributor to apartment
industry*

Anderson-Dubose Co.
6575 Davis Industrial Pkwy.
Solon, OH 44139
(216) 248-8800
Food distributor

Automated Sciences Group Inc.
1010 Wayne Ave., #700
Silver Spring, MD 21910
(301) 587-8750
*Maker of information and sensor
technology*

Barden Communications, Inc.
243 W. Congress, 10th Floor
Detroit, MI 48226
(313) 953-5010
*Communications and real estate
development*

Beauchamp Distributing Company
1911 S. Santa Fe Ave.
Compton, CA 90221
(310) 639-5320
Beverage distributor

The Bing Group
1130 W. Grand Blvd.
Detroit, MI 48208
(313) 895-3400
*Steel processing and metal stamping
distribution*

Bronner Brothers
600 Bronner Brothers Way
Atlanta, GA 30310
(404) 577-4321
Hair care products and manufacturer

Brooks Sausage Co., Inc.
7600 95th St.
Kenosha, WI 53142
(414) 947-0320
Sausage manufacturer

Burns Enterprises
822 S. 125th St.
Louisville, KY 40210
(502) 585-0400
Janitorial services and supermarkets

Burrell Communications Group
20 N. Michigan Ave.
Chicago, IL 60602
(312) 443-8600
*Advertising, public relations,
consumer promotions*

C. H. James and Co.
3990 Dunbar Ave.
Dunbar, WV 25064
(304) 744-0880
Wholesale food distributor

Calhoun Enterprises
4155 Lomac St. #G
Montgomery, AL 36106
(205) 272-4400
Supermarket chain

Capsonic Group
460 S. 2nd St.
Elgin, IL 60123
(708) 888-7300
Composite components for auto and computer control systems

Cimarron Express Inc.
21883 State Rt. 51
PO Box 185
Genoa, OH 43430
(419) 855-7012
Interstate trucking company

Community Foods Inc.
2936 Remington Ave.
Baltimore, MD 21211
(410) 235-9800
Supermarket chain

Consolidated Beverage Corp.
235 W. 154th St.
New York, NY 10039
(212) 926-5865
Beverage importer and exporter

Crest Computer Supply
7855 Gross Point Rd.
Skokie, IL 60077
(708) 982-1030
Computer hardware and software supplier

D-Orum Hair Products
1075 Grant St.
Gary, IN 46404
(219) 882-2922
Hair care products manufacturer

Drew Pearson Marketing
155006 Beltway Dr.
Addison, TX 75244
Sports licensing and sportswear manufacturer

Dual Inc.
2101 Wilson Blvd, #600
Arlington, VA 22201
(703) 527-3500
Engineering and technical services

Dudley Products Inc.
7856 McCloud Rd.
Greensboro, NC 27409
(919) 668-3000
Beauty products manufacturer

Earl G. Graves Ltd.
130 5th Ave.
New York, NY 10011
(212) 242-8000
Magazine publishing company

Essence Communications Inc.,
1500 Broadway
New York, NY 10036
(212) 642-0600
Magazine publishing company

Garden State Cable TV
PO Box 5025
Cherry Hill, NJ 08034
(609) 354-1660
Cable television operator

Gold Line Refining Ltd.
7324 S.W. Freeway, #600
Houston, TX 77074
(713) 271-3550
Oil refinery

The Gourmet Companies
1100 Spring St., #450
Atlanta, GA 30309
(404) 876-5700
Food service, golf facilities management

Granite Broadcasting Corp.
1767 3rd Ave., 28th Floor
New York, NY 10017
(212) 826-2530
Network TV affiliates

Grimes Oil Co., Inc.
165 Norfolk St.
Boston, MA 02124
(617) 825-1200
Petroleum products distributor

H.F. Henderson Industries
45 Fairfield Pl.
West Caldwell, NJ 07006
(201) 227-9250
Industrial process controls and electronics

H.J. Russell and Co.
504 Fair St. SW
Atlanta, GA 30313
(404) 330-1000
Construction and development, food services

Inner City Broadcasting Corp.
801 2nd Ave.
New York, NY 10017
(212) 661-3311
Radio, television, cable franchises

Input Output Computer Services Inc.
400 Totten Pond Rd.
Waltham, MA 02254
(617) 890-2299
Computer software and systems integrations

Integrated Steel Inc.
12301 Hubbell St.
Detroit, MI 48227
(313) 273-4020

Integrated Systems Analysts Inc.
Shirlington Rd., #1100
Arlington, VA 22206
(703) 824-0700

Systems engineering, computer systems services

J.E. Ethridge Construction Inc.
2740 E. Pine St.
Fresno, CA 93727
(209) 454-0500
Commercial construction

Johnson Publishing Company Inc.
820 S. Michigan Ave.
Chicago, IL 60605
(312) 322-9200
Publishing, broadcasting, television production, hair care manufacturer, and cosmetics

Lockhart and Pettus
79 5th Ave., 10th Floor
New York, NY 10003
(212) 366-3200
Advertising Agency

Luster Products, Inc.
1625 S. Michigan Ave.
Chicago, IL 60616
(312) 431-1150
Hair care products manufacturer and distributor

The Maxima Corp.
4200 Parliament Pl.
Lanham, MD 20706
(301) 459-2000
Systems engineering and computer facilities management

Mays Chemical Co., Inc.
7760 E. 89th St.
Indianapolis, IN 46256
(317) 842-8722
Industrial chemical distributor

Metters Industries Inc.
8200 Greensboro Dr., #500
McLean, VA 22102
(703) 821-3300
Systems engineering, telecommunications

Mid-Delta Home Health Inc.
PO Box 373
Belzoni, MS 39038
(601) 247-1254
*Home health care medical equipment
and supplies*

The Mingo Group
228 E. 45th St., 2nd Floor
New York, NY 10017
(212) 697-4515
Advertising and public relations agency

Minority Entity Inc.
PO Box 397
Norco, LA 70079
(504) 287-8561
Janitorial and food services

Network Solutions Inc.
505 Huntmar Park Dr.
Herndon, VA 22070
(703) 742-0400
Systems integration

Ozone Construction Co., Inc.
1635 E. 25th St.
Cleveland, OH 44114
(216) 696-2876
*General construction and
construction management*

Parks Sausage Company
330 Henry G. Parks Circle
Baltimore, MD 21215
(410) 664-5050
Sausage manufacturer

Pepsi-Cola of Washington
PO Box 10520
Washington, DC 20020
(202) 337-3774
Soft drink distributor

**Premium Distributors Inc. of
Washington, D.C.**
3350 New York Ave., SE
Washington, DC 20002
Beverage distributor

Pro-Line Corp.
2121 Panoramic Circle
Dallas, TX 75212
(214) 631-4247
*Hair care products manufacturer and
distributor*

Pulsar Systems Inc.
2 Reads Way, #218
New Castle, DE 19720
(302) 325-3484
*Systems integration office automation
computer resaler*

Queen City Broadcasting, Inc.
7 Broadcast Plaza
Buffalo, NY 14202
(716) 845-6190
Network television affiliates

R.O.W. Sciences Inc.
1700 Research Blvd, #400
Rockville, MD 20850
(301) 294-5400
Biomedical and health services

Restoration Supermarket Corp.
1360 Fulton St.
Brooklyn, NY 11216
Supermarket and drugstore

RMS Technologies Inc.
5 Eves Dr.
Marlton, NJ 08053
(609) 596-5775
Computer and technical services

RMP Supply Co., Inc.
621 N. 2nd St.
Philadelphia, PA 19123
(215) 627-7106
General supply contractor

Rush Communications Inc.
298 Elizabeth St.
New York, NY 10001
(212) 388-0012
*Music publishing, television, film,
radio production*

Soft Sheen Products
1000 E. 87th St.
Chicago, IL 60619
(312) 978-0700
Hair care products manufacturer and distributor

Solo Construction Corp.
15251 N.E. 18th Ave., #12
North Miami, FL 33162
(305) 944-3922
General engineering and construction

Specialized Packaging International Inc.
3190 Whitney Ave., Bldg. 1
Hamden, CT 06518
(203) 287-8561
Packaging design, engineering, brokerage

Stephens Engineering Company
4601 Forbes Blvd., #300
Lanham, MD 20706
(301) 306-9355
Engineering firm

Stop, Shop and Save
770 W. North Ave.
Baltimore, MD 21217
(410) 225-7900
Supermarket chain

Surface Protection Industries Inc.
3411 E. 15th St.
Los Angeles, CA 90023
(213) 269-9224
Paint and specialty coatings manufacturer

Systems Engineering and Management Associates Inc.
2000 N. Beauregard St., #600
Alexandria, VA 22311
(703) 845-1200
Technical support services

Systems Management American Corp.
254 Monticello Ave.
Norfolk, VA 23510
(804) 627-9331
Systems management, technical support services

Technology Applications Inc.
6101 Stevenson Ave.
Alexandria, VA 22304
(703) 461-2000
Systems integration and software engineering

Terry Manufacturing Co., Inc.
PO Box 648
Roanoke, VA 36274
(205) 863-2171
Apparel manufacturing

Thacker Engineering Company
10 Marietta St. NW, #3402
Atlanta, GA 30303
(404) 223-3404
Construction management

Threads 4 Life Corp.
PO Box 91–1091
Commerce, CA 90091
(213) 890-4700
Apparel manufacturer

TLC Beatrice International Holdings Inc.
9 W. 57th St.
New York, NY 10019
(212) 756-8900
International food processor and distributor

Tresp Associates Inc.
4900 Seminary Rd., #700
Alexandria, VA 22311
(703) 845-9400
Military logistics systems, engineering, computers

Trumark
1820 Sunset Ave.
Lansing, MI 48917
Metal stampings, manufacturing, welding

UBM Inc.
212 W. Van Buren St.,
8th Floor
Chicago, IL 60607
(312) 226-1696
General contracting and construction management

Uniworld Communications Group
100 Avenue of the Americas
New York, NY 10013
(212) 219-1600
Advertising Agency

Urban Organization
4128 N. Miami Ave.
Miami, FL 33127
(305) 576-1408
General contracting and construction management

Watiker and Sons Inc.
PO Box 2688
Zanesville, OH 43702
(614) 454-7958
Heavy highway bridges, mine reclamation

Wesley Industries Inc.
c/o Flint Coatings Inc.
40221 James P. Cole Blvd.
Flint, MI 48505
Makers of industrial and foundry products

William-Russell and Johnson Inc.
771 Spring St. NW
Atlanta, GA 30308
(404) 853-6800
Engineers, architect, and planners

Wise Construction Co. Inc.
1705 Guenther Rd.
Dayton, OH 45417
(513) 854-0281
Construction company

Yancy Minerals
1768 Litchfield Turnpike
Woodbridge, CT 06525
(203) 624-8067
Industrial metals, minerals, and coal distributor

5. AFRICAN AMERICAN–OWNED INSURANCE COMPANIES

ALABAMA

Booker T. Washington
Insurance Company
PO Box 697
Birmingham, AL 35201
(205) 328-5454

Lovett's Life and Burial
Insurance Company
PO Box 364
Mobile, AL 36603

Protective Industrial
Insurance Company of
Alabama, Inc.
PO Box 2744
Birmingham, AL 35204

CALIFORNIA

Golden State Mutual Life
Insurance Company
PO Box 2332
Terminal Annex
Los Angeles, CA 90018

FLORIDA

Central Life Insurance
Company of Florida
PO Box 3286
Tampa, FL 33607
(813) 251-1897

George F. Carter Insurance
Agency, Inc.
PO Box 12337
Jacksonville, FL 32209
(904) 764-0025

GEORGIA

Atlanta Life Insurance
Company
PO Box 897
Atlanta, GA 30301

Pilgrim Health and Life
Insurance Company
PO Box 1897
Augusta, GA 30901

ILLINOIS

Chicago Metropolitan
Assurance Company
4455 Martin Luther King Jr. Dr.
Chicago, IL 60653
(312) 285-3030

Supreme Life Insurance
Company of America
3501 Martin Luther King Jr. Dr.
Chicago, IL 60714
(312) 538-5100

KENTUCKY

Mammoth Life and Accident
Insurance Company
PO Box 2099
Louisville, KY 40201

LOUISIANA

Benevolent Life Insurance
Company
1624 Milam St.
Shreveport, LA 71103

Gertrude Geddes Willis Life
Insurance Company
2128 Jackson Ave.
New Orleans, LA 70153
(504) 522-2525

Lighthouse Life Insurance
Company
1544 Milam St.
Shreveport, LA 71103

Majestic Life Insurance
Company
1833 Dryades St.
New Orleans, LA 70113

National Service Industrial
Life Insurance Company
1716 N. Claiborne Ave.
New Orleans, LA 70116

People's Progressive
Insurance Company
109 Harrison St.
Rayville, LA 71269

Purple Shield Life Insurance
Company
PO Box 3157
Baton Rouge, LA 70802

Reliable Life Insurance
Company
108 N. 23rd St.
Monroe, LA 71201

MICHIGAN

Wright Mutual Insurance
Company
2995 E. Grand Blvd.
Detroit, MI 48202

MISSISSIPPI

Security Life Insurance of the
South
PO Box 159
Jackson, MS 39203

NEW YORK

Goodrich Johnson Brokerage
271 W. 125th St., #208
New York, NY 10027
(212) 865-6444

United Mutual Life Insurance
Company
310 Lenox Ave.
New York, NY 10027
(212) 369-4200

NORTH CAROLINA

North Carolina Mutual Life
Insurance Company
Mutual Plaza
Durham, NC 27701
(919) 682-9201

Winston Mutual Life
Insurance Company
PO Box 998
Winston-Salem, NC 27102

TENNESSEE

Golden Circle Life Insurance
Company
39 Jackson Avenue
Brownsville, TN 38012

University Life Insurance
Company
PO Box 241
Memphis, TN 38101

VIRGINIA

Southern Aid Life Insurance
Company
PO Box 12024
Richmond, VA 23241

6. SMALL BUSINESS ADMINISTRATION LOANS

BUSINESS LOANS FOR SBA PROGRAM PARTICIPANTS

Small Business Administration
Loan Policy and Procedures Branch
409 Third Street, SW
Washington, DC 20416
(202) 205-6570

DESCRIPTION: Loans to small businesses for construction, development, expansion, renovation, and acquisition of equipment. Limited to small businesses owned by socially and economically disadvantaged persons.

$ GIVEN: Nationwide FY 93 est. $5 million. Average direct loan: $113,636; guaranteed loans up to $750,000.

APPLICATION INFORMATION: Applications for direct loans are filed by the loan applicant; guaranteed loans are filed by financial institution through SBA field office.

DEADLINE: N/A

CONTACT: Regional Small Business Administration office for your state.

SMALL BUSINESS LOANS

Small Business Administration Loan
Policy and Procedures Branch
409 Third Street, SW
Washington, DC 20416
(202) 205-6570

DESCRIPTION: Guaranteed and insured loans to small, independently owned businesses not dominant in their field to construct, expand, or convert facilities, to purchase building equipment, or for working capital. Excluded are gambling establishments, publishing media, nonprofit enterprises, property speculators, lending or investment enterprises, and financing of real property held for investment.

$ GIVEN: Loans up to $750,000; average: $192,126.

APPLICATION INFORMATION: Applications should be filed by lender in field office serving territory in which applicant's business is located.

DEADLINE: None

CONTACT: Your state and/or regional office.

MINORITY BUSINESS DEVELOPMENT

Small Business Administration (SBA)
409 Third Street, SW
Washington, DC 20416
(202) 205-6410

DESCRIPTION: Provision of specialized services to foster business ownership and competitive viability to individuals who are both socially and economically disadvantaged. Limited to small business with at least 51 percent ownership by an American citizen who is disadvantaged but demonstrates potential for success.

$ GIVEN: N/A

APPLICATION INFORMATION: Written application to SBA district offices. Assistance given in completing forms.

DEADLINE: None

CONTACT: See appropriate field office.

7. SMALL BUSINESS ADMINISTRATION REGIONAL AND DISTRICT OFFICES

ALABAMA

Regional Office
1375 Peachtree Street, NE,
5th floor
Atlanta, GA 30367-8102
(404) 347-2797

District Office
Birmingham District Office
2121 8th Avenue North,
Suite 200
Birmingham, AL 35203-2398
(205) 731-1344

ALASKA

Regional Office
2615 4th Avenue,
Room 440
Seattle, WA 98121
(206) 442-5676

District Office
Anchorage District Office
222 West 8th Avenue,
Room A36
Anchorage, AK 99513
(907) 271-4022

ARIZONA

Regional Office
71 Stevenson Street, 20th floor
San Francisco, CA 94105-2939
(415) 744-6402

District Office
Phoenix District Office
2828 North Central Avenue,
Suite 800
Phoenix, AZ 85004-1025
(602) 379-3732

ARKANSAS

Regional Office
8625 King George Drive,
Building C
Dallas, TX 75235-3391
(214) 767-7643

District Office
Little Rock District Office
Post Office and Court House
Building, Room 601
320 West Capitol Avenue
Little Rock, AR 72201
(501) 378-5781

CALIFORNIA

Regional Office
71 Stevenson Street
20th floor
San Francisco, CA 94105-2939
(415) 744-6402

District Offices

Santa Ana District Office
901 West Civic Center Drive,
Suite 160
Santa Ana, CA 92703-2352
(714) 836-2494

San Diego District Office
880 Front Street, Room 4-S-29
San Diego, CA 92188-0270
(619) 557-5440

San Francisco District Office
211 Main Street, 4th floor
San Francisco, CA 94105-1988
(415) 744-6804

Fresno District Office
2719 North Air Fresno Drive
Fresno, CA 93727-1547
(209) 487-5189

Los Angeles District Office
330 North Grand Boulevard,
Suite 1200
Glendale, CA 91203-2304
(213) 894-2956

COLORADO

Regional Office
999 18th Street, Suite 701
Denver, CO 80202
(303) 294-7001

District Office
Denver District Office
721 19th Street, Room 407
Denver, CO 80201-0660
(303) 844-3984

CONNECTICUT

Regional Office
155 Federal Street, 9th floor
Boston, MA 02110
(617) 451-2023

District Office
Hartford District Office
Federal Building, 2nd floor
330 Main Street
Hartford, CT 06106
(203) 240-4700

DELAWARE

Regional Office
475 Allendale Road, Suite 201
King of Prussia, PA 19406
(215) 962-3700

FLORIDA

Regional Office
1375 Peachtree Street, NE, 5th floor
Atlanta, GA 30367-8102
(404) 347-2797

District Offices

Jacksonville District Office
7825 Baymeadows Way,
Suite 100-B
Jacksonville, FL 32256-7504
(904) 443-1900

Miami District Office
1320 South Dixie Highway,Suite 501
Coral Gables, FL 33146
(305) 536-5521

GEORGIA

Regional Office
1375 Peachtree Street, NE, 5th floor
Atlanta, GA 30367-8102
(404) 347-2797

District Office
1720 Peachtree Road, NW, 6th floor
Atlanta, GA 30309
(404) 347-4749

HAWAII

Regional Office
71 Stevenson Street, 20th floor
San Francisco, CA 94105-2939
(415) 744-6402

District Office
Honolulu District Office
300 Ala Moana Boulevard,
Room 2213
Honolulu, HI 96850-4981
(808) 541-2990

IDAHO

Regional Office
2615 4th Avenue, Room 440
Seattle, WA 98121
(206) 442-5676

District Office
Boise District Office
1020 Main Street, Suite 290
Boise, ID 83702
(208) 334-9635

ILLINOIS

Regional Office
Federal Building, Room 1975
300 South Riverside Plaza
Chicago, IL 60606-6611
(312) 353-0359

District Office
Chicago District Office
500 West Madison Street,
Room 12550
Chicago, IL 60661
(312) 353-4528

INDIANA

Regional Office
Federal Building, Room 1975
300 South Riverside Plaza
Chicago, IL 60606-6611
(312) 353-0359

District Office
Indianapolis District Office
429 North Pennsylvania Street,
Suite 100
Indianapolis, IN 46204-1873
(317) 226-7272

IOWA

Regional Office
911 Walnut Street, 13th floor
Kansas City, MO 64106
(816) 426-3608

District Offices

Des Moines District Office
New Federal Building, Room 749
210 Walnut Street
Des Moines, IA 50309
(515) 284-4762

Cedar Rapids District Office
373 Collins Road, NE,
Room 100
Cedar Rapids, IA 52402-3147
(319) 393-8630

KANSAS

Regional Office
911 Walnut Street, 13th floor
Kansas City, MO 64106
(816) 426-3608

District Office
Wichita District Office
110 East Waterman Street, 1st floor
Wichita, KS 67202
(316) 269-6616

KENTUCKY

Regional Office
1375 Peachtree Street, NE, 5th floor
Atlanta, GA 30367-8102
(404) 347-2797

District Office
Louisville District Office
Federal Building, Room 188
600 Martin Luther King Jr. Place
Louisville, KY 40202
(502) 582-5976

LOUISIANA

Regional Office
8625 King George Drive, Building C
Dallas, TX 75235-3391
(214) 767-7643

District Office
New Orleans District Office
1661 Canal Street, Suite 2000
New Orleans, LA 70112
(504) 589-6685

MAINE

Regional Office
155 Federal Street, 9th floor
Boston, MA 02110
(617) 451-2023

District Office
Augusta District Office
Federal Building, Room 512
40 Western Avenue
Augusta, ME 04330
(207) 622-8378

MASSACHUSETTS

Regional Office
155 Federal Street, 9th floor
Boston, MA 02110
(617) 451-2023

District Office
Boston District Office
10 Causeway Street, Room 265
Boston, MA 02222-1093
(617) 565-5590

MICHIGAN

Regional Office
Federal Building, Room 1975
300 South Riverside Plaza
Chicago, IL 60606-6611
(312) 353-0359

District Office
Detroit District Office
477 Michigan Avenue, Room 515
Detroit, MI 48226
(313) 226-6075

MINNESOTA

Regional Office
Federal Building, Room 1975
300 South Riverside Plaza
Chicago, IL 60606-6611
(312) 353-0359

District Office
Minneapolis District Office
100 North 6th Street, Suite 610
Minneapolis, MN 55403-1563
(612) 370-2324

MISSISSIPPI

Regional Office
1374 Peachtree Street, NE, 5th floor
Atlanta, GA 30367-8102
(404) 347-2797

District Office
Jackson District Office
100 West Capitol Street, Suite 400
Jackson, MS 39201
(601) 965-5325

MISSOURI

Regional Office
911 Walnut Street, 13th floor
Kansas City, MO 64106
(816) 426-3608

District Offices

St. Louis District Office
815 Olive Street, Room 242
St. Louis, MO 63101
(314) 539-6600

Kansas City District Office
323 West 8th Street, Suite 501
Kansas City, MO 64105
(816) 374-6762

MONTANA

Regional Office
999 18th Street, Suite 701
Denver, CO 80202
(303) 295-7001

District Office
Helena District Office
301 South Park Avenue,
Room 528
Helena, MT 59626
(406) 449-5381

NEBRASKA

Regional Office
911 Walnut Street, 13th floor
Kansas City, MO 64106
(816) 426-3608

District Office
Omaha District Office
11145 Mill Valley Road
Omaha, NB 64154
(402) 221-3604

NEVADA

Regional Office
71 Stevenson Street,
20th floor
San Francisco, CA 94105-2939
(415) 744-6402

District Office
Las Vegas District Office
301 East Steward Street,
Room 301
Las Vegas, NV 89125-2527
(702) 388-6611

NEW HAMPSHIRE

Regional Office
155 Federal Street, 9th floor
Boston, MA 02110
(617) 451-2023

District Office
Concord District Office
143 North Main Street,
Suite 202
Concord, NH 03302-1257
(603) 225-1400

NEW JERSEY

Regional Office
26 Federal Plaza,
Room 31-08
New York, NY 10278
(212) 264-7772

District Office
Newark District Office
Military Park Building,
4th floor
60 Park Place
Newark, NJ 07102
(201) 341-2434

NEW MEXICO

Regional Office
8625 King George Drive,
Building C
Dallas, TX 75235-3391
(214) 767-7643

District Office
Albuquerque District Office
625 Silver Avenue, SW,
Suite 320
Albuquerque, NM 87102
(505) 766-1870

NEW YORK

Regional Office
26 Federal Plaza, Room 31-08
New York, NY 10278
(212) 264-7772

District Offices

Buffalo District Office
Federal Building 1311
111 West Huron Street
Buffalo, NY 14202
(716) 846-4301

Syracuse District Office
100 South Clinton Street,
Room 1071
Syracuse, NY 13260
(315) 423-5383

NORTH CAROLINA

Regional Office
1375 Peachtree Street, NE, 5th floor
Atlanta, GA 30367-8102
(404) 347-2797

District Office
Charlotte District Office
200 North College Street
Charlotte, NC 28202
(704) 344-6563

NORTH DAKOTA

Regional Office
999 18th Street, Suite 701
Denver, CO 80202
(303) 294-7001

District Office
Federal Building, Room 218
657 2nd Avenue, North
Fargo, ND 58108-3086
(701) 239-5131

OHIO

Regional Office
Federal Building, Room 1975
300 South Riverside Plaza
Chicago, IL 60606-6611
(312) 353-0359

District Office
Columbus District Office
85 Marconi Boulevard, Room 512
Columbus, OH 43215
(614) 469-6860

OKLAHOMA

Regional Office
8625 King George Drive,
Building C
Dallas, TX 75235-3391
(214) 767-7643

District Office
Oklahoma City District Office
200 NW 5th Street, Suite 670
Oklahoma City, OK 73102
(405) 231-4301

OREGON

Regional Office
2615 4th Avenue, Room 440
Seattle, WA 98121
(206) 442-5765

District Office
Portland District Office
222 SW Columbia Street, Suite 500
Portland, OR 97201-6605
(503) 326-2682

PACIFIC ISLANDS

Regional Office
71 Stevenson Street, 20th floor
San Francisco, CA 94105-2939
(415) 744-6402

District Office
Agana Branch Office
Pacific Daily News Building,
Room 508
238 Archbishop F.C. Flores Street
Agana, GM 96910
(671) 472-7277

PENNSYLVANIA

Regional Office
475 Allendale Road, Suite 201
King of Prussia, PA 19406
(215) 962-3700

District Office
Pittsburgh District Office
960 Penn Avenue, 5th floor
Pittsburgh, PA 15222
(412) 644-2780

PUERTO RICO

Regional Office
26 Federal Plaza, Room 31-08
New York, NY 10278
(212) 264-7772

District Office
Federico Degetau Federal
Building, Room 691
Carlos Chardon Avenue
Hato Rey, PR 00918
(809) 766-5002

RHODE ISLAND

Regional Office
155 Federal Street, 9th floor
Boston, MA 02110
(617) 451-2023

District Office
Providence District Office
380 Westminster Mall, 5th floor
Providence, RI 02903
(401) 528-4561

SOUTH CAROLINA

Regional Office
1375 Peachtree Street, NE,
5th floor
Atlanta, GA 30367-8102
(404) 347-2797

District Office
Columbia District Office
1835 Assembly Street, Room 358
Columbia, SC 29202
(803) 765-5376

SOUTH DAKOTA

Regional Office
999 18th Street, Suite 701
Denver, CO 80202
(303) 294-7001

District Office
Sioux Falls District Office
101 South Main Avenue, Suite 101
Sioux Falls, SD 57102-0527
(605) 336-4231

TENNESSEE

Regional Office
1375 Peachtree Street, NE,
5th floor
Atlanta, GA 30367-8102
(404) 347-2797

District Office

Nashville District Office
50 Vantage Way, Suite 201
Nashville, TN 37338-1500
(615) 736-7176

TEXAS

Regional Office

8625 King George Drive,
Building C
Dallas, TX 75235-3391
(214) 767-7643

District Offices

San Antonio District Office
7500 Blanco Road,
Suite 200
San Antonio, TX 78216
(512) 229-4535

Dallas District Office
1100 Commerce Street,
Room 3C36
Dallas, TX 75242
(214) 767-0608

El Paso District Office
10737 Gateway West,
Suite 320
El Paso, TX 79935
(915) 541-5586

UTAH

Regional Office

999 18th Street, Suite 701
Denver, CO 80202
(303) 294-7001

District Office

Salt Lake City District Office
Federal Building, Room 2237
125 South State Street
Salt Lake City, UT 84138-1195
(801) 524-5800

VERMONT

Regional Office

155 Federal Street, 9th floor
Boston, MA 02110
(617) 451-2023

District Office

Montpelier District Office
Federal Building, Room 205
87 State Street
Montpelier, VT 05602
(802) 828-4474

VIRGIN ISLANDS

Regional Office

26 Federal Plaza, Room 31-08
New York, NY 10278
(212) 264-7772

District Offices

Federico Degetau Federal
Building, Room 691
Carlos Chardon Avenue
Hato Rey, PR 00918
(809) 766-5002

St. Croix Post-of-Duty
United Shopping Plaza
4C & 4D Este Sion Farm,
Room 7
Christiansted, St. Croix, VI 00820
(809) 778-5380

St. Thomas Post-of-Duty
Federal Office Building, Room 283
Veterans Drive
St. Thomas, VI 00801
(809) 774-8530

VIRGINIA

Regional Office

475 Allendale Road, Suite 201
King of Prussia, PA 19406
(215) 962-3700

District Office
Richmond District Office
Federal Building, Room 3015
400 North 8th Street
Richmond, VA 23240
(804) 771-2400

WASHINGTON

Regional Office
2615 4th Avenue, Room 440
Seattle, WA 98121
(206) 442-5676

District Offices

Spokane District Office
West 601 First Avenue
Tenth Floor East
Spokane, WA 99204
(509) 353-2807

Seattle District Office
915 Second Avenue, Room 1792
Seattle, WA 98174-1088
(206) 553-1420

WASHINGTON, DC

Regional Office
475 Allendale Road, Suite 201
King of Prussia, PA 19406
(215) 962-3700

District Office
Washington District Office
1111 18th Street, NW, 6th floor
Washington, DC 20036
(202) 634-1500

WEST VIRGINIA

Regional Office
475 Allendale Road, Suite 201
King of Prussia, PA 19406
(215) 962-3700

District Office
Clarksburg District Office
168 West Main Street,
5th floor
Clarksburg, WV 26301
(304) 623-5631

WISCONSIN

Regional Office
Federal Building,
Room 1975
300 South Riverside Plaza
Chicago, IL 60606-6611
(312) 353-0359

District Office
Madison District Office
212 East Washington Avenue,
Room 213
Madison, WI 53703
(608) 264-5261

WYOMING

Regional Office
999 18th Street,
Suite 701
Denver, CO 80202
(303) 294-7001

District Office
Casper District Office
Federal Building,
Room 4001
100 East B Street
Casper, WY 82602-2839
(307) 261-5761

Washington
Regional Administrator
1111 Third Avenue,
Room 885
Seattle, WA 98101-3211
(206) 553-1534

Washington, DC
Regional Administrator
Gateway Building,
Room 13280
3535 Market Street
Philadelphia, PA 19104
(215) 596-1183

West Virginia
Regional Administrator
Gateway Building,
Room 13280
3535 Market Street
Philadelphia, PA 19104
(215) 596-1183

Wisconsin
Regional Administrator
280 South Dearborn Street,
Room 1022
Chicago, IL 60604
(312) 353-6985

Wyoming
Regional Administrator
Federal Office Building,
Room 1452
1801 California Street,
Suite 905
Denver, CO 80202-2614
(303) 391-6755

8. MINORITY BUSINESS DEVELOPMENT CENTERS

Department of Commerce
Minority Business Agency
14th and Constitution Avenue, NW
Washington, DC 20230
(202) 377-8015

DESCRIPTION: Project grants to provide business development services for a minimal fee to minority firms and individuals interested in entering, expanding, or improving their efforts in the marketplace.
$ GIVEN: Range: $165,000–$622,000; average: $212,000.
APPLICATION INFORMATION: Standard application forms as furnished by the federal agency.
DEADLINE: See Federal Register and Commerce Business Daily.
CONTACT:
Assistant Director
Office of Operations
Room 5063

ALABAMA
Director
401 West Peachtree Street, NW
Room 1930
Atlanta, GA 30308–3516
(404) 730-3300

ALASKA
Director
221 Main Street,
Room 1280
San Francisco,CA 94105
(415) 744-3001

ARIZONA
Director
221 Main Street, Room 1280
San Francisco, CA 94105
(415) 744-3001

ARKANSAS
Director
1100 Commerce Street, Room 7B23
Dallas, TX 75242
(214) 767-8001

AMERICAN SAMOA
Director
221 Main Street, Room 1280
San Francisco, CA 94105
(415) 744-3001

CALIFORNIA

Director
221 Main Street, Room 1280
San Francisco, CA 94105
(415) 744-3001

District Officer
977 North Broadway, Suite 201
Los Angeles, CA 90012
(213) 894-7157

COLORADO
Director
1100 Commerce Street, Room 7B23
Dallas, TX 75242
(214) 767-8001

CONNECTICUT
Director
26 Federal Plaza, Room 3720
New York, NY 10278
(212) 264-3262

DELAWARE
Director
14th and Constitution Avenue, NW,
Room 6711

Washington, DC 20230
(202) 377-8275

DISTRICT OF COLUMBIA
Director
14th and Constitution Avenue, NW,
Room 6711
Washington, DC 20230
(202) 377-8275

FLORIDA

Director
401 West Peachtree Street, NW,
Room 1930
Atlanta, GA 30308-3516
(404) 730-3300

District Officer
Federal Building,
Room 928
51 SW First Avenue
P.O. Box 25
Miami, FL 33130
(305) 536-5054

GEORGIA
Director
401 West Peachtree Street, NW,
Room 1930
Atlanta, GA 30308-3516
(404) 730-3300

GUAM
Director
221 Main Street,
Room 1280
San Francisco, CA 95105
(415) 744-3001

HAWAII
Director
221 Main Street, Room 1280
San Francisco, CA 95105
(415) 744-3001

IDAHO
Director
221 Main Street, Room 1280
San Francisco, CA 95105
(415) 744-3001

ILLINOIS
Director
55 East Monroe Street, Suite 1440
Chicago, IL 60603
(312) 353-0182

INDIANA
Director
55 East Monroe Street, Suite 1440
Chicago, IL 60603
(312) 353-0182

IOWA
Director
55 East Monroe Street, Suite 1440
Chicago, IL 60603
(312) 353-0182

KANSAS
Director
55 East Monroe Street,
Suite 1440
Chicago, IL 60603
(312) 353-0182

KENTUCKY
Director
401 West Peachtree Street, NW,
Room 1930
Atlanta, GA 30308-3516
(404) 730-3300

LOUISIANA
Director
1100 Commerce Street,
Room 7B23
Dallas, TX 75242
(214) 767-8001

MAINE
Director
26 Federal Plaza,
Room 3720
New York, NY 10278
(212) 264-3262

MARYLAND
Director
14th and Constitution Avenue,
NW, Room 6711
Washington, DC 20230
(202) 377-8275

MASSACHUSETTS

Director
26 Federal Plaza, Room 3720
New York, NY 10278
(212) 264-3262

District Officer
10 Causeway Street, Room 418
Boston, MA 02222-1041

MICHIGAN
Director
55 East Monroe Street,
Suite 1440
Chicago, IL 60603
(312) 353-0182

MINNESOTA
Director
55 East Monroe Street,
Suite 1440
Chicago, IL 60603
(312) 353-0182

MISSISSIPPI
Director
401 West Peachtree Street, NW,
Room 1930
Atlanta, GA 30308-3516
(404) 730-3300

MISSOURI
Director
55 East Monroe Street, Suite 1440
Chicago, IL 60603
(312) 353-0182

MONTANA
Director
1100 Commerce Street,
Room 7B23
Dallas, TX 75242
(214) 767-8001

NEBRASKA
Director
55 East Monroe Street,
Suite 1440
Chicago, IL 60603
(312) 353-0182

NEVADA
Director
221 Main Street, Room 1280
San Francisco, CA 94105
(415) 744-3001

NEW HAMPSHIRE
Director
26 Federal Plaza, Room 3720
New York, NY 10278
(212) 264-3262

NEW JERSEY
Director
26 Federal Plaza, Room 3720
New York, NY 10278
(212) 264-3262

NEW MEXICO
Director
1100 Commerce Street,
Room 7B23
Dallas, TX 75242
(214) 767-8001

NEW YORK
Director
26 Federal Plaza, Room 3720
New York, NY 10278
(212) 264-3262

NORTH CAROLINA
Director
401 West Peachtree Street, NW,
Room 1930
Atlanta, GA 30308-3516
(404) 730-3300

NORTH DAKOTA
Director
1100 Commerce Street,
Room 7B23
Dallas, TX 75242
(214) 767-8001

OHIO
Director
55 East Monroe Street, Suite 1440
Chicago, IL 60603
(312) 353-0182

OKLAHOMA
Director
1100 Commerce Street, Room 7B23
Dallas, TX 75242
(214) 767-8001

OREGON
Director
221 Main Street, Room 1280
San Francisco, CA 94105
(415) 744-3001

PENNSYLVANIA
Director
14th and Constitution Avenue,
NW, Room 6711
Washington, DC 20230
(202) 377-8275

District Officer
Federal Office Building,
Room 10128
600 Arch Street
Philadelphia, PA 19106
(215) 597-9236

District Officer
614–16 Federal Office Building
1000 Liberty Avenue
Pittsburgh, PA 15222
(412) 722-6659

PUERTO RICO
Director
26 Federal Plaza, Room 3720
New York, NY 10278
(212) 264-3262

RHODE ISLAND
Director
26 Federal Plaza, Room 3720
New York, NY 10278
(212) 264-3262

SOUTH CAROLINA
Director
401 West Peachtree Street, NW,
Room 1930
Atlanta, GA 30308-3516
(404) 730-3300

SOUTH DAKOTA
Director
1100 Commerce Street,
Room 7B23
Dallas, TX 75242
(214) 767-8001

TENNESSEE
Director
401 West Peachtree Street, NW,
Room 1930
Atlanta, GA 30308-3516
(404) 730-3300

TEXAS
Director
1100 Commerce Street,
Room 7B23
Dallas, TX 75242
(214) 767-8001

UTAH
Director
1100 Commerce Street,
Room 7B23
Dallas, TX 75242
(214) 767-8001

VERMONT
Director
26 Federal Plaza, Room 3720
New York, NY 10278
(212) 264-3262

VIRGIN ISLANDS
Director
26 Federal Plaza, Room 3720
New York, NY 10278
(212) 264-3262

VIRGINIA
Director
14th and Constitution Avenue,
NW, Room 6711
Washington, DC 20230
(202) 377-8275

WASHINGTON
Director
221 Main Street, Room 1280
San Francisco, CA 94105
(415) 744-3001

WEST VIRGINIA
Director
14th and Constitution Avenue,
NW, Room 6711
Washington, DC 20230
(202) 377-8275

WISCONSIN
Director
55 East Monroe Street, Suite 1440
Chicago, IL 60603
(312) 353-0182

WYOMING
Director
1100 Commerce Street, Room 7B23
Dallas, TX 75242
(214) 767-8001

9. HISTORICALLY BLACK COLLEGES AND UNIVERSITIES

Alabama A&M University
PO Box 1387
Normal, AL 35762
(205) 851-5000
Public. Founded 1875
DEGREES OFFERED: associate,
    bachelor's, masters, doctorate
1994–95 EXPENSES: tuition: $1,600
    in-state; $3,150 out-of-state;
    room/board: $2,550

Alabama State University
915 S. Jackson Street
Montgomery, AL 36101
(205) 293-4100
Public. Founded 1866
DEGREES OFFERED: associate,
    bachelor's, masters
GRADUATE SCHOOL PATTERNS: 13%
    enter graduate study within one
    year of graduation.
1994–95 EXPENSES: tuition: $1,500
    in-state; $3,000 out-of-state;
    room/board: $2,813.

Albany State College
504 College Drive
Albany, GA 31705
(912) 430-4600
Public. Founded 1903.
DEGREES OFFERED: bachelor's.
1994–95 EXPENSES: tuition: $1,422
    in-state; $4,266 out-of-state;
    room/board: $2,854.

Alcorn State University
Lorman, MS 39096
(601) 877-6100
Public. Founded 1871
DEGREES OFFERED: associate,
    bachelor's, master's.
GRADUATE SCHOOL PATTERNS: 1%
    enter law school, 1% enter
    MBA programs, 2% enter medical
    school, 8% enter other graduate
    study within one year of
    graduation.
1994–95 EXPENSES: tuition: $4,474
    in-state, $6,616 out-of-state.

Allen University
1530 Harden Street
Columbia, SC 29204
(803) 376-5701
Private. Founded 1870.
DEGREES OFFERED: associate,
    bachelor's.
1994–95 EXPENSES: tuition: $4,650;
    room/board: $3,910.

Arkansas Baptist College
1600 Bishop Street
Little Rock, AR 72202
(501) 374-7856
Private. Founded 1884.
DEGREES OFFERED: associate,
    bachelor's
1994–95 EXPENSES: tuition: $1,838;
    room/board: $2,420.

Barber Scotia College
145 Cabarrus Avenue, W
Concord, NC 28025
(704) 786-5171
Private. Founded 1867.
GRADUATE SCHOOL PATTERNS: 10%
enter graduate study within one
year of graduation.
1994–95 EXPENSES: tuition: $3,969;
room/board: $2,612.

Benedict College
Harden and Blanding Streets
Columbia, SC 29204
(803) 256-4220
Private. Founded 1870.
DEGREES OFFERED: associate
GRADUATE SCHOOL PATTERNS: 15%
enter graduate study within one
year of graduation.
1994–95 EXPENSES: tuition: $5,084;
room/board: $2,892.

Bennett College
900 E. Washington Street
Greensboro, NC 27401
(919) 273-4431
Private. Founded 1873.
DEGREES OFFERED: bachelor's
GRADUATE SCHOOL PATTERNS: 4%
enter law school, 5% enter MBA
programs, 12% enter medical
school, 16% enter other graduate
study within one year of graduation.

Bethune Cookman College
Dr. Mary McLeod Bethune
Boulevard
Daytona Beach, FL 32115
(904) 255-1401
Private. Founded 1904.
DEGREES OFFERED: bachelor's.
GRADUATE SCHOOL PATTERNS: 1%
enter law school, 10% enter MBA
programs, 1% enter medical school,
7% enter other graduate study
within one year of graduation.

1994–95 EXPENSES: tuition: $5,188;
room/board: $3,396

Bluefield State College
219 Rock Street
Bluefield, WV 24701
(304) 327-4000
Public. Founded 1895.
DEGREES OFFERED: associate,
bachelor's
GRADUATE SCHOOL PATTERNS: 1%
enter law school, 3% enter MBA
programs, 1% enter medical school,
2% enter other graduate study
within one year of graduation.
1994–95 EXPENSES: tuition: $1,832
in-state; $4,202 out-of-state.

Bowie State University
14000 Jericho Park Road
Bowie, MD 20715
(301) 464-3000
Public. Founded 1865.
DEGREES OFFERED: bachelor's,
master's.
1994–95 EXPENSES: tuition: $2,514
in-state; $4,689 out-of-state;
room/board: $3,607.

Central State University
1400 Brush Row Road
Wilberforce, OH 45384
(513) 376-6011
Public. Founded 1887.
DEGREES OFFERED: associate,
bachelor's, master's.
1994–95 EXPENSES: tuition: $1,513
in-state, $4,731 out-of-state;
room/board $4,293.

Cheyney University
Cheyney and Creek Roads
Cheyney, PA 19319
(215) 399-2000
Public. Founded 1837.
DEGREES OFFERED: associate,
bachelor's, master's.

1994–95 EXPENSES: tuition: $2,954 in-state, $7,352 out-of-state; room/board: $4,804.

Chicago State University
95th Street at King Drive
Chicago, IL 60628
(312) 995-2000
Public. Founded 1867.
DEGREES OFFERED: bachelor's, master's.
1994–95 EXPENSES: tuition: $1,848 in-state, $5,544 out-of-state.

Claflin College
Orangeburg, SC 29115
(803) 534-2710
Private. Founded 1866.
DEGREES OFFERED: bachelor's.
1994–95 EXPENSES: tuition: $4,412; room/board: $2,200.

Clark Atlanta University
James P. Brawley Drive at Fair Street
Atlanta, GA 30314
(404) 880-8000
Private. Founded 1988.
DEGREES OFFERED: bachelor's master's, doctorate.
1994–95 EXPENSES: tuition: $7,460; room/board: $2,193.

Coppin State College
2500 W. North Avenue
Baltimore, MD 21216
(301) 383-4500
Public. Founded 1900.
DEGREES OFFERED: bachelor's, master's.
1994–95 EXPENSES: tuition: $2,600 in-state, $5,000 out-of-state; room/board: $4,540.

Delaware State College
1200 N. Dupont Highway
Dover, DE 19901
(302) 739-4917

Public. Founded 1891.
DEGREES OFFERED: bachelor's, master's.
GRADUATE SCHOOL PATTERNS: 1% enter law school, 3% enter MBA programs, 1% enter medical school, 10% enter other graduate study within one year of graduation.
1994–95 EXPENSES: tuition: $1,788 in-state, $4,346 out-of-state; room/board: $2,650.

Dillard University
2601 Gentilly Boulevard
New Orleans, LA 70122
(504) 283-8822
Private. Founded 1869.
DEGREES OFFERED: bachelor's.
1994–95 EXPENSES: tuition: $6,400; room/board: $3,550.

Edward Waters College
1658 Kings Road
Jacksonville, FL 32209
(904) 355-3030
DEGREES OFFERED: bachelor's.
1994–95 EXPENSES: tuition: $3,570; room/board: $3,760.

Elizabeth City State University
1704 Weeksville Road
Elizabeth City, NC 27909
(919) 335-3400
Public. Founded 1891.
DEGREES OFFERED: bachelor's.
GRADUATE SCHOOL PATTERNS: 20% enter graduate study within one year of graduation.
1994–95 EXPENSES: tuition: $556 in-state, $5,030 out-of-state; room/board: $2,648.

Fayetteville State University
Newbold Station
Fayetteville, NC 28301
(919) 486-1111

Public. Founded 1867.
DEGREES OFFERED: associate,
bachelor's, master's.
GRADUATE SCHOOL PATTERNS: 20%
enter graduate study within one
year of graduation.
1994–95 EXPENSES: tuition: $740
in-state, $6,806 out-of-state;
room/board: $2,550.

Fisk University
1000–17th Avenue N.
Nashville, TN 37208
(615) 329-8665
Private. Founded 1856.
DEGREES OFFERED: bachelor's,
master's.
1994–95 EXPENSES: tuition: $6,240;
room/board: $3,690.

Florida A&M University
Tallahassee, FL 32307
(904) 599-3000
Public. Founded 1877
DEGREES OFFERED: associate,
bachelor's, master's, doctorate.
GRADUATE SCHOOL PATTERNS: 25%
enter graduate study within one
year of graduation.
1994–95 EXPENSES: tuition: $1,749
in-state, $6,651 out-of-state;
room/board: $2,668.

Florida Memorial College
15800 N.W. 42nd Avenue
Miami, FL 33054
(305) 625-4141
Private. Founded 1879.
DEGREES OFFERED: bachelor's.
1994–95 EXPENSES: tuition: $3,800;
room/board: $2,800.

Fort Valley State College
State College Drive
Fort Valley, GA 31030
(912) 825-6211
Public. Founded 1902.

DEGREES OFFERED: associate,
bachelor's, master's.
GRADUATE SCHOOL PATTERNS: 1%
enter law school, 7% enter MBA
programs, 7% enter medical school,
31% enter other graduate study
within one year of graduation.
1994–95 EXPENSES: tuition: $1,341
in-state, $2,682 out-of-state;
room/board: $2,370.

Grambling State University
Box 583
Grambling, LA 71245
(318) 274-2000
Public. Founded 1901.
DEGREES OFFERED: associate,
bachelor's, master's, doctorate.
GRADUATE SCHOOL PATTERNS: 33%
enter graduate study within one
year of graduation.
1994–95 EXPENSES: tuition: $4,728
in-state, $6,374 out-of-state;
room/board: $2,612.

Hampton University
Hampton, VA 23668
(804) 727-5000
Private. Founded 1868.
DEGREES OFFERED: bachelor's,
master's, doctorate.
1994–95 EXPENSES: tuition: $11,282;
room/board: $3,518.

Huston-Tillotson College
900 Chicon Street
Austin, TX 78702
(512) 505-3000
Private. Founded 1875.
DEGREES OFFERED: bachelor's.
1994–95 EXPENSES: tuition: $5,180;
room/board: $3,624.

Jackson State University
1400 JR Lyncy Street
Jackson, MS 39217
(601) 968-2121

Public. Founded 1877.
DEGREES OFFERED: bachelor's,
   master's, doctorate.
GRADUATE SCHOOL PATTERNS: 6%
   enter law school, 7% enter medical
   school within one year of
   graduation.
1994–95 EXPENSES: tuition: $2,230 in-
   state, $4,190 out-of-state;
   room/board: $2,446.

Jarvis Christian College
PO Drawer G
Hawkins, TX 75765
(903) 769-2174
Private. Founded 1913.
DEGREES OFFERED: bachelor's
GRADUATE SCHOOL PATTERNS: 8%
   enter graduate study within one
   year of graduation.
1994–95 EXPENSES: tuition: $4,200;
   room/board: $3,485.

Johnson C. Smith University
100 Beatties Ford Road
Charlotte, NC 28216
(704) 378-1000
Private. Founded 1867.
DEGREES OFFERED: bachelor's.
GRADUATE SCHOOL PATTERNS: 2%
   enter law school, 5% enter MBA
   programs, 3% enter medical school,
   10% enter other graduate study
   within one year of graduation.
1994–95 EXPENSES: tuition: $5,453;
   room/board: $2,191.

Kentucky State University
Frankfort, KY 40601
(502) 227-6000
Public. Founded 1886.
DEGREES OFFERED: associate,
   bachelor's, master's.
1994–95 EXPENSES: tuition: $1,340
   in-state, $4,120 out-of-state;
   room/board: $2,682.

Knoxville College
901 College Street
Knoxville, TN 37921
(615) 524-6500
Private. Founded 1875.
DEGREES OFFERED: associate,
   bachelor's.
1994–95 EXPENSES: tuition: $5,470;
   room/board: $3,150.

Lane College
545 Lane Avenue
Jackson, TN 38301
(901) 426-7500
Private. Founded 1882.
DEGREES OFFERED: bachelor's.
GRADUATE SCHOOL PATTERNS: 2%
   enter law school, 5% enter MBA
   programs, 9% enter medical school,
   10% enter other graduate study
   within one year of graduation.
1994–95 EXPENSES: tuition: $4,566;
   room/board: $2,862.

Langston University
PO Box 907
Langston, OK 73050
(405) 466-2231
Public. Founded 1897.
DEGREES OFFERED: bachelor's, master's.
1994–95 EXPENSES: tuition: $1,212
   in-state, $2,062 out-of-state;
   room/board: $2,380.

LeMoyne-Owen College
807 Walker Avenue
Memphis, TN 38126
(901) 774-9090
Private. Founded 1862.
DEGREES OFFERED: bachelor's
1994–95 EXPENSES: tuition: $4,200;
   room/board: $1,700.

LeTourneau University
PO Box 7001
Longview, TX 75607
(903) 753-0231
Private. Founded 1946.

DEGREES OFFERED: associate,
bachelor's, master's.

GRADUATE SCHOOL PATTERNS: 1%
enter law school, 1% enter medical
school, 1% enter other graduate
study within one year after
graduation.

1994–95 EXPENSES: tuition: $8,840;
room/board: $4,240.

Lincoln University
820 Chestnut
Jefferson City, MO 65102
(314) 681-5000
Public. Founded 1866.
DEGREES OFFERED: associate,
bachelor's, master's.
1994–95 EXPENSES: tuition: $1,800
in-state, $3,600 out-of-state;
room/board: $2,728.

Lincoln University
P.O. Box 179
Lincoln University, PA 19352
(610) 932-8300
Public. Founded 1854.
DEGREES OFFERED: bachelor's, master's.
GRADUATE SCHOOL PATTERNS: 10%
enter MBA programs, 1% enter
medical school, 40% enter other
graduate study within one year of
graduation.
1994–95 EXPENSES: tuition: $2,800
in-state, $4,000 out-of-state;
room/board: $3,527.

**Livingstone College/Hood
Theological Seminary**
701 W. Monroe Street
Salisbury, NC 28144
(704) 638-5500
Private. Founded 1879.
DEGREES OFFERED: bachelor's,
master's.
GRADUATE SCHOOL PATTERNS: 5% enter
law school, 15% enter MBA programs, 5% enter medical school,

25% enter other graduate study
within one year of graduation.
1994–95 EXPENSES: tuition: $4,700;
room/board: $3,400.

Miles College
PO Box 3800
Birmingham, AL 35208
Private. Founded 1905
DEGREES OFFERED: associate
GRADUATE SCHOOL PATTERNS: 1%
enter law school. 2% enter other
graduate study within one year of
graduation.
1994–95 EXPENSES: tuition: $3,760;
room/board: $2,300.

Mississippi Valley State University
14000 Highway 82, W.
Itta Bena, MS 38941
(601) 254-9041
Public. Founded 1950.
DEGREES OFFERED: bachelor's,
master's.
GRADUATE SCHOOL PATTERNS: 2% enter
law school, 1% enter MBA programs, 3% enter medical school,
25% enter other graduate study
within one year of graduation.
1994–95 EXPENSES: tuition: $2,164
in-state, $4,306 out-of-state;
room/board: $1,900.

Morehouse College
830 Westview Drive, SW
Atlanta, GA 30314
(404) 681-2800
Private. Founded 1867.
DEGREES OFFERED: bachelor's.
GRADUATE SCHOOL PATTERNS: 6% enter
law school, 10% enter MBA programs, 14% enter medical school,
22% enter other graduate study
within one year of graduation.

Morgan State University
Cold Spring Lane and Hillen Road

Baltimore, MD 21239
(410) 319-3333
Public. Founded 1867
DEGREES OFFERED: bachelor's,
   master's, doctorate.
1994–95 EXPENSES: tuition: $1,794
   in-state, $4,136 out-of-state;
   room/board: $4,640.

Morris College
100 W. College Street
Sumter, SC 29150
(803) 775-9371
Private. Founded 1908.
DEGREES OFFERED: bachelor's.
GRADUATE SCHOOL PATTERNS: 1%
   enter law school, 1% enter MBA
   programs, 10% enter other
   graduate study within one year of
   graduation.
1994–95 EXPENSES: tuition: $4,515;
   room/board: $2,550.

Morris Brown College
634 Martin Luther King Dr,
NW
Atlanta, GA 30314
(404) 220-0270
Private. Founded 1881.
DEGREES OFFERED: bachelor's.
GRADUATE SCHOOL PATTERNS: 2%
   enter law school, 5% enter MBA
   programs, 2% enter medical school
   within one year of graduation.
1994–95 EXPENSES: tuition: $6,770;
   room/board: $4,438.

Norfolk State University
2401 Corprew Avenue
Norfolk, VA 23504
(804) 683-8600
Public. Founded 1935.
DEGREES OFFERED: associate,
   bachelor's, master's
1994–95 EXPENSES: tuition: $2,710
   in-state, $5,090 out-of-state;
   room/board: $3,600.

**North Carolina A&T State
University**
1601 E. Market Street
Greensboro, NC 27411
(919) 334-7500
Public. Founded 1891.
DEGREES OFFERED: bachelor's,
   master's.
GRADUATE SCHOOL PATTERNS: 1%
   enter law school, 1% enter MBA
   programs, 2% enter medical
   school, 6% enter other graduate
   study within one year of
   graduation.
1994–95 EXPENSES: tuition: $740
   in-state, $6,806 out-of-state;
   room/board: $1,780.

North Carolina Central University
Fayetteville Street
Durham, NC 27707
(919) 560-6100
Public. Founded 1789.
DEGREES OFFERED: bachelor's,
   master's.
1994–95 EXPENSES: tuition: $676
   in-state, $5,730 out-of-state;
   room/board: $3,136.

Oakwood College
Huntsville, AL 35896
(205) 726-7000
Private. Founded 1896.
DEGREES OFFERED: associate,
   bachelor's.
1994–95 EXPENSES: tuition: $6,639;
   room/board: $3,999.

Paine College
1235 15th Street
Augusta, GA 30910
(706) 821-8200
Private. Founded 1882.
DEGREES OFFERED: bachelor's.
1994–95 EXPENSES: tuition: $5,460;
   room/board: $2,814.

Paul Quinn College
3837 Simpson Stuart Road
Dallas, TX 75241
(214) 376-1000
Private. Founded 1872.
DEGREES OFFERED: bachelor's
1994–95 EXPENSES: tuition: $3,400;
room/board: $2,950.

Philander Smith College
Little Rock, AR 72203
(501) 370-5217
Private. Founded 1877.
DEGREES OFFERED: bachelor's.
1994–95 EXPENSES: tuition: $2,370;
room/board: $1,260.

Savannah State College
Savannah, GA 31404
(912) 356-2181
Public. Founded 1890.
DEGREES OFFERED: associate,
bachelor's, master's.
GRADUATE SCHOOL PATTERNS: 7%
enter graduate study within one
year of graduation.
1994–95 EXPENSES: tuition: $1,818
in-state, $4,662 out-of-state;
room/board: 2,520.

Prairie View A&M
PO Box 2610
University Drive
Prairie View, TX 77446
(409) 857-3311
Public. Founded 1878.
DEGREES OFFERED: bachelor's,
master's.
1994–95 EXPENSES: tuition: $6,215
in-state, $10,585 out-of-state;
room/board: $1,817.

Rust College
150 Rust Avenue
Holly Springs, MS 38635
(601) 252-8000
Private. Founded 1866.

DEGREES OFFERED: associate,
bachelor's.
GRADUATE SCHOOL PATTERNS: 2% enter
law school, 1% enter MBA programs, 1% enter medical school,
27% enter other graduate study
within one year of graduation.
1994–95 EXPENSES: tuition: $4,500;
room/board: $2,100.

St. Augustine's College
1315 Oakwood Avenue
Raleigh, NC 27610
(919) 828-4451
Private. Founded 1867.
DEGREES OFFERED: bachelor's
GRADUATE SCHOOL PATTERNS: 2%
enter law school, 2% enter MBA
programs, 30% enter other
graduate study within one year of
graduation.
1994–95 EXPENSES: tuition: $4,100;
room/board: $3,600.

St. Paul College
406 Windsor Avenue
Lawrenceville, VA 23868
(804) 848-3111
Private. Founded 1888.
DEGREES OFFERED: bachelor's.
1994–95 EXPENSES: tuition: $5,256;
room/board: $3,834.

Selma University
1501 Lapsley Street
Selma, AL 36701
(205) 872-2533
Private. Founded 1878.
DEGREES OFFERED: associate,
bachelor's.
1994–95 EXPENSES: tuition: $4,340;
room/board: $3,700.

Shaw University
118 E. South Street
Raleigh, NC 27611
(919) 546-8200

Private. Founded 1865.
DEGREES OFFERED: associate,
bachelor's, master's.
1994–95 EXPENSES: tuition: $5,112;
room/board: $3,374.

Southern University at New Orleans
6400 Press Drive
New Orleans, LA 70126
(504) 286-5000
Public. Founded 1959.
DEGREES OFFERED: associate,
bachelor's.
GRADUATE SCHOOL PATTERNS: 6% enter
law school, 30% enter MBA programs, 3% enter other graduate
study within one year of graduation.
1994–95 EXPENSES: tuition: $1,451
in-state, $3,009 out-of-state.

Spelman College
350 Spelman Lane, SW
Atlanta, GA 30314
(404) 681-3643
Private. Founded 1881.
DEGREES OFFERED: bachelor's
GRADUATE SCHOOL PATTERNS: 6% enter
law school, 3% enter MBA programs, 5% enter medical school,
18% enter other graduate study
within one year of graduation.
1994–95 EXPENSES: tuition: $7,000;
room/board: $5,565.

Stillman College
PO Box 1430
Tuscaloosa, AL 35403
(205) 349-4240
Private. Founded 1876.
DEGREES OFFERED: bachelor's
1994–95 EXPENSES: tuition: $4,460;
room/board: $2,754.

Talladega College
627 W. Battle Street
Talladega, AL 35160

(205) 362-0206
Private. Founded 1867.
DEGREES OFFERED: bachelor's.
1994–95 EXPENSES: tuition: $4,166;
room/board: $2,364.

Tennessee State University
3500 John Merritt Boulevard
Nashville, TN 37209
(615) 320-3131
Public. Founded 1912.
DEGREES OFFERED: associate,
bachelor's, master's, doctorate.
1994–95 EXPENSES: tuition: $1,706
in-state, $5,488 out-of-state;
room/board: $2,920.

Tougaloo College
500 W. County Line Road
Tougaloo, MS 39174
(601) 977-7700
Private. Founded 1869.
DEGREES OFFERED: associate,
bachelor's.
1994–95 EXPENSES: tuition: $4,795;
room/board: $3,185.

Texas College
2404 N. Grand Avenue,
Box 4500
Tyler, TX 75702
(214) 593-8311
Private. Founded 1894.
DEGREES OFFERED: bachelor's.
GRADUATE SCHOOL PATTERNS: 7%
enter graduate study within one
year of graduation.
1994–95 EXPENSES: tuition: $3,605;
room/board: $2,430.

Texas Southern University
3201 Wheeler Avenue
Houston, TX 77004
(713) 527-7011
Public. Founded 1949.
DEGREES OFFERED: bachelor's,
master's, doctorate.

GRADUATE SCHOOL PATTERNS: 15% enter law school, 11% enter MBA programs, 3% enter medical school, 17% enter other graduate study within one year of graduation.

1994–95 EXPENSES: tuition: $720 in-state, $7,860 out-of-state; room/board: $3,360.

Tuskegee University
Suite 101. Old Admin. Bldg.
Tuskegee, AL 36088
(205) 727-8011
Private. Founded 1881.
DEGREES OFFERED: bachelor's, master's, doctorate.
GRADUATE SCHOOL PATTERNS: 2% enter law school, 4% enter MBA programs, 3% enter medical school, 11% enter other graduate study within one year of graduation.

1994–95 EXPENSES: tuition: $6,735; room/board: $3,395.

University of Arkansas at Pine Bluff
1100 N. University Drive
Pine Bluff, AR 71601
(501) 541-6500
Public. Founded 1873.
DEGREES OFFERED: associate, bachelor's, master's.
1994–95 EXPENSES: tuition: $1,392 in-state, $3,216 out-of-state; room/board: $2,328.

University of Maryland Eastern Shore
Princess Anne, MD 21853
(301) 651-2200
Public. Founded 1886.
DEGREES OFFERED: bachelor's, master's, doctorate.
GRADUATE SCHOOL PATTERNS: 2% enter law school, 4% enter MBA programs, 2% enter medical

school, 7% enter other graduate study within one year of graduation.

1994–95 EXPENSES: tuition: $2,741 in-state, $7,401 out-of-state; room/board: $3,730.

University of Washington
Seattle, WA 98195
(206) 543-2100
Public. Founded 1861.
DEGREES OFFERED: bachelor's, master's, doctorate.
1994–95 EXPENSES: tuition: $2,907 in-state, $8,199 out-of-state; room/board: $4,218.

Virginia State University
1 Hayden Place
PO Box 9013
Petersburg, VA 23806
(804) 524-5000
Public. Founded 1882.
DEGREES OFFERED: bachelor's, master's.
1994–95 EXPENSES: tuition: $1,894 in-state, $5,787 out-of-state; room/board: $4,845.

Virginia Union University
1500 N. Lombardy Street
Richmond, VA 23220
(804) 257-5600
Private. Founded 1865.
DEGREES OFFERED: bachelor's, doctorate.
1994–95 EXPENSES: tuition: $6,646; room/board: $3,494.

Voorhees College
1411 Voorhees Road
Denmark, SC 29042
(803) 793-3351
Private. Founded 1897.
DEGREES OFFERED: bachelor's.
GRADUATE SCHOOL PATTERNS: 1% enter law school, 3% enter MBA

programs, 12% enter other graduate study within one year of graduation.
1994–95 EXPENSES: tuition: $4,250; room/board: $2,522.

West Virginia State College
PO Box 1000
Institute, WV 25112
(304) 766-3221
Public. Founded 1891.
DEGREES OFFERED: associate, bachelor's
GRADUATE SCHOOL PATTERNS: 1% enter law school, 1% enter MBA programs, 1% enter medical school, 3% enter other graduate study within one year of graduation.
1994–95 EXPENSES: tuition: $1,894 in-state, $4,294 out-of-state; room/board: $3,150.

Wilberforce University
1055 N. Buckett Road
Wilberforce, OH 45384
(513) 376-2911
Private. Founded 1856.
DEGREES OFFERED: bachelor's.
1994–95 EXPENSES: tuition: $6,760; room/board: $3,720.

Wiley College
711 Wiley Avenue
Marshall, TX 75670
(903) 927-3300

Private. Founded 1873.
DEGREES OFFERED: associate, bachelor's.
GRADUATE SCHOOL PATTERNS: 1% enter medical school, 10% enter other graduate study within one year of graduation.
1994–95 EXPENSES: tuition: $3,550; room/board: $2,672.

Winston-Salem State University
601 Martin Luther King Jr. Drive
Winston-Salem, NC 27110
(910) 750-2000
DEGREES OFFERED: bachelor's.
1994–95 EXPENSES: tuition: $1,254 in-state, $6,272 out-of-state; room/board: $2,762.

Xavier University of Louisiana
7325 Palmetto Street
New Orleans, LA 70125
(504) 486-7411
Private. Founded 1915.
DEGREES OFFERED: bachelor's, master's, doctorate.
GRADUATE SCHOOL PATTERNS:7% enter law school, 1% enter MBA programs, 16% enter medical school, 16% enter other graduate study within one year of graduation.
1994–95 EXPENSES: tuition: $6,900; room/board: $4,000.

10. INVESTMENT ASSOCIATIONS

National Association of Investors Corporation
(810) 583-NAIC

American Association of Individual Investors
(312) 280-0170

11. WOMEN'S SPECIAL EMPLOYMENT ASSISTANCE

Department of Labor
Women's Bureau
Office of the Secretary
Room 53305
Washington, DC 20210
(202) 523-6606

DESCRIPTION: Advisory services/counseling and dissemination of technical information for expansion, training, and employment opportunities for women especially in new technology and nontraditional occupations. Available for any individual (especially women) located in the United States or its territories.
$ GIVEN: N/A
APPLICATION INFORMATION: Requests made to appropriate Department of Labor
DEADLINE: none
CONTACT:
Chief
Office of Administration Management
or Regional Administrator in respective state

ALABAMA
Regional Administrator
1371 Peachtree Street, NE,
Room 323
Atlanta, GA 30367
(404) 347-4461

ALASKA
Regional Administrator
111 Third Avenue,
Room 885
Seattle, WA 98101–3211
(206) 553-1534

ARIZONA
Regional Administrator
71 Stevenson Street,
Room 927
San Francisco, CA 94105
(415) 774-6678 .

ARKANSAS
Regional Administrator
Federal Building, Suite 731
525 Griffin Street
Dallas, TX 75202
(214) 767-6985

CALIFORNIA
Regional Administrator
71 Stevenson Street, Room 927
San Francisco, CA 94105
(415) 774-6678

COLORADO
Regional Administrator
Federal Office Building,
Room 1452
1801 California Street, Suite 905
Denver, CO 80202-2614
(303) 391-6755

CONNECTICUT
Regional Administrator
One Congress Street
Boston, MA 02214
(617) 565-1988

DELAWARE
Regional Administrator
Gateway Building, Room 13280
3535 Market Street
Philadelphia, PA 19104
(215) 596-1183

FLORIDA
Regional Administrator
1371 Peachtree Street, NE,
Room 323
Atlanta, GA 30367
(404) 347-4461

GEORGIA
Regional Administrator
1371 Peachtree Street, NE,
Room 323
Atlanta, GA 30367
(404) 347-4461

HAWAII
Regional Administrator
71 Stevenson Street, Room 927
San Francisco, CA 94105
(415) 774-6678

IDAHO
Regional Administrator
111 Third Avenue, Room 885
Seattle, WA 98101-3211
(206) 553-1534

ILLINOIS
Regional Administrator
280 South Dearborn Street,
Room 1022
Chicago, IL 60604
(312) 353-6985

INDIANA
Regional Administrator
280 South Dearborn Street,
Room 1022
Chicago, IL 60604
(312) 353-6985

IOWA
Regional Administrator
Federal Building, Room 2511
911 Walnut Street
Kansas City, MO 64106
(816) 426-6108

KANSAS
Regional Administrator
Federal Building, Room 2511
911 Walnut Street
Kansas City, MO 64106
(816) 426-6108

KENTUCKY
Regional Administrator
1371 Peachtree Street, NE, Room 323
Atlanta, GA 30367
(404) 347-4461

LOUISIANA
Regional Administrator
Federal Building, Suite 731
525 Griffin Street
Dallas, TX 75202
(214) 767-6985

MAINE
Regional Administrator
One Congress Street
Boston, MA 02214
(617) 565-1988

MARYLAND
Regional Administrator
Gateway Building, Room 13280
3535 Market Street
Philadelphia, PA 19104
(215) 596-1183

MASSACHUSETTS
Regional Administrator
One Congress Street
Boston, MA 02214
(617) 565-1988

MICHIGAN
Regional Administrator
280 South Dearborn Street,
Room 1022
Chicago, IL 60604
(312) 353-6985

MINNESOTA
Regional Administrator
280 South Dearborn Street,
Room 1022
Chicago, IL 60604
(312) 353-6985

MISSISSIPPI
Regional Administrator
1371 Peachtree Street, NE
Room 323
Atlanta, GA 30367
(404) 347-4461

MISSOURI
Regional Administrator
Federal Building, Room 2511
911 Walnut Street
Kansas City, MO 64106
(816) 426-6108

MONTANA
Regional Administrator
Federal Office Building,
Room 1452
1801 California Street, Suite 905
Denver, CO 80202-2614
(303) 391-6755

NEBRASKA
Regional Administrator
Federal Building, Room 2511

911 Walnut Street
Kansas City, MO 64106
(816) 426-6108

NEVADA
Regional Administrator
71 Stevenson Street,
Room 927
San Francisco, CA 94105
(415) 774-6678

NEW HAMPSHIRE
Regional Administrator
One Congress Street
Boston, MA 02214
(617) 565-1988

NEW JERSEY
Regional Administrator
201 Varick Street,
Room 601
New York, NY 10014
(212) 337-2389

NEW MEXICO
Regional Administrator
Federal Building,
Suite 731
525 Griffin Street
Dallas, TX 75202
(214) 767-6985

NEW YORK
Regional Administrator
201 Varick Street,
Room 601
New York, NY 10014
(212) 337-2389

NORTH CAROLINA
Regional Administrator
1371 Peachtree Street, NE,
Room 323
Atlanta, GA 30367
(404) 347-4461

NORTH DAKOTA
Regional Administrator
Federal Office Building, Room 1452
1801 California Street, Suite 905
Denver, CO 80202-2614
(303) 391-6755

OHIO
Regional Administrator
280 South Dearborn Street,
Room 1022
Chicago, IL 60604
(312) 353-6985

OKLAHOMA
Regional Administrator
Federal Building, Suite 731
525 Griffin Street
Dallas, TX 75202
(214) 767-6985

OREGON
Regional Administrator
1111 Third Avenue, Room 885
Seattle, WA 98101-3211
(206) 553-1534

PENNSYLVANIA
Regional Administrator
Gateway Building, Room 13280
3535 Market Street
Philadelphia, PA 19104
(215) 596-1183

PUERTO RICO
Regional Administrator
201 Varick Street, Room 601
New York, NY 10014
(212) 337-2389

RHODE ISLAND
Regional Administrator
One Congress Street
Boston, MA 02214
(617) 565-1988

SOUTH CAROLINA
Regional Administrator
1371 Peachtree Street, NE,
Room 323
Atlanta, GA 30367
(404) 347-4461

SOUTH DAKOTA
Regional Administrator
Federal Office Building, Room 1452
1801 California Street, Suite 905
Denver, CO 80202-2614
(303) 391-6755

TENNESSEE
Regional Administrator
1371 Peachtree Street, NE, Room 323
Atlanta, GA 30367
(404) 347-4461

TEXAS
Regional Administrator
Federal Building, Suite 731
525 Griffin Street
Dallas, TX 75202
(214) 767-6985

UTAH
Regional Administrator
Federal Office Building, Room 1452
1801 California Street, Suite 905
Denver, CO 80202-2614
(303) 391-6755

VERMONT
Regional Administrator
One Congress Street
Boston, MA 02214
(617) 565-1986

VIRGIN ISLANDS
Regional Administrator
201 Varick Street, Room 601
New York, NY 10014
(212) 337-2389

VIRGINIA
Regional Administrator
Gateway Building, Room 13280
3535 Market Street
Philadelphia, PA 19104
(215) 596-1183

WEST VIRGINIA
Director
14th and Constitution Avenue, NW,
Room 6711
Washington, DC 20230
(202) 377-8275

WISCONSIN
Director
55 East Monroe Street,
Suite 1440
Chicago, IL 60603
(312) 353-0182

WYOMING
Director
1100 Commerce Street,
Room 7B23
Dallas, TX 75242
(214) 767-8001

12. THE IRA

HOW IT WORKS: You can open an Individual Retirement Account (IRA) and each year deposit up to 100 percent of your wages or earned income up to a maximum of $2,000. The $2,000 limit can be increased to $2,250 if you cover your *non-working spouse*. Two separate savings accounts, one in your name and the other in the name of your spouse, must be used. The $2,250 can be divided any way you choose. However, one account cannot exceed the $2,000 limit. If both husband and wife work—meet IRA income limit and file a joint return, the deduction can total $4,000. This money need not come out of current income. You can transfer the amount from an existing savings account. In effect what you do is take up to $4,000 from your left pocket, put it in your right pocket, and get a deduction on your federal income tax return. In addition, the interest will accumulate tax free.

WHO BENEFITS MOST

The full deduction of your IRA contribution is available for three groups of workers:
- Self-employed individuals.
- Employees who are not overed by an employer's pension plan.
- Employees covered by an employer's pension plan whose *Adjusted Gross Income (AGI)* does not exceed $25,000 if filing single or $40,000 if filing jointly.

Individuals in the above categories, in effect, enjoy the following special tax advantages:
1. Their contributions are *tax deductible*.
2. Their IRA earnings accumulate *tax free* until they retire.

3. A deduction can be taken in one year, and payment made in the next (by due date of return).

COVERED INDIVIDUAL

SINGLE FILER		MARRIED FILING JOINTLY	
AGI	**Amount Deductible**	**AGI**	**Amount Deductible**
$25,000	$2,000	$40,000	$4,000
$30,000	$1,000	$45,000	$2,000
over $35,000	$0	over $50,000	$0

$2,000 EACH YEAR	
10% Interest	**Effective Rate Years**
$ 35,062	10
126,005	20
361,887	30
973,704	40

13. AFRICAN AMERICAN CPA FIRMS

**NATIONAL ASSOCIATION OF BLACK ACCOUNTANTS—
DIVISION OF FIRM MEMBERS**

Abrams, Foster, Nola, &
Williams, CPAs
The Quadrangle-Suite 272B
The Village of Cross Keys
Baltimore, MD 21210
(410) 433-6830
Fax (410) 433-8871
Contact: Alicia J. Foster, CPA

Anderson & Associates
7203 C. Hanover Parkway
Greenbelt, MD 20770-2000
(301) 330-3086
Fax (301) 474-0145
Contact: Lloyd G. Anderson, CPA

R.E. Bassie & Company, CPAs
7100 Regency Square Blvd.
Suite 135
Houston, TX 77035
(713) 286-0591
Fax (713) 286-0691
Contact: Roosevelt E. Bassie, CPA

Bolling & Hill, CPAs
8527 S. Stony Island
Chicago, IL 60617
(312) 734-7133
Fax (312) 734-8512
Contact: Howard E. Hill, CPA

Branch, Richards & Co.
2201 6th Ave., Suite 1009
Seattle, WA 98121-1899
(206) 626-4723
Fax (206) 626-0377
Contact: Andrew L. Branch

Charles R. Brown & Company, P.C.
2990 W. Grand Blvd,
Suite 201
Detroit, MI 48202
(313) 871-4030
Fax (313) 871-4081
Contact: Charles R. Brown, CPA

Carr & Associates
CPAs & Consultants
175 W. Jackson Blvd, WA-2107
Chicago, IL 60604
(312) 341-1009
Fax (317) 341-0694
Contact: Bonnie Carr, CPA

Coleman & Coleman
1008 Corporate Pointe,
Suite 103
Culver City, CA 90230
(310) 215-3500
Fax (310) 215-9893
Contact: Ken M. Coleman, CPA

Coleman & Williams, LTD.
Certified Public Accountants
316 N. Milwaukee St.,
Suite 350
Milwaukee, WI 53202
(414) 278-0170
Fax (414) 278-1169
Contact: William B. Coleman, CPA

Coleman & Williams, LTD
Certified Public Accountants
413 E. Locust, Suite 102
Des Moines, IA 50309
(515) 246-0100
Fax (515) 246-0106
Contact: William B. Coleman, CPA

Anita T. Conner & Assocaites, P.C.
6000 Old York Road
Elkins Park, PA 19117
(215) 782-8833
Fax (215) 782-8933
Contact: Anita T. Conner, CPA

Mario J. Daniels & Assocaites, P.C.
Certified Public Accountants
432 N. Saginaw Street,
Suite 404
Flint, MI 48502
(313) 232-1551
Fax (313) 232-1562
Contact: Mario J. Daniels, CPA

Shaun M. Davis, CPA
2131 Hollywood Blvd,
Suite 204
Hollywood, FL 33020
(305) 927-5900
Fax (305) 927-5927
Contact: Shaun M. Davis, CPA

Daniel Dennis & Company
116 Huntington Avenue,
3rd Floor
Boston, MA 02116
(617) 262-9898
Fax (617) 437-9837
Contact: Daniel Dennis, CPA

Francis & Company
701 Ouster Ave., North,
Suite 404
Seattle, WA 98109
(206) 282-3720
Fax (206) 282-3949
Contact: Horace C. Francis, CPA

Frye, Williams & Co., PA, CPAs
43 Halsey St.
Newark, NJ 03102-3030
(201) 643-3236
Fax (201) 843-5170
Contact: Walter K. Frye, CPA
H. O'Neil Williams, CPA

Grant, Smith, Vincent & Co.
505 14th St., Suite 950
Oakland, CA 94612
(510) 832-0257
Fax (510) 272-9757
Contact: Ralph J. Grant, CPA

Grant, Smith, Vincent & Co.
1998 Tuclurnne St., Suite 914
Fresno, CA 92721
(209) 265-6738
Fax (208) 266-8739
Contact: Marshall Kelly, CPA

John L. Green, CPA
4348 Loop Central Drive, #960
Houston, TX 77081
(713) 650-7400
Fax (713) 680-9921
Contact: John L. Green, CPA

Hoskins & Company
Certified Public Accountants
Germantown Center
1314 5th Avenue N,
Suite 100
Nashville, TN 37205
(615) 244-CPAS
Fax (615) 244-2812
Contact: Harvey Hoskins, CPA

J. L. Howard, CPA
139 Fulton St. Suite 605
New York, NY 10038
(212) 227-3730
Fax (212) 227-3485
Contact: John L. Howard, CPA

Ralph C. Johnson and Company
106 West 11th Street,
Suite 1830
Kansas City, KS 64104
(816) 472-8900
Fax (816) 472-4633
Contact: Ralph C. Johnson, CPA

Benjamin L. King, CPA
4804 York Rd.

Baltimore, MD 21212
(410) 433-9173
Fax (410) 433-9176
Contact: Benjamin L. King, CPA

King, King & Associates, P.A.
CPAs and Management Consultants
4604 York Road
Baltimore, MD 21212
(410) 433-9173
Fax (410) 433-9176
Contact: Pamela King Smith, CPA

Sandford Loyd, CPA, P.C.
360 Bay Street, Suite 100
Augusta, GA 30901
(708) 722-8105
Contact: Sanford Loyd, CPA

Management Control Systems
Crenshaw Office Professional
Building
P.O. Box 2302
8443 S. Crenshaw Blvd, Suite 206
Inglewood, CA 90305
(213) 778-1324
Contact: Wanda M. Brown, CPA

Middleton & Middleton
5959 Estates Dr
Oakland, CA 94641
(510) 339-6680
Fax (510) 339-6850
Contact: Dennis N. Middleton, CPA

Floyd E. Miller, CPA
508 Franklin St.
Clarksville, TN 37040
(615) 552-0156
Fax (615) 452-7656
Contact: Floyd E. Miller, CPA

Mitchell/Titus & Co
One Battery Park Plaza
New York, NY 10004
(212) 709-4500
Fax (212) 709-4680
Contact: Robert P. Titus, CPA

Mitchell/Titus & Co.
1625 K St. NW, Suite 515
Washington, DC 20808
(202) 293-7500
Fax (202) 822-1826
Contact: Phillip P. Williams, CPA

Mitchell/Titus & Co.
1 Logan Square
Philadelphia, PA 19103
(215) 581-7300
Fax (215) 589-8709
Contact: Wayne O. Leavy, CPA

Deatrice Russell & Company
12621 MacDuff Drive
Fort Washington, MD 20744
(301) 292-0508
Fax (301) 292-1439
Contact: Deatrice Russell, CPA

Bert Smith & Company
1401 New York Avenue, NW,
Suite 540
Washington, DC 20005
(202) 393-5680
Fax (202) 393-5680
Contact: George S. Willie, CPA

Bert Smith & Company
5485 Harpers Farm Road,
Suite 240
Columbia, MD 21044
(301) 596-3344
Fax (202) 393-5606
Contact: George S. Wilie, CPA

Charles A. Stewart, Jr.
Certified Public Accountants
1019 Market St., Ste. #2023
St. Louis, MO 63101
(314) 444-6750
Fax (314) 444-1470
Contact: Charles A. Stewart Jr., CPA

George W. Stewart, Jr., CPA
464 12th Ave, Suite #410
Seattle, WA 98122-5571

(206) 328-8554
Fax (206) 726-8912
Contact: George W. Stewart, Jr. CPA

Thompson, Curtis, Bazilio &
Associates, P.C.
CPAs and Management Consultants
4400 MacArthur Blvd,
5th Floor
Newport Beach, CA 92660
(714) 955-7905
Fax (714) 955-4980
Contact: Michael J. De Castro

Thompson, Curtis, Bazilio &
Associates, P.C.
CPAs and Management Consultants
185 Asylum Street
31st Floor—City Place
Hartford, CT 07163
(203) 249-7248
Fax (203) 276-6504
Contact: Tanya R. Curtis, CPA

Thompson, Curtis, Bazilio &
Associates, P.C.
CPAs and Management Consultants
1010 Vermont Avenue, N.W.,
Suite 308
Washington, DC 20005
(202) 737-3300
Fax (202) 737-2684
Contact: Jeffrey E. Thompson, CPA

Emma S. Walker, CPA
610 Texas Street
Fort Worth, TX 76102
(817) 332-3049
Fax (817) 870-1851
Contact: Emma S. Walker, CPA

Walker & Company, CPAs
5100 Wisconsin Avenue, N.W.,
Suite 401
Washington, DC 20016
(202) 363-9308
Fax (202) 363-0531
Contact: Jacqueline G. Walker, CPA

Watson, Rice & Company
246 Fifth Avenue—6th Floor
New York, NY 10001
(212) 447-7300
Fax (212) 683-8031
Contact: Bennie L. Hadnoti, CPA

Watson, Rice & Company
1375 Eucid Avenue, Suite 400
Cleveland, OH 44115
(216) 696-0767
Fax (216) 696-1145
Contact: Bennie L. Hadnoti, CPA

Watson, Rice & Company
1010 Vermont Avenue NW. Suite 710
Washington, DC 20005
(202) 371-9005
Fax (202) 371-1699
Contact: Bennie L. Hadnoti, CPA

Watson, Rice & Company
506 N.W. 185th Street, Suite 205
Miami, FL 33159
(305) 947-1638
Fax (305) 944-6225
Contact: Bennie L. Hadnoti, CPA

Clarence White, CPA
Certified Public Accountants
312 9th Street
Richmond, CA 94801
(510) 234-8983
Fax (510) 234-9005
Contact Clarence White, CPA

Donald R. White, CPA
505 14th St. Suite 905
Oakland, CA 94612
(510) 832-2008
Fax (510) 272-9757
Contact: Donald R. White, CPA

Williams, Adley & Company
1300 I St. N.W.
Suite 260 East
Washington, DC 20005
(202) 371-1397
Fax (202) 371-9161
Contact: Henry L. Adley. CPA

Williams, Adley & Company
155 Sansome SL.
Suite 810
San Francisco, CA 94101
(415) 958-6133
Fax (510) 893-2803
Contact: Tom W. Williams, Jr. CPA

Wright, Richardson & Co., Inc.
13855 Superior Rd.
Suite 1901
East Cleveland, OH 44118
(216) 397-0093
Fax (216) 397-9843
Contact: John R. Wright, CPA
James P. Richardson, CPA

Wyatt & Associates
5534 Martin Luther King Jr. Way
Oakland, CA 94609
(510) 658-3540
Fax (510) 658-0463
Contact: Jesse Wyatt, CPA

Ida E. Yarbrough, CPA
6709 La Tijera Blvd,
Suite 449
Los Angeles, CA 90045
(213) 295-0816
Fax (213) 299-0803
Contact: Ida E. Yarbrough, CPA

14. A++ RATED INSURANCE COMPANIES

Company Name	State	1992 Rating
Aetna Life & Ann	CT	A++
Aid Assn For Luth	WI	A++
Allstate Life	IL	A++
Allstate Life of	NY	A++e
Amer Franklin	IL	A++e
Amer Genl L & A	TN	A++
Amer Genl Life	TX	A++
Amer Natl Ins	TX	A++
Amer Natl Life	TX	A++e
Canada Life Amer	MI	A++e
Canada Life Assur	CN	A++
Conn General Life	CT	A++
Contin Assurance	IL	A++p
Criterion Life	MD	A++e
First Colony	VA	A++
Franklin Life	IL	A++
Glenbrook L&A	IN	A++r
Glenbrook Life	OK	A++r
Globe L & A	DE	A++
Great West the of	CN	A++
Guardian Ins. & Ann	DE	A++
Guardian Life	NY	A++
Hartford Life	CT	A++
ITT Life Ins	WI	A++r
Jefferson-Pilot	NC	A++
John Hancock Life	MA	A++
John Hancock Var	MA	A++
Knights of Colum	CT	A++
Liberty Natl	AL	A++
Lincoln Benefit	NE	A++r
Lutheran Bro Var	MN	A++e
Lutheran Brother	MN	A++
M M L Bay State	MO	A++e
M M L Pension Ins	DE	A++
Manufacturers L	CN	A++
Manufacturers L	PA	A++e
Manufacturers USA	ME	A++e
Mass Mutual Life	MA	A++
Metropolitan Life	NY	A++
Metropolitan Tow	DE	A++e
Minn Mutual Life	MN	A++
New York L & Ann	DE	A++
New York Life	NY	A++
Northbrook Life	IL	A++r
Northwestern Mut	WI	A++

Company Name	State	1992 Rating
Principal Mutal	IA	A++
Principal Natl	IA	A++
Pruco Life Ins Co	AZ	A++e
Pruco Life Ins Co	NJ	A++e
Prudential Ins	NJ	A++
State Farm L&A	IL	A++
State Farm Life	IL	A++
Sun Life Ins Ann	NY	A++e
Sun Life Ins Co	CN	A++
Sun Life of CN US	DE	A++e
Surety Life	UT	A++r
Teachers Ins & Ann	NY	A++
U S A A Life	TX	A++
United Investors	MO	A++
Valley Forge Life	PA	A++p
Variable Annuity	TX	A++
Western & Souther	OH	A++
Western-Southern	OH	A++e

15. AFRICAN AMERICAN WOMEN PROFESSIONAL GROUPS

African American Women's Clergy Association
P.O. Box 1493
Washington, DC 20013
Phone: (202) 797-7460

Alliance of Minority Women for Business and Political Development
c/o Brenda Alford
P.O. Box 13933
Silver Spring, MD 20911–3933
Phone: (301) 565-0258

Association of African American Women Business Owners
c/o Brenda Alford
P.O. Box 13933
Silver Springs, MD 20911–3933
Phone: (301) 565-0258

Black Women's Forum
P.O. Box 01702
Los Angeles, CA 90001
Phone: (213) 292-3009

International Black Women's Congress
1081 Bergen St.
Newark, NJ 07112
Phone: (201) 926-0570
Fax: (201) 926-0818

League of Black Women
18 S. Michigan Ave.
Chicago, IL 60603
Phone: (312) 368-1329

Minority-Women Business Enterprise
201 S. Rosalind Ave.
Orlando, FL 32801
Phone: (407) 836-7317

National Coalition of 100 Black Women
300 Park Ave., 2nd Floor
New York, NY 10022
Phone: (212) 974-6140
Fax: (212) 838-0542

Operation Sisters United
1104 Allison St. NW
Washington, DC 20011
Phone: (202) 726-7365

Women for Racial and Economic Equality
198 Broadway, Room 606
New York, NY 10038
Phone: (212) 385-1103

National Association of Black Women Entrepreneurs
P.O. Box 1375
Detroit, MI 48231
Phone: (313) 871-4660

16. IMPORTANT PHONE NUMBERS

Federal National Mortgage Association (Fannie Mae)
1-800-732-6643

Housing and Urban Development
1-800-775-7167

National Association of Personal Financial Advisors
1-800-366-2732

National Association of Investment Corporations
(DRIP) 1-810-583-6242

International Association for Financial Planning
404-395-1605

National Foundation for Consumer Credit
1-800-388-2227

Institute of Certified Financial Planners
1-800-282-7526

17. LIFE EXPECTANCY AT BIRTH, BY RACE AND GENDER, SELECTED YEARS, 1940–1991

Year	ALL RACES Both sexes	Male	Female	WHITE Both sexes	Male	Female	ALL OTHER Total Both sexes	Male	Female	ALL OTHER Black Both sexes	Male	Female
1940	62.9	60.8	65.2	64.2	62.1	66.6	53.1	51.5	54.9	NA	NA	NA
1950	68.2	65.6	71.1	69.1	66.5	72.2	60.8	59.1	62.9	NA	NA	NA
1960	69.7	66.6	73.1	70.6	67.4	74.1	63.6	61.1	66.3	NA	NA	NA
1970	70.8	67.1	74.7	71.7	68.0	75.6	65.3	61.3	69.4	64.1	60.0	68.3
1975	72.6	68.8	76.6	73.4	69.5	77.3	68.0	63.7	72.4	66.8	62.4	71.3
1980	73.7	70.0	77.4	74.4	70.7	78.1	69.5	65.3	73.6	68.1	63.8	72.5
1981	74.1	70.4	77.8	74.8	71.1	78.4	70.3	66.2	74.4	68.9	64.5	73.2
1982	74.5	70.8	78.1	75.1	71.5	78.7	70.9	66.8	74.9	69.4	65.1	73.6
1983	74.6	71.0	78.1	75.2	71.6	78.7	70.9	67.0	74.7	69.4	65.2	73.5
1984	74.7	71.1	78.2	75.3	71.8	78.7	71.1	67.2	74.9	69.5	65.3	73.6
1985	74.7	71.0	78.2	75.3	71.8	78.7	71.0	67.0	74.8	69.3	65.0	73.4
1986	74.7	71.2	78.2	75.4	71.9	78.8	70.9	66.8	74.9	69.1	64.8	73.4
1987	74.9	71.4	78.3	75.6	72.1	78.9	71.0	66.9	75.0	69.1	64.7	73.4
1988	74.9	71.4	78.3	75.6	72.2	78.9	70.8	66.7	74.8	68.9	64.4	73.2
1989	75.1	71.7	78.5	75.9	72.5	79.2	70.9	66.7	74.9	68.8	64.3	73.3
1990	75.4	71.8	78.8	76.1	72.7	79.4	71.2	67.0	75.2	69.1	64.5	73.6
1991	75.5	72.0	78.9	76.3	72.9	79.6	71.5	67.3	75.5	69.3	64.6	73.8

Note: Values for 1981–1989 have been revised using intercensal population estimates based on the 1990 census. They are not comparable to any previous NCHS reports.
NA: Not available.
Source: National Center for Health Statistics, unpublished data, July 1994.

18. N.A.I.C.
DIVIDEND REINVESTMENT PROGRAM COMPANIES

COMPANIES INVESTED MONTHLY

AFLAC (NYSE:AFL)
ALLIED GROUP (OTC:ALGR)
AMERICAN BUSINESS PRODUCTS
   (NYSE:ABP)
AMERICAN GENERAL CORP.
   (NYSE:AGC)
AMOCO CORPORATION (NYSE:AN)
AQUARION (NYSE:WTR)
ASHLAND COAL (NYSE:ACI)
ATMOS ENERGY (NYSE:ATO)
AT&T (NYSE:T/10 SHR. MIN. + $50
   FLUCT.)
AVERY DENNISON (NYSE:AVY)
BARNETT BANK (NYSE:BBI)
BAY STATE GAS CO. (NYSE:BCG)
BEARINGS INC. (NYSE:BER)
BELL ATLANTIC CORP. (NYSE:BEL/10
   SHR. MIN. + $50 FLUCT.)
BENEFICIAL CORP. (NYSE:BNL)
BOB EVANS (NASDAQ:BOBE)
BROWN-FORMAN (NYSE:BFD.B)
CENTRAL ME POWER (NYSE:CTP)
CENTRAL & SW CORP. (NYSE:CSR)
CENTRAL VT PUBLIC SERV. (NYSE:CV)
CENTURY TELEPHONE ENTERP.
   (NYSE:CTL)
CHASE MANHATTAN (NYSE:CMB) (U.S.
   RESIDENCE ONLY)
CHESAPEAKE UTILITIES CORP.
   (NYSE:CPK)
CINCINNATI BELL (NYSE:CSN)
CINERGY CORP. (NYSE:CIN)
CITIZENS UTILITIES A (NYSE:CZNA/
   5 SHR. MIN.)
CITIZENS UTILITIES B (NYSE:CZNB/
   5 SHR. MIN.)
CLAYTON HOMES, INC. (NYSE:CMH)
CMS ENERGY CORPORATION
   (NYSE:CMS)
CNB BANCSHARES, INC. (OTC:CNBE)
COLGATE-PALMOLIVE (NYSE:CL/10
   SHR. MIN. + $50 FLUCT.)
COLONIAL GAS CO. (NASDAQ:CGES)

CONNECTICUT ENERGY (NSE:CNE)
CONNECTICUT NATURAL GAS
   (NYSE:CTG)
CONSUMERS WATER CORP.
   (OTC:CONW)
DANA CORP. (NYSE:DCN)
DELTA NATURAL GAS CO.
   (NASDAQ:DGAS)
DIAL CORPORATION (NYSE:DL)
DIEBOLD, INC. (NYSE:DBD)
D&N FINANCIAL CORP. (OTC:DNFC)
DOW CHEMICAL CO. (NYSE-DOW)
DQE, INC. (NYSE:DQE)
DUKE REALTY INVEST'S., INC.
   (NYSE:DRE)
EASTERN UTILITIES (NYSE:EUA)
ENERGEN CORP. (NYSE:EGN)
EQUITABLE COMPANIES INC.
   (NYSE:EQ)
EQUITABLE RESOURCES (NYSE:EQT)
FEDERAL-MOGUL (NYSE:FMO)
FEDERAL REALTY TRUST (NYSE:FRT)
FIGGIE INT'L. A (OTC:FIGIA)
FIGGIE INT'L. B (OTC:FIGI)
FIRST UNION CORP. (NYSE:FTU)
FIRST WESTERN BANCORP, INC.
   (NASDAQ:FWBI)
FRONTIER CORPORATION (NYSE:FRO)
FULLER (H.B.) CO. (OTC:FULL)
GENERAL SIGNAL (NYSE:GSX)
GREEN MOUNTAIN PWR. CORP.
   (NYSE:GMP)
HANNA (M.A.) (NYSE:MAH)
HANNAFORD BROS. (NYSE:HRD)
HANSON IND. (NYSE:HAN)
   (U.S. RESIDENCE ONLY)
HAWAIIAN ELECTRIC (NYSE:HE)
HOUSTON IND. (NYSE:HOU/3 SHR.
   MIN.)
HUNTINGTON BANCSHARES
   (OTC:HBAN)
ILLINOIS CENTRAL CORP. (NYSE:IC)
INSTEEL INDUSTRIES, INC. (NYSE:III)

ITT CORPORATION (NYSE:ITT)
JOHN DEERE (NYSE:DE)
JOHN H. HARLAND (NYSE:JH)
JOHNSON CONTROLS (NYSE:JCI)
KAMAN CORPORATION (OTC:KAMNA)
KEITHLEY INSTRU., INC. (AMEX:KEI)
KELLOGG CO. (NYSE:K)
KERR-MCGEE (NYSE:KMG)
KEYCORP (NYSE:KEY)
KNAPE & VOGT MFG. (OTC:KNAP)
KN ENERGY (NYSE:KNE)
LA-Z-BOY CHAIR (NYSE:LZB)
LINCOLN NATIONAL (NYSE:LNC)
LUKENS (NYSE:LUC)
MAYTAG CORPORATION (NYSE:MYG)
MCDONALD'S CORP. (NYSE:MCD)
MCN CORPORATION (NYSE:MCN)
MINNESOTA POWER & LIGHT CO.
    (NYSE:MPL)
MOBIL CORPORATION (NYSE:MOB)
MODINE MANUFACTURING CO.
    (OTC:MODI)
MOTOROLA (NYSE:MOT)
NATIONAL CITY CORP. (NYSE:NCC)
NEWELL CO. (NYSE:NWL)
NEW JERSEY RESOURCES (NYSE:NJR)
NICOR INC. (NYSE:GAS)
NW NATURAL GAS CO. (OTC:NWNG)
NORAM ENERGY CORP. (NYSE:NAE)
NORWEST CORP. (NYSE:NOB)
OM GROUP, INC. (NASDAQ:OMGI)
ONEOK, INC. (NYSE:OKE)
OTTER TAIL PWR. CO. (NASDAQ:OTTR)
OWENS & MINOR (NYSE:OMI)
PACIFIC ENTERPRISES (NYSE:PET)
PACIFIC TELESIS GRP. (NYSE:PAC/
    2 SHR. MIN.)
PANHANDLE EASTERN (NYSE:PEL)
PEOPLES ENERGY CORP. (NYSE:PGL)
PINNACLE WEST (NYSE:PNW)
PIONEER-STANDARD ELECTRONICS
    (NASDAQ:PIOS)
PLY GEM INDUSTRIES, INC. (NYSE:PGI)
PMC CAPITAL (ASE:PMC)
PROVIDENCE ENERGY (ASE:PVY)
PUBLIC SERVICE CO. OF COLO.
    (NYSE:PSR)
PUBLIC SERVICE CO. OF NC, INC.
    (NYSE:PGS)

QUAKER OATS COMPANY (NYSE:OAT)
QUANEX CORPORATION (NYSE:NX)
QUESTAR (NYSE:STR)
RLI CORP. (NYSE:RLI)
RPM, INC. (NASDAQ:RPOW)
RYDER SYSTEM (NYSE:R)
SBC COMMUNICATIONS (NYSE:SBC)
SCECORP (NYSE:SCE)
SERVICEMASTER (NYSE:SVM)
ST. PAUL COMPANIES (NYSE:SPC)
SOUTHEASTERN MI GAS ENTERP.
    (NASDAQ:SMGS)
SOUTHERN NATIONAL (NYSE:SNB)
STX CORPORATION (NYSE:STW)
SYNOVUS FINANCIAL CORP.
    (NYSE:SNV)
TEXACO INC. (NYSE:TX)
TRIBUNE COMPANY (NYSE:TRB)
UNITED CITIES GAS (OTC:UCIT)
UPJOHN CO. (NYSE:UPJ)
USBANCORP, INC. (NASDAQ:UBAN)
US WEST, INC. (NYSE:USW/4 SHR. MIN.)
VALLEY RESOURCES, INC. (AMEX:VR)
VOLVO (AB) (OTC:VOLVY)
WASHINGTON GAS (NYSE:WGL)
WENDY'S INT'L, INC. (NYSE:WEN)
WESTERN RESOURCES, INC.
    (NYSE:WR)
WHIRLPOOL CORP. (NYSE:WHR)

COMPANIES INVESTED QUARTERLY

AMERICAN GREETINGS
    (NASDAQ:AGREA/10 SHR.
    MIN + $50 FLUCT.)
ASHLAND INC. (NYSE:ASH)
CML GROUP, INC. (NYSE:CML)
CONN. WATER SERVICE, INC.
    (NASDAQ:CTWS)
CONSOLIDATED NATURAL GAS CO.
    (NYSE:CNG)
EMC INSURANCE GROUP (OTC:EMCI)
GUARDSMAN PROD. INC. (NYSE:GPI)
IDAHO POWER (NYSE:IDA)
INTEL CORPORATION (NASDAQ:INTC)
MDU RESOURCES GROUP, INC.
    (NYSE:MDU)
MID AM. INC. (NASDAQ:MIAM)
OLD NAT'L BANCORP (NASDAQ:OLDB)

INDEX

ABOUT THE AUTHOR

Kelvin Boston, a former financial planner with IDS/American Express, currently serves as a director of the Calvert New Africa Mutual Fund, and is chief executive officer of Boston Media, a multimedia company that produces *The Color of Money* for PBS and cable television. He also publishes the *Color of Money Journal* and *Corporate Detroit* magazine, an award-winning regional business publication. *Corporate Detroit* is also one of the few major business publications owned by an African American investment group.